Gordon Kahl was a hard-working farmer, a war hero, a religious patriot who had obeyed and respected the government for most of his life. He was also a leading member of the ultra-right-wing Posse Comitatus and a fierce tax protestor. Imprisoned once for IRS evasion, he vowed never to go back to jail. When Kahl broke probation, federal marshals came to arrest him again, and there was a shootout. Kahl and his son killed two marshals and Kahl became a fugitive from justice, finding refuge in the homes of sympathizers throughout the Midwest.

The violence in Medina, North Dakota, wounded an entire community. Lifelong bonds were broken over conflicting sympathies about Kahl; families were ruptured. Some thought Kahl was a cold-blooded murderer, a terrorist taking the law into his own hands. Others thought he had given those representing a gluttonous, interfering government precisely what they deserved. Kahl had been a charismatic spokesman, raging against the IRS, the federal courts, the Federal Reserve Board, and the Eastern banking interests that conspired, he said, to take from him and his fellow believers their farms, their land, their way of life. The trial of Kahl's wife and son became a battle for the soul of the heartland, as the chief of counterinsurgence for the Posse Comitatus threatened to storm the courtroom and "finish the job Kahl started."

James Corcoran grew up in North Dakota not far from Gordon Kahl's farm, and covered the tragedy for the Fargo *Forum*. Torn between his loyalties to farmers no longer able to survive and his despair and outrage at the violence that some have turned to, he is extraordinarily eloquent about a crisis that has ruined millions of lives and altered the American landscape.

0590

BITTER HARVEST

BITTER HARVEST

Gordon Kahl and the Posse Comitatus: Murder in the Heartland

JAMES CORCORAN

VIKING

VIKING
Published by the Penguin Group
Viking Penguin, a division of Penguin Books USA Inc.,
40 West 23rd Street, New York, New York 10010, U.S.A.
Penguin Books Ltd, 27 Wrights Lane, London W8 5TZ, England
Penguin Books Australia Ltd, Ringwood, Victoria, Australia
Penguin Books Canada Ltd, 2801 John Street,
Markham, Ontario, Canada L3R 1B4
Penguin Books (N.Z.) Ltd, 182–190 Wairau Road,
Auckland 10, New Zealand

Penguin Books Ltd, Registered Offices:
Harmondsworth, Middlesex, England

First published in 1990 by Viking Penguin,
a division of Penguin Books USA Inc.

1 3 5 7 9 10 8 6 4 2

Page one of photograph insert:
top and inset—Bruce Crummy/Fargo *Forum*,
bottom—Colburn Hvidston III/Fargo *Forum*;
page five: top—Bruce Crummy/Fargo *Forum*;
page eight: Dave Wallis/Fargo *Forum*;
all other photos, Wide World Photos.

LIBRARY OF CONGRESS CATALOGING IN PUBLICATION DATA
Corcoran, James.
Bitter Harvest / James Corcoran.
p.   cm.
ISBN 0-670-81561-6
I. Title.
PS3553.06445M8   1990
813'.54—dc20   89-40311

Printed in the United States of America
Set in Primer

90. 5 - 242

To my parents,
Kenneth and Brenda,
with a special thanks to
my teachers, Maggie,
Bev, and Jonathan

Acknowledgments

The material in this book was derived from my own observations, interviews, and initial stories on the subject while working as a reporter for *The Forum* of Fargo-Moorhead, as well as the review of thousands of pages of court documents and trial transcripts, official law enforcement reports, confidential FBI and U.S. Marshal investigative reports, news stories, books, and research papers.

I am most grateful to Lois Muir, Shauna Faul, and Joan Kahl, who, without exception, answered the most painful of questions. And to Bradley Kapp, Darrell Graf, Paul Benson, Rodney Webb, Lynn Crooks, Richard Blay, Irv Nodland, Warren Sogard, Ralph Vinje, Jonathan Garaas, and the many other individuals involved on both sides of this tragedy, I offer thanks for the time and assistance provided me. I am also deeply indebted to Daniel Levitas, the former research director for Prairiefire Rural Action and now with the Center for Democratic Renewal; Leonard Zeskind, research director for the CDR; and Sarah Vogel, North Dakota's commissioner of agriculture. Their expertise helped me to better understand the crisis facing rural America and the danger posed by the right-wing extremist organizations. I also want to thank Kevin Rafferty, who provided me with taped Identity sermons that proved invaluable.

This book also could not have been written without the aid, comfort, and support of my family, friends, and colleagues: Mike Olson, Kevin Carvell, Andrea Halgrimson, Jim Neumann, Steve Singer, Eve Stern, Lucinda Ballantyne, Mike Mahlum, Becky Jones, Lisa Mullins, and Vaughn Sills. I also wish to extend a most heartfelt thanks to Gail Ross, who is both my agent and friend. And last, but far from least, thanks to Nan Graham and Kathryn Harrison for their patience, support, and deft editorial judgment.

Contents

BITTER HARVEST

Prologue

The shooting stopped.

Bradley Kapp knelt on the wet, cool ground, his head bowed slightly as if in prayer. He pressed his left hand hard against the wound in his forehead, partly to ease the intense pain, partly to stem the flow of blood that filled his left eye and blurred his vision. Finally, the silence, like a hard slap to the face, jarred Kapp to his senses. He lifted his head and, with his one good eye, peered over the edge of the ditch onto the narrow, blacktop country road. There was no movement revealed by the fast-fading light of day. There was no sound that disturbed the still February air.

Where did everyone go? he asked himself, bewildered.

Kapp's shotgun rested against his legs. It was empty. He groped in the right-hand pocket of his windbreaker for shells, but his hand wasn't working properly. He couldn't get a grip on the shells. Kapp pulled his right hand out of his pocket. "Jesus Christ," he muttered out loud.

His trigger finger was hanging from his hand by a sliver of skin. He could see the white, jagged bone. And blood, a lot of blood. Kapp held what remained of his index finger between his middle and ring fingers. He tried to comfort himself. "Maybe the doctor can sew it back on."

Kapp again looked to see if there was anyone moving around on the road. He had been one of six; six cops to arrest one sixty-three-year-old dirt farmer who had refused to obey the terms of his probation and pay his damn taxes. Where was everybody?

Twenty yards away a pair of eyes fixed on Kapp. They gazed steadily at him and locked onto Kapp's one good eye. Kapp froze. He had the answer to his question.

We lost, Kapp thought. Everyone else is dead. I'm the only one left.

The eyes studied Kapp for what seemed like hours, but were only seconds. Evidently having determined that Kapp was no longer a threat, the eyes turned their attention northward.

Kapp knew what he had to do. Run. Fast.

That wouldn't be easy. Not blessed with sprinter's speed, the twenty-six-year-old Kapp had to move 210 pounds that were unevenly distributed over a five-foot ten-inch frame.

Run, his mind ordered.

Kapp shook off his pain. He struggled to his feet and turned. His first couple of strides were awkward. His cowboy boots spun out from under him on the soggy, lumpy terrain, and he stumbled forward. His eye focused on the gentle rise of Cheese Plant Hill, three hundred yards to the south. On the other side of the hill, which was little more than a speed bump on the prairie, was the town of Medina and help.

Zigzag, he told himself. Zigzag.

The maneuver wasn't something Kapp had been taught at the North Dakota Law Enforcement Academy. Nor was it something he learned during his year as police chief of Streeter, or in his two years as a deputy with the Stutsman County sheriff's office. He learned it from a TV cop show.

Zigzag, zigzag. He didn't want to die from a bullet in the back in a drainage ditch in the middle of the North Dakota prairie. He wanted to live. He wanted to see and hold Shelly, his high school sweetheart and wife of nine years. And there was Amanda, their eight-year-old daughter. She would get moody and sick when he was gone for only a couple days on a hunting trip. What would happen to her if he were no longer around? Who would watch her play baseball and be on hand to assure her that the boys were just jealous of her ability when they told her she wasn't good enough to play?

Zigzag, zigzag.

On the road, the pair of eyes returned and watched Kapp snake his way through the ditch. The left eye closed slowly. The right eye looked down the sights of a Ruger mini-14 rifle, the civilian version of the U.S. Army's M-16, and took aim at the large, white sheriff's badge insignia that stood out on the back of Kapp's black windbreaker like a huge bull's-eye. It would be an easy shot, just like target practice.

Especially for a man like Gordon Kahl, who, friends claimed, could shoot a duck out of flight with a .22-caliber rifle. No mean feat.

Kahl didn't look like a killer. Rather, he looked like someone's grandfather, which he was five times over. On the outside there was little that was distinctive about Kahl. He was of average height, five feet seven inches tall, and his 160 pounds were beginning to settle into a paunch. His receding hair was gray and cropped short. His nose was a bit large for his face, and his ears flared out from the sides of his head.

But inside Gordon Kahl, an ideological fire raged. Kahl was a Believer. He believed that the government, manipulated by the Jews through the Internal Revenue Service, the federal courts, and the Federal Reserve Board, with the support of minorities, communists, and eastern banking interests, had conspired to take from him and his fellow believers their farms, their land, and their way of life.

The man he watched stagger through the ditch was a *Shabbas goy,* an agent doing the dirty work of his enemies. But to Kahl, the man was more than a Christian hired to do the menial tasks Jews were forbidden to perform on the Holy Day of the Sabbath. He was an agent hired to kill Kahl, his wife, Kahl's son, and three of his friends. That man didn't deserve to live. He deserved to be sent down that broad road that ends at the Lake of Fire.

Kahl steadied his aim.

Maybe it was too easy a shot. Kahl lowered his rifle, but continued to follow Kapp's movements. Was he stopping? Was he turning around to shoot? Kahl again raised his rifle and his right eye took its bead on Kapp. No, the man had just stumbled. Once more the rifle was lowered and the pair of eyes watched until Kapp crested the hill.

Kapp was nearly out of breath when he reached the top of the hill. His legs were weak and he could barely keep his balance. But he was alive. He had made it. Several hundred feet in front of him, Kapp saw Darrell Graf, Medina's chief of police, standing next to his cruiser with a member of the town's volunteer ambulance service. Kapp waved for them to come up the hill. Within the minute it took Graf and the volunteer to reach him, Kapp's fear had turned into vengeance.

"Go down there and kill those motherfuckers!" Kapp screamed at Graf, his boyish, round face contorted by the mix of anger and pain. "Look at what they did to my hand."

Graf looked at Kapp's right hand. He winced. A shudder raced through Graf's body, and straightened him up. The trigger finger on Kapp's hand was gone.

Graf waved the ambulance crew, waiting at the foot of the hill, to come up. What about everyone else? Graf thought to himself. The ambulance crew arrived and Kapp climbed into the back of the ambulance to be taken to the clinic in town.

1

A Gathering Storm

That Sunday, the thirteenth of February 1983, had been a good day for North Dakota, a land where winter is harsh.

The sky, a brilliant, clear blue, seemed to stretch without limit over the vast expanse of empty, snow-dusted fields. The southwest wind was gentle to the skin, not biting. The sun warmed the rich, fertile soil, and the state's 686,000 inhabitants, with record-setting temperatures of fifty degrees. It felt warm. The air was fresh, clean, and invigorating. It was the perfect tonic for the cabin fever, brought on by months of the shortest, most colorless, bitter cold winter days in America. Here, at the geographical center of the North American continent (a stone monument that marks the exact spot is located inside its borders at Rugby), and the most northern of the Plains states, it gets so cold that undertakers place the dead in unheated concrete buildings at local cemeteries to await burial in the spring, after the ground thaws.

But on that Sunday it was spring, if only for a day. It was the kind of day that served as an exclamation point for national studies that rated North Dakota first among states in quality of life, and one of the least stressful places to live in the United States. Those study findings are a source of pride for North Dakotans, who feel they are often overlooked, or worse, ignored, by the rest of the country except when serving as the butt for a national joke. Once, two disc jockeys in Washington, D.C., suggested that the state was a figment of South Dakota's imagination and asked their listeners to provide proof the state existed.

In the nation's mind, Alaska is the last frontier, Iowa is the site of the first presidential caucus, and Montana is the country's link to its romantic past, the Old West. And North Dakota . . . well, it's somewhere "out there." A bleak and barren land buffeted by blizzards, floods, droughts, tornadoes, and hailstorms, seasonal tantrums that strike randomly, but with equally lethal and destructive results. A windswept land that is cold, dull, boring, and lonesome. A land, writes native son Eric Sevareid, that is a "large rectangular blank spot in the nation's mind."

Of course, that isn't a view shared by most North Dakotans, who refer to their home as the Peace Garden State and consider it the nation's best-kept secret. Not that North Dakotans don't enjoy a good joke, even if it's at their own expense. Anyone driving along either of the state's two interstate highways can see billboards that display prairie landscapes and inform the motorist the "North Dakota Mountain Removal Project completed," or suggest that the vehicle's occupants "Stay in North Dakota. Custer was healthy when he left." Or, a person can purchase a T-shirt or poster that bears an image of the state tree—a telephone pole—or the state bird, a mosquito.

But to those people who come to the land, endure nature's punishments, and stay—at first it was mostly Scandinavian and German-Russian immigrants whose egalitarian, pragmatic character and rock-ribbed, conservative faith was well suited to meet challenges—North Dakota is a tranquil land.

It is a quiet, wholesome place, uncorrupted by crime, pollution, or other big-city ills. It is a place where people, while driving along the highway, pass friends, neighbors, and acquaintances, not strangers; where children attend the same elementary and high schools their parents attended and, in all likelihood, are taught by some of the same teachers; where a farmer, if felled by illness, will have his crop planted, cared for, and harvested by neighbors. It is a place where most people lead quiet lives—they go to work in the morning, have sit-down suppers at the dining room table at night, and attend church on Sunday—and take seriously their civic duties: the state's citizens consistently rank at, or near, the top in voter turnout during presidential elections and its sons have the highest rate of compliance with the draft.

The citizens of North Dakota hold fast to small-town values that reflect much of what was good about America: common sense, fairness, enterprise, hard work, loyalty, friendship, and patriotism, and are intolerant, writes Sevareid, ". . . of snobbery, of callousness, of crookedness, of men who kicked other men around."

For those who come, endure, and stay, North Dakota is a land of bounty. A lush prairie garden that produces more wheat, rye, barley, sunflowers, honey, and flax than any other state in the union, as well as a good share of the nation's soybeans and sugar beets. Nor is farming the only successful enterprise. In western North Dakota, where farming is more of a gamble because of the irratic rainfall, ranchers raise cattle, and corporate America exploits the state's plentiful oil, coal, and natural gas resources.

In essence, North Dakota seems to be the kind of land, populated by the kind of people, Norman Rockwell captured on canvas countless times: life as it should be, peaceful and bucolic.

On that Sunday, however, the thirteenth of February 1983, not all was as Norman Rockwell would have painted it. Something terrible, and terribly important, was taking place. Not only in North Dakota, but throughout the agrarian midsection of the country known as the American Heartland. Seeds of desperation, mistrust, anger, and hatred had been nurtured by low crop prices, high interest rates, foreclosures, and bankruptcies and were beginning to sprout like weeds throughout the region, threatening to choke off and kill a way of life.

Hard times had hit the Heartland. They hit with a punch that was nearly as powerful as the one delivered to the region in the 1930s, when years of drought, strong winds, and sky-darkening hordes of grasshoppers turned the country's breadbasket into a dust bowl. Only this time, the rains had come, and each year gave life to fields of wheat, corn, soybean, and beet crops that seemed more lush and abundant than the crops harvested the previous year. Grain elevators and silos overflowed. Farmers were forced to store the excess bushels of wheat and corn on the ground.

The world was hungry, but nobody wanted what they had to sell, at least not at a price that would keep the tractors in the fields, pay the taxes on the land, and cover the loan payments to the bank. What farmers had once counted a blessing—a bountiful harvest—had now become a curse.

And, it was a curse that was as destructive and devastating as any disaster wrought by the powerful, incomprehensible, and irrational forces of nature.

Few, if any, voices had predicted such a state of affairs ten years earlier, when, in the mid-seventies, the government urged a change in farm policy. After the stock market crash of 1929, and the drought of the 1930s, farm production had been targeted mainly for domestic markets. In the 1970s, however, a world food crisis and the resulting foreign demand for U.S. corn, wheat, and soybeans sent crop prices soaring. Plant fencerow-to-fencerow, Secretary of Agriculture Earl Butz urged the farmers. The world was a hungry place, and Butz and others in the government envisioned America becoming the farmer's market for the world.

Also a period of high inflation when land values increased threefold, the 1970s witnessed many farmers attain, on paper at least, millionaire status. In fact, by 1980 North Dakota had the second-highest number of millionaires per capita in the United States. And the new "landed gentry" were encouraged to use their paper wealth as equity for loans to pay for the modernization and expansion of their farming operations. "Get big or get out," said Butz. The idea to expand both crop production and farm size was strongly endorsed by private lenders, who had money to borrow at interest rates that would climb from 12 percent to 18 percent. But those interest rates shouldn't be a concern, said pundits and prophets, who preached that farmers could leverage their way out of debt.

Many farmers didn't need much encouragement. The 1970s

brought them wealth—each year new farm export records were set—and something more: the respect of their fellow countrymen. The rest of America had seen the farm programs of the previous forty years as little more than a public dole. Now, as exports of other goods shrank and imports increased, the farmers provided the country with much of its foreign exchange earnings. Not only were the farmers now paying their own way, they also were feeding the hungry, both here and abroad. Many farmers took Butz's advice. Some went on a buying binge. They bought new tractors and combines, irrigation equipment, and, of course, more land. They tried to get big in a hurry, and bought land by the section, 640 acres at a time. One, two, or three, however many sections were available.

Some expanded modestly, purchasing 80 acres to bring a son or daughter into the operation. The land didn't come cheap—some of it sold for more than $2,100 an acre—and often the price a farmer paid for the land didn't cost out, even at the inflated grain prices of the 1970s. Yet, it was still seen as a good investment. God no longer made fertile farmland, and times were only going to get better. And they did. In the decade of the 1970s, the country's farm exports nearly tripled and crop prices stayed high. The question posed to farmers was whether they could produce enough to meet the world's demand.

Then, in 1981, the bubble burst. The world fell into a recession. Interest rates climbed. The money that Third World nations had used to buy America's grains was now needed to service their debts to international banks. Crop prices tumbled and, more significantly, the value of land dropped, then plummeted. Once valued at $2,100 an acre, land prices fell to less than $700 an acre. This reduced land value resulted in reduced equity. Worse still, inflation continued to roar along, driving up the costs of everything needed to plant a crop in the spring and the money needed to cover those higher costs became harder to come by. Bankers, who had been so generous just a few short years earlier, grew cautious. They took a more realistic look at what a farmer's land and machinery were worth: they valued it with an eye to what it would bring at an auction sale.

What bankers saw in the early to mid-1980s, they didn't like. A survey by the American Bankers Association revealed that nearly one-third of the country's farms—many of them midsize family farms—were deteriorating seriously. Another one-third of the farms, while stable, could be pushed into serious problems by interest rate increases or weather setbacks. And the future didn't hold any hope for better times. A congressional report estimated that more than 1 million of the nation's 2.2 million farmers would be driven off the land by the year 2000. While some of that land would be purchased by neighboring farmers, much of it would be passed into the hands of huge agricultural-industrial combines. By the end of the century, predicted the report, fewer than 50,000 large, corporate farms would provide three-quarters of the country's food needs.

In the morning mail, delivered to rural mailboxes by circuit-riding postmen, farmers who were either behind on their payments or viewed by the bankers as a poor risk, received official-looking documents that notified them that their repayment schedules had been accelerated. They had ninety days—in some cases no more than thirty days—to make good on their outstanding loans. Farmers with unencumbered land had to put it up as additional collateral to cover their debts. Even the family homestead, which had been inherited free and clear, was not safe. Those without land had to put up their machinery. Liens were placed against living and operating expenses, and bank accounts were frozen. In some cases, farmers didn't discover their accounts had been frozen until they entered the bank and found that their personal checks were no longer honored. Where, in the past, their handshakes were good enough to seal a loan agreement, farmers were now required to get the bank to cosign checks for the purchase of seed, fertilizer, and even food.

Farmers unable to satisfy their lenders were forced to quit: to sell off their land, their machinery, their home. Those who refused to quit were torn from their corn, soybean, and wheat fields through foreclosure and bankruptcy proceedings.

Not all left the land quietly. In fact, many farmers appealed the foreclosures. Couldn't the private and government lenders see that farmers had done everything those very same people had asked of the farmers just ten years earlier? That farmers were unable to meet their payments because of situations outside their control? Couldn't they see the impact their decisions had on rural America? That the forced sales of farm assets placed land and machinery on already weak farm markets and made them weaker still? Couldn't the lenders see that the foreclosures and bankruptcies robbed small towns of residents, retail sales, and public services? In desperation the farmers argued for a temporary moratorium on the foreclosures and repossessions, just a little extra time so that when the economy turned around, as the federal government insisted it would, they would still be on the land and could once again become productive members of society.

Most often, the answer to those questions was no. In nearly all cases, the appeals were heard by the same people who made the initial decision to foreclose, and in nearly all the cases, the appeals were denied. These appeal proceedings ended with the farmer losing more than his livelihood. Land doesn't only serve as a farmer's collateral for operational loans, the ability to buy the seed, fertilizer, and chemicals to plant his fields—land is a farmer's identity. It is his connection to God; it is his religion, his nationality, his family's heritage, and his legacy to his children. Land is a farmer's way of life, and in the early 1980s he was losing it. Like the people he replaced on the land—the American Indian—the farmer became a modern exile, forced to migrate to strange cities and states in search of a new life.

The sharp report of the auctioneer's gavel echoed across the prairie. It served as the death knell to a way of life.

The sale lasted until nightfall when Roger Drevlow retreated to the solitude of his barn. "I avoided people all day. I knew I couldn't talk without falling apart. It is just like a part of me died. I went walking through the barn. It was almost eerie. It was empty. I thought, 'It doesn't seem like a barn anymore,' " Drevlow remembered.

The barn was part of the dream Roger and Joanne Drevlow held of owning their own farm. It was a dream that had room for an apple orchard and raspberry bushes, a cornfield to walk through for relaxation, and a clean, freshly painted barn that housed a prized dairy herd. It was a dream of nurturing a lifestyle the couple could bequeath to their children. "Ever since I was a kid I dreamt of owning my own farm and of raising my family in that kind of environment. I thought it was a very noble profession," said the thirty-two-year-old Drevlow.

But each year of bad weather, low prices, and high interest rates drained a bit more life from the dream until on September 20, 1984, ten miles southwest of Maddock, North Dakota, the Drevlows' equipment and livestock were auctioned.

"It was a terrible sale. When I watched them sell the lariat and nose pliers—you may think I'm crazy, but to see those things go affected me more than the big machinery," recalled Drevlow. "There is this kind of feeling this really isn't happening. This is a bad dream. But toward the end of the day you had to let it sink in that it is over. That finally you have to say good-bye."

The dream was born on a small, 40-acre farm near Ada, Minnesota. A Lutheran minister, Drevlow's father enjoyed working the land and instilled in his son a similar love. "To walk through the cornfields was just the best form of relaxation there was for my father," said Drevlow.

Upon graduation from high school, Drevlow attended the University of Minnesota at Crookston, where he majored in animal science. There, he also married Joanne, whom he had met at a 4-H Club function in Ada. (4-H—Head, Heart, Hands, and Health—is a national organization whose purpose is to help people living in rural areas, particularly children, develop practical skills and moral character.)

After college, the couple moved to Maddock where Drevlow was employed by the Grain Terminal Association Elevator. In 1977, the opportunity to realize the dream of owning their own farm presented itself in the form of a 200-acre farm that was for sale. The couple jumped at it. But their foray into farming brings to mind the words of a John Prine song: "If it wasn't for bad luck, I'd have no luck at all. Gloom, despair and agony on me."

In their first year of operation the Drevlows suffered through a drought, and their entire crop totaled 160 small bales of hay. The next year, 1978, brought a slight improvement, but a December fire destroyed the couple's hog operation. In 1979, they expanded their dairy herd in an attempt to offset the earlier losses and rented an additional 140 acres of cropland. A hailstorm wiped out the crop, and later in the year their house, along with all their belongings, burned to the ground. They rebuilt with insurance money and the help of their neighbors. But now, farm prices tumbled and interest rates on operating loans skyrocketed. The couple was spending $15 to produce 100 pounds of milk that would only return to them $12.

The couple tried to tap into the farm subsidy pipeline, but found that the programs were geared more toward the large producers than the family-size operation. One farm program, for example, required that he reduce his dairy herd from seventy cows to twenty-five, which would have been akin to economic suicide.

By that time, however, it didn't much matter.

"In the last two years we were simply surviving. You do what you do to keep the cows alive, to survive. But that isn't living," said Drevlow.

The couple decided to quit. They were more than $200,000 in debt. After the sale, Drevlow moved his family to Highland, Wisconsin, where he took a job as manager of a dairy operation and Joanne returned to school. At times at his new job, Drevlow has walked out into the morning darkness to the barn, turned on the light and "for an instant" thought he was home. But he denied he harbors any dream of again owning his own farm. "I would love to if it was just me. But I would never subject my family to that kind of torment again. I have five children and a wife. They have to come first," he said.

He recalled how he watched his nine-year-old and twelve-year-old sons "do the jobs of men. While other kids in class had time to do other things, they [his sons] had to work. I never even took them into town for a basketball game because we had to work.

"They didn't grow up loving the farm like I did," he said.

Nor, he believed, would other farmers' children.

"The whole system is in trouble. The lending agencies don't know how to handle a situation like this because it has never been so bad," said Drevlow. "And the farmers can't stay out there with the prices the way they are, the interest rates the way they are.

"Our rural communities are going to die. There is no way to keep them alive."

At first, farmers like Roger Drevlow, faced with bankruptcy or foreclosure, could expect little sympathy or support for their views. Least of all from the choir of county farm agents, bankers, and government officials, who sang the refrain that the downturn—it wasn't a crisis—was only weeding out the bad managers, ridding the bloated calf of excess fat.

It was true. Up to a point. Farmers who didn't have debt, and resisted the call to expand their operations and upgrade their machinery during the high inflation of the 1970s, or who were large enough to take advantage of the government's subsidy programs, or operated hobby farms and supplemented their incomes with Main Street jobs, survived. At first.

But with each new year the lists of auction ads and bankruptcy notices grew longer. They appeared daily, like obituaries, in the newspapers. The "bad manager" refrain grew fainter. The farm situation—still not named a crisis—was no longer a matter of survival of the fittest, but of imminent extinction. Farmers who for years had run profitable operations, like their fathers and grandfathers before them, now found their account sheets covered with ink as red as the paint on their barns. No matter how many times a "successful" farmer sat at his kitchen table and ran the numbers through his calculator, or sat in a plush, overstuffed chair and ran the numbers by his banker, they didn't change. He spent more money to plant, fertilize, and harvest the food than he got for it at market. He had become one of the bad managers.

In the early 1980s, the depressed farm situation—*not* crisis— was never long outside of local talk. It had replaced the weather as the number one topic of conversation at the counters and tables of the Prairie Inn, the Galaxy Steakhouse, English's Café and a host of other small-town restaurants where the sons and daughters, grandsons and granddaughters of Scandinavian and German-Russian immigrants met worriedly over cups of weak coffee and pieces of homemade pie.

They had reason to be concerned. Farming is the cornerstone of an industry that provides some 20 million jobs for Americans. When the farmer doesn't have money, neither does the tractor builder, the seed producer, the petrochemical company; nor does the grocery store owner, the implement dealer or the lumberyard operator. For every ten farmers who left the land, a business in the small towns—that existed almost solely to serve the farmers—closed its doors and boarded shut its windows. Each farmer and shopkeeper who left took away part of the tax base needed to support a school and some of the children needed to attend it. The school served as the social center for the community, with its sporting events, class plays, band concerts, and PTA meetings. It gave a community its hometown feel, its quaintness. When it closed, the town started to die. It wasn't a sudden death, like a wheat crop battered into the ground by golfball-size hail. Instead, it was a slow, painful, withering death. Each year a bit more life was drained—the hardware store, the post office, the grain elevator, the tavern. Finally, the town, its residents gone, disappeared. All that remained were a few weathered gray buildings that stared blankly at each other and awaited reclamation by the one unwavering constant: the prairie.

During those conversations, which sometimes moved from the coffee shop to a nearby bar for something a bit more consoling to drink, the question always was raised: Who was to blame?

The answers, sometimes simple, sometimes complex, included plenty of villains—some imagined, others quite real—not the least of which was the federal government. It was the federal government that adopted subsidy programs that favored corporate farming and abandoned family farm agriculture; that pursued a policy of import expansion, which increased production, lowered income, and was based on the assumption that what the farmers lost in income, they would make up in volume. It was the federal government that maintained a huge deficit which forced fierce competition for credit. And it was the federal government, with the aid of the Federal Reserve Board, that was determined to kill inflation by adopting policies that kept money tight and interest rates high.

But the federal government wasn't the only villain. There was the growing list of former customers—China, India, Brazil, and a host of other nations—now more self-sufficient in food production. There was the Third World, too deep in debt to purchase significant amounts of grain. And, there were the American farmers who had become too efficient at growing food.

Unable to make a living, the farmers made jokes. They told of the farmer who won a $1-million lottery and, when asked what he was going to do with the money, said he would farm until it was gone. And what about the farmer who was arrested on charges of child abuse after he left the farm to his son. When the jokes stopped being funny, some farmers quit. The people who prided themselves on being the last to give up, gave up.

Other farmers dug in their heels, hunkered down, and stayed in the fields. They did what they knew how to do: they worked sixteen-hour days, seven days a week, believing the work ethic would help them weather the storm. They took second jobs in town, if they could find them. Their wives and their children took jobs. They bagged groceries, drove school buses, moved furniture, and painted houses. They scratched and clawed to save a way of life that placed them below the poverty line. They sold what they could to raise money, even a daughter's bicycle. Some went so far as to take the most degrading of steps: they accepted food baskets from private charities, applied for government food stamps, and learned to live with shame. The people who fed the world couldn't feed their own families.

In church basements, where in the past they had gathered with friends and neighbors for wedding receptions, socials, and bingo games, some farmers broke with the rural tradition of silent stoicism and talked about personal and financial problems with counselors, social workers, and psychologists. They talked with journalists and legislators, anyone who would listen. When talk wasn't enough to make people listen, they swallowed hard, set aside their pride and begged for legal and government help to save their land.

In the past, such groveling would have been unheard of. Farmers would have said to hell with the policymakers and politicians and taken matters into their own hands, just as North Dakota farmers had done at the turn of the twentieth century. After it was granted statehood in 1889, North Dakota's government and economy was largely controlled by railroad barons, grain buyers, and bankers, headquartered in Minneapolis–St. Paul, and farther east in Chicago, who viewed the state as a resource to be exploited, relegating the farmers to little more than serfdom. The railroads set high, discriminatory freight rates to transport crops to markets which were controlled and manipulated by large grain elevators that offered low, fixed prices, forcing the farmers to operate the next year on credit extended by the bankers. By 1915, tired of the exploitation, farmers organized under the banner of the Nonpartisan League, a party strongly influenced by the socialist movement. A year later, voters swept into office a slate of league candidates who ran against "Big Biz," bankers, and other eastern interests. The league governed the state for nearly seven years, and left as its legacy two thriving institutions: the Bank of North Dakota, which served as the depository for all state and local government funds and offered low-cost rural and business loans, and the State Mill and Elevator Association, which created a system of state-owned elevators, flour mills, and warehouses. During its time in office, the NPL also revamped the state's hail crop insurance, toughened the state's grain-grading and inspection laws, and enacted statutes aimed at reducing freight rates. According to journalist John Gunther, many of the league's reforms served as a foundation for President Franklin Roosevelt's New Deal. "The ever normal granary is an extension of [the] . . . idea for a state elevator; the Federal Crop Insurance Law embodies the League's ideas on hail insurance; the Federal Deposit Insurance Corporation and the Federal Housing Administration applied on the national level what had already been worked out locally in North Dakota," wrote Gunther in his book *Inside U.S.A.*

In the early 1930s, farmer activism again was stirred by a ten-year-long farm depression that forced thousands of people off the land. In May of 1932, farmers gathered in Des Moines, Iowa, and formed the Farm Holiday Association, which pledged not to sell any agricultural products below the cost of production, and to take whatever action was necessary, including violence, to stop foreclosures and evictions. Those were not idle words. In February of 1933, one thousand farmers forcibly stopped a sheriff's sale at a farm near Finley, North Dakota. A similar demonstration of force took place two weeks later at a farm outside Minot, North Dakota. Farmers also flexed their political muscle. More than eighty farmers were elected to the 1933 North Dakota legislature. In rapid succession, the legislature enacted laws that declared an embargo on the shipment of wheat out-of-state, placed a moratorium on foreclosures and evictions, and allowed persons foreclosed upon to remain in possession of their homes or farms for at least two years and to keep all profits earned during that period. Although some of the reforms, such as the embargo and right of redemption laws, were later declared unconstitutional by both the state and U.S. supreme courts, the lengthy process needed to settle the legal questions provided many farmers with the necessary time to save their land. In fact, between 1933 and 1940, the number of farms in North Dakota actually increased by nearly 10 percent from 78,000 to 85,600. After 1940, however, the number of farms in the state started its steady decline.

Like their predecessors, farmers in the late 1970s and early 1980s organized to press their demands. The American Agricultural Movement, and later Groundswell, called for higher commodity prices, guaranteed loans for spring planting, and long-term debt restructuring. They also demanded a moratorium on farm, home, and small business foreclosures as a way to stop the hemorrhaging that was bleeding the rural economy dry. Buoyed by the success of those before them, farm leaders expressed optimism. In 1978,

Elmo Olson, head of the North Dakota chapter of the AAM, told a reporter for *The Forum* of Fargo-Moorhead that he was certain the government would take notice and bring farm prices in line with production costs. But except for some headline-grabbing farm rallies, a short-lived blockade of Canadian beef shipments into the United States, and a tractorcade on Washington, D.C., that snarled the capital's traffic for a few days, the efforts proved futile. The hard truth was that unlike their predecessors, the farmers didn't have the political clout. As early as 1960, nearly 20 million people lived on farms. But twenty years later, that number had been reduced by 80 percent, and the farm vote comprised less than 4 percent of the electorate. The optimism once held by farm leaders turned to bitterness. "People my age refer to the Depression as the Dirty '30s," the sixty-six-year-old Olson told *The Forum*. "But the '30s is going to be a picnic compared to what it could be. I believe we could see tougher times yet."

He was right, times did get tougher.

By 1983, North Dakota alone was losing three farmers a day, as its farm debt nearly doubled from $2.5 billion to $4.9 billion, and the interest paid on that debt tripled to $555 million. Foreclosure or debt reduction accounted for nearly 40 percent of all land sales. Other states in the farm belt were harder hit, losing ten, twelve, up to fifteen farmers a day and a bank a month. The farm debt for the nation exceeded $215 billion, a quarter of that deemed uncollectable. And by 1987, reported the Center on Budget and Policy Priorities, nearly 17 percent of rural Americans lived below the poverty line, a rate that was nearly as high as the 18.5 percent in the inner cities.

The auctioneer's gavel continued to fall. Again. And again. And again.

The unwillingness, or inability, of politicians, bankers, and economists to address the farm crisis stirred others to action. Local and state governments, private charities, church-sponsored organizations, and individuals tried to ease the farmers' sense of isolation and offer a flicker of hope. Groups such as Prairiefire Rural Action and the Iowa Interchurch Forum, both based in Des Moines, and

FACTS, a Manhattan, Kansas–based farm advocacy group, established food pantries, and set up twenty-four-hour crisis hot lines to provide financial and psychological counseling; and attorneys like Bismarck, North Dakota's Sarah Vogel offered legal help. But, like the light of fireflies that dart across the prairie night, the hope they provided was only glancing. The scope of the problem was too large, the budgets too tight, and the number of trained personnel too few. Even when the farmers won battles to save their land, the victories, in most cases, proved bittersweet.

Sarah Vogel returned to North Dakota in 1981, fourteen years after she had left the state to study law at New York University in New York City. Immediately upon graduation from law school, Vogel accepted the position of assistant counsel of the New York City Department of Consumer Affairs, under Bess Myerson. She later became the legal advisor for consumer issues at Manufacturers Hanover Trust Company, and then, in 1976, accepted a job in Washington, D.C., with the Federal Trade Commission, where she was responsible for managing the Equal Credit Opportunity Act program and supervising civil rights enforcement under the program. But now, a divorced mother of one, Vogel wanted to come home. She wanted a more leisurely lifestyle and a more healthy environment in which to raise her son, Andrew. Vogel bought a house that had a picture window overlooking the Missouri River, and started her own practice.

One of Vogel's first cases involved a farmer's appeal of a foreclosure by the federal government's Farmers Home Administration. In banking circles, the FmHA is known as the lender of last resort. It's where farmers go when they've been denied credit everywhere else. As in the private sector, the only appeal a farmer could make was to the FmHA itself, and the appeal was often heard by the same person who made the decision to foreclose. Vogel lost the appeal. Nevertheless, another farmer requested her help. And another, and another. Like her first case, Vogel lost most of those appeals, too. But she had fought hard for her clients and started to gain a reputation as an advocate for the farmers, a reputation that extended beyond North Dakota's borders. Farmers in Minnesota, Iowa, Nebraska, Kansas, and Texas called her for help, and she went to their aid. She didn't work for free. However, since most of her clients were unable to pay her, in return for her services they offered tomatoes, corn, and other produce. One farmer even proffered $1,500 worth of bull sperm. Unfortunately, such compensation wasn't accepted by the telephone company, which cut off her service for nonpayment, or the bank, which, after three notices of foreclosure, readily accepted the "voluntary" conveyance of her dream home along the Missouri River.

Still, Vogel refused to quit. There was, she said, "just too much suffering going on out there," and her sense of fair play and decency was offended by FmHA practices that included freezing a farmer's income, seizing a farmer's machinery, and liquidating a farmer's property without prior notice or due process.

Vogel's father, Robert, a former state supreme court justice, provided her with an office in his Grand Forks law firm and encouraged her to continue her fight. When still in Washington, D.C., one of the last acts Vogel took before she left the Federal Trade Commission was to prepare a report that urged legal action against the FmHA's lending practices. No action was taken.

In March of 1983, Vogel took the action she had recommended three years earlier, and filed a class-action lawsuit against the FmHA on behalf of nine North Dakota farmers. The lawsuit asked the federal court to order the FmHA to implement a 1978 law that allowed the agency's state directors to hold off foreclosures when farmers were unable to meet loan payments due to circumstances outside their control. The lawsuit also demanded that the FmHA release lien money for minimum living and farm operational expenses, and that the agency grant farmers due process in all portions of the appeal hearings, so that farmers could understand their rights and therefore exercise them. On the day the lawsuit went to trial in September, it was expanded to include each of the FmHA's 245,000 customers in forty-five states.

More than one year later, federal judge Bruce M. Van Sickle of Bismarck ordered the FmHA to comply basically with each of the

points outlined in Vogel's lawsuit. The farmers had won and their
rights under the law and constitution would be protected. Unfortunately the continued deterioration of the farm economy weakened
the ruling's significance. Prices were still too low, costs too high,
and there was no improvement in sight. The farmers' rights would
be protected, but unless they got paid for their crops, what it cost
to grow them, it would only be a matter of time before they'd drown
in a sea of red ink. "The biggest disappointment is that when the
suit was filed, [U.S. Secretary of Agriculture John] Block said,
'Times will be better.' Now, they are saying things are worse,"
Vogel, who is now the agriculture commissioner for North Dakota,
told a reporter with the *Grand Forks Herald,* shortly after the court's
order was issued.

It seemed that no matter how hard the farmers worked, or prayed,
or fought, the hard times on the farm wouldn't go away. A deep
sense of hopelessness and failure settled over the Heartland. The
fabric of the rural community started to unravel. Crisis hot lines
were deluged with desperate calls as more and more farmers unleashed their anger and frustrations on their spouses and children,
sought refuge and solace in alcohol and drugs, and tried to escape
through divorce, suicide, and murder. Many incidents passed without notice and casualties to anger, frustration, and lost hope were
mourned quietly by only family members and a few friends. But,
as the crisis deepened in the 1980s, a few incidents were so sen-
sational that they grabbed attention throughout the region and, in
some cases, the country.

   In Chattanooga, Oklahoma, a fifty-four-year-old farm wife, despondent over the mounting debts on her family's 1,280-acre wheat
farm, climbed atop a barrel of burning trash and killed herself. In
Elk Point, South Dakota, thirty-eight-year-old Bruce Litchfield, a
Farmers Home Administration county supervisor, was informed of
new government regulations that might force him to foreclose on
many borrowers. A week later, Litchfield killed his wife, daughter,
and son, and then himself. In Ruthton, Minnesota, a forty-six-year-
old farmer and his eighteen-year-old son, who lost their 10-acre

dairy operation to foreclosure, ambushed and killed two bank officers. The farmer later committed suicide and his son was found guilty of murder. In Hills, Iowa, sixty-four-year-old Dale Burr, more than $800,000 in debt, killed his wife, banker, and a neighbor, before he turned his shotgun on himself.

In a region not known for violence, each outburst sent a tremor through the Middle West, and left many of its residents shocked. The violence, however, came as little surprise to the individuals who listened daily to the desperation in the voices of people who called the crisis hot lines. "A lot of people are on the edge, and it doesn't take much to push them over," said Daniel Levitas, a spokesman for Prairiefire, a Des Moines–based farm advocacy group. "There are thousands of Dale Burrs out here."

There also was a growing number of farmers like Gordon Kahl.

2

Sowers of Hate

In January of 1983, North Dakota farmer Gordon Kahl traveled to Springfield, Colorado. There, Kahl joined more than 250 other farmers at a meeting to protest the foreclosure sale of a farm owned by Jerry Wright, a leader in the American Agriculture Movement.

Although he wasn't a member of the AAM, Kahl went to Springfield for the same reasons he earlier had gone to Halstead, Kansas; Little Eagle, South Dakota; Mena, Arkansas; Crane, Texas; Benton, Tennessee, and Boulder, Colorado. He went to Springfield to show support for his angry and frustrated farm cousins, and to deliver a message.

It wasn't a message Kahl was asked to give from the podium. Instead, it was one he delivered to individual farmers as he worked the crowd. It was a message he carried to other AAM-sponsored farm protests and rallies, and outlined in interviews with news reporters.

What Kahl had to say was simple: The farmers had done no wrong, but were victims. The victims of a Jewish-led, communist-supported conspiracy that had infiltrated the U.S. government, the judicial system and law enforcement, and was bent on destroying the Christian Republic that had been established by the Founding Fathers. Kahl told of a speech allegedly given by Benjamin Franklin at the Constitutional Convention in 1787. In that speech, said Kahl, Franklin warned against granting citizenship to Jews because wherever they settled, the Jews created a state within a state and tried to strangle that nation to death financially. "If you do not exclude them, in less than two hundred years your descendants will be working in the fields to furnish the substance while the Jews will be in the counting house rubbing their hands. I warn you, gentlemen, if you do not exclude the Jews for all time, your children will curse you in your grave," Kahl quoted Franklin as saying.

"This has happened exactly as was predicted," Kahl told his listeners. "These enemies of Christ have taken their Jewish Communist manifesto and incorporated it into the statutory laws of our country, and have thrown our Constitution and our Christian Common Law—which is nothing other than the laws of God as set forth in the Scriptures—into the garbage can.

"We are a conquered and occupied nation; conquered and occupied by the Jews and their hundreds, maybe thousands, of front organizations doing their un-Godly work."

The front organizations, claimed Kahl, included the Internal Revenue Service, which collected the illegal income tax (Did you know the income tax is the second plank of the Communist manifesto?), and the Federal Reserve System, which placed the control of the country's money and credit into the hands of private bankers. Now, said Kahl, the conspirators were set to erase the last vestiges of independence and individualism in the nation . . . the farmer. They would rob the farmer of his land through manipulation of land values, grain prices, and credit, which would result in either bankruptcy or foreclosure. Once they controlled the land, they controlled the food supply. When they controlled the food supply, they controlled the people. It would then be a short step for them to reach their ultimate goal: the establishment of a one-world government.

Want proof? asked Kahl. Look no further than the billions of tax dollars given each year to Israel, and yet not one dollar can be found to help the farmer.

"If you've been paying tithes to the Synagogue of Satan, under the second plank of the Communist Manifesto to finance your own destruction, stop right now and tell Satan's tithing collectors, as I did many years ago, never again will I give aid and comfort to the enemies of Christ," said Kahl.

The next day in Springfield, the farmers tried to stop the sale of Wright's land by storming the steps of the county courthouse, and were turned back by tear gas and sheriff's deputies dressed in riot gear and armed with nightsticks and rifles.

Kahl, however, wasn't on hand to give aid and comfort to the protestors. He, along with his traveling companions, son Yorie and fellow North Dakota farmer Scott Faul, was well on his way home to North Dakota when the first tear gas canister was fired. Kahl had completed his work the previous night. The seeds had been sown, and only after they were nourished by more foreclosures and confrontations like the one in Springfield, would Kahl, or someone like him, return to reap the bitter harvest.

Kahl was a member of the Posse Comitatus, a right-wing extremist group that contended that the true intent of the country's founders was to establish a Christian Republic where the individual is sovereign and that has as its first duty to promote, safeguard, and protect the Christian faith.

"The government is nothing but an expansion of the Christian church . . . it was founded by a compact . . . known as the Articles of Confederation, Perpetual, which have their source in the Holy Bible. Since the Constitution was lifted from the Articles of Confederation, the source of the Constitution is the Bible," wrote William Potter Gale, a Posse leader in Mariposa, California.

In a democracy, contended the Posse, the majority was sovereign. And since the majority of people in the United States were nonproductive welfare recipients and idlers, the democratic form of government allowed those parasites to vote themselves the wealth generated by the productive minority. But in a republic, stated the Posse, the individual was sovereign and the government had no power to enact laws that "will loot and plunder the wealth produced by the sovereign individual."

The Posse encouraged people to reclaim their sovereignty by returning their driver's licenses, birth certificates, Social Security cards, and any other government-issued documents, contending they gave heed to "Jewish fables, and commandments of men, that turn from the truth."

The group, which takes its name from the Latin for "power of the county," traces its lineage to Old English Common Law, which stated that all power rested with the people and their duly elected Reave of the Shire. In its American form, that translated to mean there is no legitimate form of government beyond the county level, no higher law enforcement authority than the county sheriff. The people were sovereign, however, and should the sheriff fail to carry out the will of the county's citizens—or should he allow state and federal officials to come into the county and impose illegal laws, regulations, or other government controls—"he shall be removed by the Posse to the most populated intersection of streets in the township and at high noon be hung by the neck, the body remaining until sundown as an example to those who would subvert the law."

And the law, stated Posse doctrine, was set out by God and not some Jewish-influenced legislature. "There shall be no legislative body since God himself has already legislated the only laws necessary to our preservation and prosperity and he cannot be improved upon. The chief executive of this government, now and forever, is Yahweh, Yahshua, Jesus Christ," read the preamble of a Posse's government charter.

The Posse placed all power to interpret God's laws with common-law associations and Christian grand juries, composed of only white, Christian males. (Jews, minorities, and women have no legal standing in a Posse government.)

Because they believed the Constitution was derived from the Bible, and was given to the country's forefathers by God himself, Posse members fashioned themselves as constitutional purists, and held to strict interpretations of the document. The Posse, for example, believed the Second Amendment not only guaranteed a person's right to bear arms, including automatic weapons, but also granted an individual the right to carry those guns anywhere he wanted, whether it be into a grocery store, a doctor's office, or a church.

But the Posse's faith in the Constitution wasn't absolute. According to Posse theorists, all amendments ratified after the Bill of Rights were unconstitutional because they were endorsed and supported by illegal legislative bodies that were doing the bidding of a Jewish-led conspiracy. The Sixteenth Amendment, which allows the federal government to tax a personal income, was particularly onerous to Posse members because, as they see it, it plays into the hands of the conspirators. "Karl Marx . . . said that one of the things that will bring about the downfall of a nation is to impose a heavy progressive income tax on the working class of people," said Len Martin, the author of numerous Posse-related books and pamphlets.

The year 1913 was seen by the Posse as the time at which the conspirators tipped their hand to what they had in store for the rest of the country. Not only was the Sixteenth Amendment ratified then, but the Federal Reserve Act, which created the Federal Reserve System, also was passed.

"The year, 1913, was a good one for the Money Czars. The federal income tax gave them the right to steal from us; and the Federal Reserve Act gave them the right to create money with the stroke of a pen," stated one Posse tract.

Although 1913 was considered the year of the "Great Betrayal," it was not the only significant date in Posse conspiracy lore. Other red-letter dates include:

—1933's passage of the Gold Act, which prohibited private citizens from owning gold. To the Posse, only gold and silver coins were lawful money, and Federal Reserve notes, which they referred to as the Federal Fraud, were worthless.

—1945's creation of the United Nations, which the Posse believed would become the seat of government for the one-world conspirators.

—1954's desegregation of public schools, which the Posse contended was designed to encourage race-mixing.

The Posse also viewed the Korean and Vietnam wars as blatant attempts by the conspirators to get white American soldiers involved in drugs and sex with other races, which would lead to the destruction of the white race and Christianity.

The Posse was founded in 1969 in Portland, Oregon, by Henry L. Beach, a retired dry cleaner and one-time member of the Silver Shirts, a Nazi-inspired organization that was established in America after Hitler took power in Germany. The group existed in relative obscurity until 1975, when the Little Rock, Arkansas, office of the FBI was alerted to a possible assassination attempt against then vice-president Nelson Rockefeller, who was viewed by the Posse as one of the major "Money Czars."

A subsequent FBI probe uncovered seventy-eight Posse chapters in twenty-three states. Those states included Oregon, Washington, California, Texas, Colorado, Kansas, Wisconsin, North and South Dakota, Minnesota, Nebraska, and Virginia. Many of the chapters were similar to the one Kahl organized in North Dakota, where two or three dozen people met once or twice a month at the home or business of a member and discussed the evils of the Federal Reserve System and the income tax, and planned the formation of their own Posse-style county government.

But there were other, more elaborate, chapters.

In a placid corner of the northeastern woodlands of Wisconsin, along the banks of the Embarrass River, James Wickstrom, the self-proclaimed national director of counterinsurgency for the Posse Comitatus, established his Christian Identity ministry and the Constitutional Township of Tigerton Dells. The 570-acre compound— rimmed with signs that warned "Federal Agents Keep Out. Survivors will be prosecuted" and "Disturb me at your own peril"— was complete with a church, trailer park, and guerrilla warfare training ground. From his pulpit inside the Life Science Church, a one-time tavern, the forty-year-old Wickstrom preached his theology of Christian Identity, which blended the ideas of Adolf Hitler and apartheid, and urged his two hundred followers to store food, ammunition, and other supplies.

"These fools [the federal government] think we are a political organization, not realizing that we have declared a Holy War against them," Wickstrom told them.

For the Posse, secrecy was not only a virtue, but an obsession. As a result, the FBI could only guess the Posse's membership, which the bureau estimated at between twelve thousand and fifty thousand hard-core members with ten to twelve times that number of sympathizers.

"Generally speaking, the Posse appears to draw rural people . . . the movement does not appear to be declining . . . the movement will, in all likelihood, increase in certain sections of the country," the 1976 FBI report concluded.

One section of the country where it did increase was the Midwest. Like a vulture perched over a stray calf, the Posse saw the farm crisis as an opportunity to feed its hunger to create a white, Christian Republic.

It didn't take much for the Posse to incorporate the farm crisis into its crazy quilt of hate-filled theories, especially given the Federal Reserve's efforts to dampen the inflationary fires with a blanket of high interest rates. Men like Gordon Kahl and James Wickstrom jumped at the opportunity to convince farmers that the blame for their troubles rested with the Federal Reserve and the Jews. "The Jew-run banks and federal loan agencies are working hand-in-hand, foreclosing on thousands of farms right now in America. They are in essence, nationalizing farms for the Jews, as the farmer becomes a tenant slave on the land he once owned," wrote Wickstrom in his pamphlet *The American Farmer: 20th Century Slave.* "The farmers must prepare to defend their families and land with their lives, or surrender it all."

Kahl, Wickstrom, and others delivered their message wherever farmers gathered: grain elevators, feedlots, hardware stores, fields, implement dealers, churches, foreclosure sales and auctions. They delivered it on cassette tapes played in farmhouse kitchens, pickup trucks, and the cabs of combines. And on radio stations like WSM Clear Channel in Nashville, Tennessee, and KTTL-FM, a country music station in Dodge City, Kansas.

WSM was one of more than twenty-five stations that carried the syndicated show "America's Promise," which was produced and hosted by the late Sheldon Emry, who founded the Identity-steeped Lord's Covenant Church in Phoenix, Arizona. Emry, who also authored *Billions for Bankers, Debts for the People,* a pamphlet that claimed the Federal Reserve was the cause of all of America's economic problems, used the radio program to disseminate his beliefs that America was the new Promised Land, that white Christians were the true members of the House of Israel, and Jews and people of color were aliens, who threatened the racial, social, religious, and political order of the country.

And on KTTL, listeners were told by William Gale, a retired U.S. Army colonel and the author of a handbook on guerrilla warfare tactics for the Posse, that "Yes, we are going to cleanse our land. We're going to do it with a sword. And we're going to do it with violence.

"You're damn right I'm teaching violence. God said you're going to do it that way, and it's about time somebody is telling you to get violent, whitey," said Gale.

Gale also urged his listeners to "start making dossiers, names, addresses, phone numbers, car license numbers, on every damn Jew rabbi in this land, and every Anti-Defamation League leader or JDL leader in this land, and you better start doing it now. . . . You get these roadblock locations, where you can set up ambushes, and get it all working now."

Some Posse members heeded Gale's call to action.

In February of 1982, according to FBI documents, Posse arrest warrants were issued against a sheriff and his deputy in Johnson, Kansas. The two lawmen were told if they didn't appear before a Posse court for execution, a school would be blown up. School authorities dismissed classes early, the lawmen didn't show up, and the school remained standing. State officials also received more than a dozen notices of asseveration. A technical term, it was used by the Posse to announce that its members had severed their contractual relationship with the state. They had declared that they were no longer citizens of the United States.

A month later, Kansas farmer Wesley White sponsored a three-day counterinsurgency seminar, which both Wickstrom and Gale addressed, and where classes were offered on guerrilla warfare and survival tactics. Two months later White was charged with, and subsequently convicted of, illegally transporting explosives to Colorado.

Other Posse members, like former dairy farmer Roderick "Rick" Elliot of Brighton, Colorado, crisscrossed the Midwest and conducted "constitutional law seminars." Elliot advised farmers to file do-it-yourself lawsuits and offered—for a fee of $500—help in obtaining low-interest loans. At those seminars, which often drew crowds of between 40 and 250 people, Elliot told the farmers that all loans written after 1974 were invalid because the contracts violated the federal Truth-in-Lending Act and other consumer-related legislation. Elliot, who founded the National Agricultural Press Association (NAPA) and published the *Primrose and Cattlemen's Gazette,* advised his listeners to file multimillion-dollar "pro se" lawsuits against both the lender and the Federal Reserve. Such a lawsuit, said Elliot, would not only void the loan and earn the farmer millions of dollars in damages, but would also clog the courts and delay other foreclosures. He buttressed his claims with selected passages from the legal tomes of Title 15 of the U.S. Code, which he brandished before his audience like a minister waving the Bible at a revivalist meeting.

One farmer who accepted Elliot's advice was Monrad Berg of Starkweather, North Dakota. Since 1949, Berg farmed the land first owned by his parents. He taught Sunday school, was president of his Lutheran church congregation and served as vice-president of the state chapter of the National Farmers Organization. Berg didn't consider himself a radical. But in the early 1980s, he was deep in debt and just a few legal proceedings away from losing the farm he now shared with his son. With barely enough money to keep the farm operating, let alone pay for an attorney, Berg acted as his own lawyer. With Elliot's prepackaged "legal karate kit" in his hand, Berg entered the third-floor office of the clerk for the U.S. District Court in Fargo and filed a $12 million lawsuit against the

Federal Land Bank. As suggested by Elliot, Berg contended that the lender violated the truth-in-lending laws, and that the Federal Reserve, which set the interest rates, was unconstitutional. "I was brought up to believe . . . you owe a debt, you pay it. That is still my belief, [but] in the interest I have paid back, I have paid back what I borrowed," said the sixty-two-year-old Berg.

The federal judge, however, didn't see it that way and dismissed the lawsuit as being legally frivolous. In fact, *all* of the nearly one thousand "pro se" lawsuits filed throughout the country by desperate farmers have been dismissed on similar grounds.

Despite that track record, Elliot continued to draw hundreds of desperate farmers to his seminars. Even after 1986, when he was sentenced to eight years in prison for defrauding his supporters of more than $200,000 in a phony loan scheme, the Posse continued to encourage the use of do-it-yourself lawsuits. And farmers continued to file them.

The Posse also encouraged its members to use questionable legal tactics designed to get even with the government officials it viewed as its oppressors. One such tactic was the common-law lien, which Douglas Hart employed to fight what he called fifteen years of harassment by the Internal Revenue Service.

In June of 1982, he walked into the register-of-deeds offices in Cass and Richland counties and filed liens against the homes of the IRS director in North Dakota and two of his agents. The action, said Hart, fifty-seven, was an attempt to make the public aware of the illegal activities being conducted by the IRS, and to force the courts to uphold the U.S. Constitution.

According to Hart, the illegal activities included an IRS audit of his 1979 and 1980 income taxes, which resulted in Hart being assessed a $33,000 tax liability, and the government's refusal to let his challenge of the audit be heard at a jury trial, which the Posse contends is the right of every citizen no matter what is at issue.

"As a result, the liens are the only way I can fight them. I'm just trying to get them off my back," said Hart, a salesman and World War II veteran. "They have assessed me a tremendous amount of money and have threatened me with all kinds of stuff . . . including imprisonment. [But] I was born free, I'm going to die free and in between I'm going to live free.

"I'm going to nail these guys," he vowed. "They are gangsters."

But the only person who got nailed was Hart. To the muffled groans of more than sixty supporters who were in the courtroom, a federal judge issued an injunction prohibiting Hart—or any other tax protestors—from filing more fictitious liens. Hart, however, remained unruffled. "I will appeal it," he said. "The federal court has no jurisdiction. The whole thing is wrong."

What was really wrong was the increasing desperation that prompted a growing number of individuals to turn to extralegal procedures that challenged the legitimacy of established systems of justice.

In the 1970s and 1980s, the Posse Comitatus wasn't the only group that offered asylum for people dedicated to the ideas of racism and anti-Semitism, or saw in the suffering of the farmers an opportunity to enhance their image and swell their membership ranks.

In Washington, D.C., Willis Carto saw in the farm crisis the opportunity to form a new political party that would champion the causes and ideals of the Liberty Lobby, a racist and anti-Semitic organization he founded in 1957. In nearly every issue of *The Spotlight,* the Lobby's slick, thirty-two-page weekly newspaper sent to more than 100,000 subscribers, stories about the plight of the farmers were featured side by side with articles that promoted the formation of a new Populist party that would end U.S. foreign aid to Israel, repeal the income tax, abolish the Federal Reserve System, and uncover the Holocaust for what it was: a hoax.

Just south of the Missouri-Arkansas border, near Mountain Home, Arkansas, James Ellison saw the dispossessed and struggling farmers as potential "Christian survivalists" who would swell the ranks of the Covenant, Sword and Arm of the Lord. The CSA believed the Battle of Armageddon—in the form of a nuclear war between the United States and the Soviet Union and followed by a gigantic race war—was fast approaching. Once engaged in battle, contended Ellison, God would call upon CSA members to serve as

Soldier-Saints to cleanse the world of all remaining anti-Christ forces, and would then allow them to "rule and reign" with him once he established his pure, white, Christian Kingdom on earth. "We believe that God is raising up a remnant out of the nations, giving them the Spirit of Sonship, to grow them into perfection, to be manifested as mature Sons of God, who walk in his image upon this earth, and who will rule and reign upon earth as His Elect," wrote Ellison in the CSA journal.

To prepare his two hundred followers for the upcoming battle, Ellison established the Endtime Overcomer Survival Training School at the CSA's 220-acre compound on the shores of Bull Shoals Lake. The school, which nonmembers could attend for $500, included a paramilitary training ground—complete with pop-up targets of blacks, Jews, and police officers wearing Star of David badges—and offered courses in guerrilla and urban warfare, weapons training, bomb-making, and Christian military truths.

In the pine-scented mountains surrounding the small, one-time logging community of Hayden Lake, Idaho, the Reverend Richard G. Butler, founder of the neo-Nazi Aryan Nations and pastor of the Christian Identity–based Church of Jesus Christ, Christian, saw among the desperate farmers recruits for a revolution that would result in the establishment of a national racist state.

"Today, the lawful citizens are being dispossessed from farms, homes, businesses and employment while their country is being invaded by alien hordes on a scale unprecedented in all the world's history," Butler wrote in the Ayran Nations newsletter in 1982. "The farmer is being backed into a wall, and he's beginning to believe there has to be an answer for all this. The answer is revolution.

"The farmers were the first victims of the Revolution in 1776, as they are the first victims of this revolution. He's [*sic*] been dispossessed of his land. He's been used and abused. . . . He's going to get a lot more angry, and eventually he'll see that the only way to turn things around is to fight to win his country back for white Christians."

Even old-line hate groups saw the farm crisis as an opportunity for a membership drive; and the Ku Klux Klan was eager to fit new members with white sheets. In his newsletter, *The White Patriot,* Thom Robb, chaplain for the Knights of the Ku Klux Klan and leader of the Harrison, Arkansas–based White People's Committee to Restore God's Law, carried "An Open Letter to the American Farmer" that claimed no Jews were murdered by Nazis in the USSR during World War II. Instead, contended the letter, it was the Jews who killed Russian farmers. "You have seen the pictures, but you were told by the same network of conspirators that is now attempting to drive you off your land that they were Jews killed by Hitler's SS. But they weren't Jews, they weren't even ordinary anti-Communist resisters. They were farmers. The Jew plan is to steal your land. And this is exactly what they are doing time and time again," said the letter.

And there were hundreds of other like-minded groups—as many as 1,700 different organizations with more than 100,000 members, according to law enforcement authorities—peppered throughout the country. While a few of the groups maintained elaborate compounds, had hundreds, and in some cases thousands, of adherents, and used a sophisticated, nationwide computer network to communicate with each other, most of the organizations had little more than a post office box, a telephone, and a handful of members.

Although memberships sometimes overlapped, these groups fiercely maintained their independence from one another and often differed over tactics.

The more militant segments of the Posse, along with many of the Klan and neo-Nazi groups, such as the Ayran Nations and The Order, openly advocated a race war and rejected attempts to cultivate a mass following. What these groups wanted were true believers, people who were willing to die for the cause. "We intend to purge this land . . . of every non-white person, idea and influence," Louis Beam, leader of the Texas Klan, wrote in his newsletter, the *Inter-Klan and Survival Newsletter.* "It is pure fantasy to imagine the Klan as a broad-based movement that will effect peaceful change. There should be no doubt that all means short of armed conflict have been exhausted."

The blueprint for that armed conflict was contained in the novel *The Turner Diaries,* which was written in 1978 by William Pierce, a member of the neo-Nazi National Alliance. In the book, which has become to segments of the extremist movement what Hitler's *Mein Kampf* was to the National Socialist German Workers' party, white supremacists start a guerrilla war against ZOG (the Zionist Occupation Government, or the U.S. government) in 1991. After eight years of terrorist activities, which included the assassination of federal officials, lawmen, politicians, Jews, and other minorities, as well as the destruction of public utilities and the poisoning of municipal water supplies, the supremacists overthrow the government, purge the country of all Jews and other minorities, and destroy Israel with the nuclear arsenal inherited from ZOG.

There were other groups, however, which downplayed both their racist, anti-Semitic views and the need for violence to effect change in the country. Groups such as the Liberty Lobby, NAPA, the Iowa Society for Educated Citizens, segments of the Posse, and a host of other organizations that referred to themselves as Christian Patriots, sought to build a bridge between their terrorist brethren and mainstream America. They employed more insidious tactics, which were designed to cultivate a grassroots base of support. They disguised their hate for Jews, minorities, and the U.S. government with concern for the small businessman, the family farmer, and the white Christian American. Instead of sheets and swastikas, they draped themselves in the American flag. They eschewed blatant racist and anti-Semitic slogans, using code terms such as racialist, eastern and international bankers, and white civil rights. They armed members not with guns but with elaborate constitutional, legal, and religious interpretations which they were urged to carry into the courtroom. Instead of violence, they advocated the election of people who would dismantle the Federal Reserve System, abolish the income tax, and root out the conspirators who used their government positions to undermine the country's Christian ideals.

Yet, whatever their differences, the groups were tightly bound by ideological and theological threads that, in time, could be woven into the whole cloth of a unified political and social movement.

The two most common, and strongest, threads were a hatred for Jews and an adherence to the religious teachings of Christian Identity.

A quasi-religious movement, Christian Identity "provided a theological undergirding for sectors of the racist and anti-Semitic movement, including groups such as the Ayran Nations, the Ku Klux Klan, and the Posse Comitatus, and has promoted a practical working unity among geographically disparate organizations and groups," said Leonard Zeskind, a research analyst for the Atlanta-based Center for Democratic Renewal, which monitors racist and anti-Semitic activities throughout the country.

Identity allowed white-robed Klansmen to mingle with plaid-shirted Posse members, and camouflaged survivalists to rub shoulders with blue-shirted neo-Nazis. But even more frightening and dangerous, said Zeskind, it also brought religious people into contact with the racist movement.

Although founded in 1946 by Wesley Swift, a former member of the Ku Klux Klan, Christian Identity's theological roots reach back nearly a century earlier to the formulation of the religious thought called British Israelism. The origins of the religious cult, said Zeskind, can be traced to either John Wilson, a Scotsman who, in 1840, published the book *Our Israelitish Origins,* or to Edward Hines, an Englishman who, in 1871, wrote the book *Identification of the British Nation with Lost Israel.*

According to Zeskind, the essence of British Israelism belief is that the Ten Lost Tribes of Israel migrated through the centuries and eventually settled in northern Europe. The northern Europeans were, therefore, God's chosen people and America, which was colonized by the Europeans, was God's Promised Land. The largest group of believers of British Israelism in the United States is the 80,000-member Worldwide Church of God, established by the late Herbert Armstrong, said Zeskind.

But where Armstrong believed that the Jews were entitled to grace, Swift and his followers gave Identity theology a racist slant. Swift contended the struggle for the white Aryans of the Lost Tribes wasn't to maintain their religious identity, but instead was to preserve their racial purity. Swift preached that Jews were the offspring of Satan, and the descendants of the Mongolian tribe the Khazars. While blacks, and other nonwhites, said Swift, were "mud people," the mistakes of creation [false starts before God made the perfect— read white—Adam and Eve]. Swift also insisted that the Bible demanded racial and religious segregation, and that marriages and cooperation between races, as well as cooperation between Jews and Christians, were sins.

"If you believe the Bible, you are going to be a segregationist. If you believe the Bible, you are not going to work out any deal of coexistence in the devil's kingdom, because your Race was sent down here to overthrow it," wrote Swift in his pamphlet *Anti-Christ in the Pulpits*.

And, like that of many fundamentalist and cult religious groups, Christian Identity's theology extended into the secular world of politics, and it incorporated into its thought many of the beliefs held by the disparate extremist groups. Identity held that the United States was a "Christian Republic," governed by biblically derived Christian Common Law, not statutory law. It also contended that the Constitution expressly forbids citizenship to Jews and people of color, and argued that paper money and income taxes were unconstitutional. It also claimed that the Internal Revenue Service, the Federal Reserve Bank, and other federal agencies were controlled by a Jewish-led conspiracy of bankers, communists, minorities, and corrupt government officials that, as it tightened its grip on the government, the courts, the news media, and the economy, would soon realize its goal of a one-world government and result in the enslavement of all white Christians.

During the 1970s, Gale, Wickstrom, Butler, and other hucksters for Christian Identity, attempted to sell their racist and anti-Semitic cure-alls to the people of the Northwest and Midwest. Except in the prisons, where Identity was recognized by the federal courts as an official inmate religion for the white-supremacist gangs the Ayran Brotherhood and the Ayran Special Forces, few people bought them.

But as the economic crisis deepened in the 1980s, those ministers saw in the farmers, factory workers, and small-town merchants fertile ground to be tilled. They rallied their supporters to once again take their message into the countryside.

The message was carried into the Heartland by extremist apostles like Kahl who not only looked like farmers but were farmers. They wore baseball caps with a seed or grain company's logo, work shirts, blue jeans, and boots; not white sheets, swastika armbands, or jackboots. They talked like farmers and spoke passionately of subjects close to the farmers' hearts—religion, country, and family. They called themselves Christians, patriots, freemen, and citizens for a constitutional government. But the message they bore was filled with scapegoats, not solutions. It was anti-Semitic, racist, and hateful. It was a message that was as ludicrous as it was simple, and one sired by desperation.

Many farmers saw it as that and turned a deaf ear to it. Others were just too busy to be bothered; they already worked sixteen hours a day to maintain their hardscrabble existence and, if that wasn't enough, they would work twenty. They didn't have time for more meetings or organizations.

But some farmers listened. Sure the message was crazy. Sure it didn't make sense. But was it any crazier, or did it make any less sense, than what was happening in the country? People on welfare ate well with the benefit of farmers' tax dollars while the farmers themselves groveled for food and were forced from their homes. And in the schools, children were taught sex before they were taught their ABCs, and that they were descendants of apes, not Adam and Eve.

And other farmers believed. These were desperate times, and the farmers in the Heartland wanted to believe in something. They needed to believe in something. All their lives they had been told that if they worked hard, kept a strong faith in God, and served both their community and country, they would succeed. All their lives they had believed that to be true. They had done everything asked of them, often leaving their land only once—to serve in the armed forces—and yet, they were losing the very land their grandparents had settled more than seventy, eighty, ninety years earlier.

And the institutions in which they had believed and trusted—their government, church, bank, and community—were telling them that the trouble they were in was of their own making. It was their fault they were losing the farm.

The message carried by Kahl, and others like him, was more acceptable.

Kahl's appeal was not one contingent upon a kind of backwater ignorance. Instead, said Daniel Levitas of Prairiefire, it was an appeal "tied much more closely to the fact that these people feel they've lost control of their lives."

The activities of the extreme right didn't go unnoticed. Its anti-government posture—more than its racist and anti-Semitic rhetoric—had caught the FBI's interest in 1976, and again four years later, when a report warned agents that all members of the Posse should be considered armed and dangerous. The FBI hadn't heard anyone talking about revolution since 1968.

Still, admitted a federal prosecutor in North Dakota, most authorities tended to laugh off the virulent rhetoric and tough talk of the extremists. Instead of a threat, the extremists were viewed as aging juvenile delinquents who liked to play make-believe war games with real guns. People who, despite tough talk and veiled threats to the contrary, weren't violent, merely frustrated.

Private organizations, such as Prairiefire, the Center for Democratic Renewal, and the Anti-Defamation League, saw little humor in the activities of the extremists and warned against the "pernicious virus of hatred . . ." being spread throughout the Heartland.

They said the extremists shouldn't be dismissed as isolated groups that squabbled among themselves. Rather, the extremists should be viewed as a single movement composed of different groups that sometimes competed—but more often collaborated. A movement that had a military component, a political and legal intent, and a religious underpinning. And there was evidence to support their concern.

In the early 1980s, the Aryan Nations' annual congress drew more than five hundred people and included individuals affiliated with the Posse, the CSA, the Klan, and the neo-Nazis in the United States, the Western Guard in Canada, the National Front in Great Britain, and the Teutonic Unity and the Liberation of the German Reich in West Germany. At the same time, the Christian Defense League's annual Freedom Festivals attracted more than fifteen hundred participants, many with similar affiliations.

Warnings from Prairiefire and others, however, were mostly ignored. The leaders of those organizations were viewed as doomsayers with respect to the farm crisis. And, as is all too often the case when diagnosis concerns the cancer of racism and anti-Semitism, their concerns were greeted with skepticism and denial. It couldn't be happening in my backyard, they were told. Farmers weren't racists or Jew-haters.

But on February 13, 1983, those views were shattered, like a windshield struck with a bullet from a high-powered rifle. On February 13, 1983, Gordon Kahl declared a Holy War against his government.

3

A True Believer

His name was Gordon Wendell Kahl, and he was born on January 8, 1920, and grew up near Heaton, North Dakota, on a farm his father had homesteaded in 1906.

By all accounts, Gordon, the oldest of five children, had an ordinary childhood. Like most farm boys, he was introduced to the rural work ethic at a young age. Well before he reached his teens, Gordon learned to drive a tractor and, side by side with his father, Fred, he cultivated, sowed, and harvested the wheat fields on the family's 240-acre farm.

And, like most farm boys, Gordon was introduced to hunting when he was very young. At ten, Gordon was presented with his first weapon—a 16-gauge shotgun—and, when the chores were completed, father and son often walked the hills that surrounded the farm in search of pheasant, duck, prairie chicken, and most any other type of game. Gordon earned his pocket money by hunting. Each gopher he killed brought two cents a tail, and each rabbit he shot earned him five cents a pelt.

"About all he did was hunt. In those days that is about all there was to do," said his wife, Joan. "He spent more time hunting gophers than going to school."

Hunt, and play piano. Kahl, who took piano lessons at the urging of his mother, rebuffed her attempts to have him learn the works of Mozart, Chopin, Beethoven, and other classical composers. But he did have an ear for the popular songs of the day and joined a band that performed at community and wedding dances.

Despite spotty attendance, and an undistinguished academic record, Gordon graduated from high school in 1938. He joined the New Deal's Civilian Conservation Corps, worked on a construction crew for six months in eastern Montana, and then teamed up with three childhood friends and traveled to the West Coast where they worked as pickers in the fruit orchards of California. Gordon returned to North Dakota in 1940, and divided his time between his father's farm and the lumberyard in Heaton. Still restless for adventure, Gordon attempted to enlist in the U.S. Army Air Corps in the fall of 1941. He wanted to be a pilot. But a broken nose, which he suffered in a childhood accident and that left him with a breathing problem, disqualified him.

He returned to the farm and the lumberyard, which was where he met Joan Seil, a fourteen-year-old schoolgirl. The two started to date.

Love, however, would have to wait. On December 7, 1941, Pearl Harbor was bombed and war declared. This time when Gordon tried to enlist, he was accepted. While his breathing problem still prevented him from becoming a pilot, it didn't prevent him from shooting a gun, something at which he was very good. Less than two months after Pearl Harbor, Gordon was made a turret gunner on a B-25 bomber. For the next two years, Gordon fired a .50-caliber machine gun and was credited with shooting down ten enemy aircraft. He also collected a Silver Star, a Bronze Star, two air medals, a presidential unit citation, nine battle stars, and two Purple Hearts. He received the last Purple Heart during a mission over Europe, when he was severely wounded, taking shrapnel in the jaw, chest, and hip. Surgeons in North Africa were able to remove most of the metal, but not all of it.

His second-oldest daughter, Lorna, recalled a time when she was five years old and her father was teaching her how to swim. She had swung her arm around and struck Gordon along the left side of the face, and caused him a great deal of pain. Lorna said her father showed her where he still had some metal in the side of his face and allowed her to rub it. She said he told her that it was leftover scrap metal from the war and that when it was rubbed the wrong way it would hurt. Some of that scrap metal also remained in his left hip. Those injuries earned him a 30 percent disability pension from the government.

After he recuperated from his wounds, Gordon returned to duty in the Asian theater. It was there, during a mission over Burma, Gordon claimed to have shot down an American P-51 pilot who had mistaken his aircraft for a Japanese bomber.

In November of 1944, after more than fifty combat missions, Staff Sgt. Gordon Kahl returned to the United States. After he was debriefed in Santa Ana, California, Gordon was given a three-day furlough and ordered to report to Boonville, North Carolina, where he would serve out the war as a gunnery instructor. Gordon took his pass and headed home. On January 6, 1945, nearly four years after they had met over the counter at the lumberyard, Gordon and Joan were married. The next day, Gordon left for North Carolina. Joan waited until April to join him. When she arrived, Gordon presented Joan with his wedding gift to her: a 20-gauge double-barreled shotgun. He taught her to use it in the back country that surrounded the air base.

It also was there, in the land of mint juleps, Tobacco Road, and the Ku Klux Klan, that the twenty-four-year-old soldier's once normal patriotic views toward his government came under attack: The war hadn't been necessary. It had been started by the superrich. The United States could have sat out the war had it not been for the greed of a small cabal of international bankers and Zionist businessmen who wanted to profit from the manufacture and sale of war goods. And FDR was in cahoots with them, and acted at their direction. He maneuvered Japan into a position where it was forced to attack the United States, and allowed Japan to do it unchallenged. How else could Pearl Harbor be explained?

It was barracks talk. Claptrap. It was a tapestry of hatred woven with the threads of rumor, hearsay, gossip, and lies. It was tailored and offered as a blanket of truth by people like Gerald Winrod, a fundamentalist preacher from central Kansas—whose apocalyptic Christianity still resonates throughout the church pews of the Identity movement—and who were better known as "Jayhawk Nazis." And there were others: William Pelley, who founded the Nazi-inspired Silver Shirts and outlined many of the wild Jewish conspiracy theories; the Reverend Charles Coughlin, the Catholic priest whose anti-Semitic venom was carried to millions of Americans on his weekly radio show; and Gerald K. Smith, a one-time aide to Huey Long, who established the Christian Nationalist Crusade and served as a mentor to Wesley Swift, the California Klansman who later articulated and popularized the theology of the Identity movement.

A vast majority of Americans considered the sources, discerned their motives, and accepted what these men said for what it was: hate wrapped in the American flag. But Gordon was susceptible to such ideas. As a child, Gordon, with his mother, younger brother, and three younger sisters, would regularly attend the Congregational Church and Sunday school. His father, Fred, however, would remain home on Sundays. He rejected the liberal views of the Universal Christian Council for Life and Work, of which the church was a member. The council, which, in 1938, would merge with the Faith and Order Conference to form the World Council of Churches, called for social and interracial justice, denounced anti-Semitism as a sin against God, and encouraged a greater understanding between Christians and Jews. But in the Kahl household, Negroes and whites weren't meant to mix. Nor were Jews and Christians.

Still, it wasn't so much what Gordon heard, as it was what he read, that raised questions in his mind. And one book that struck Kahl particularly was *The International Jew: The World's Foremost Problem,* written by automobile magnate Henry Ford, and which first appeared in 1920 as a series in a Dearborn, Michigan, newspaper. In it, Ford outlined the Protocols of the Elders of Zion. The Protocols was an alleged account of a 1918 meeting among Russian Jews, where a plot was devised to control the world, as well as to destroy Christianity and the white race. According to Ford, the conspirators—with the aid of corrupt financiers and politicians—would seize control through the manipulation of the banking system, the farm economy, and the press. The book contended that Jews controlled most of the entertainment, sugar, and tobacco industries and more than 50 percent of the cotton, steel, banking, and liquor industries. In 1929, Ford repudiated his views contained in the book and acknowledged that the Protocols was a forgery created by czarist Russians. But by that time, the book had become part of the rich vein of Jewish conspiracy literature which extremists mined for validation.

Gordon was discharged from the armed services in September of 1945. He returned to Heaton with his medals, his wife, and a whole set of new ideas and philosophies, which having taken hold would later fester and grow more twisted in their logic.

"When Gordon returned from World War II he realized something was drastically wrong in the United States," said Joan Kahl. "But he didn't know what."

He wanted to find out. And he wanted to figure out what to do with his life. Soon after he returned home, Gordon purchased 160 acres of land adjacent to his father's farm. Between the two of them they had 400 acres, not a large operation, at least not large enough to support two families.

Kahl decided to enter college and get a degree in electrical engineering. He and Joan moved to Fargo and Kahl enrolled at the North Dakota Agricultural College (now known as North Dakota State University). During his second semester Kahl clashed with an English professor he claimed was a communist. Convinced that communists were running the college, Gordon quit school. Anyway, Gordon told Joan, why did he have to take English if what he wanted was to become an engineer. Gordon and Joan moved to Bowdon, where he got a job as a mechanic at a farm implement dealership, and where, in October of 1947, the first of the couple's six children was born—a daughter they named Linda.

In the spring, Kahl moved his family back to his parents' farm. It was still no easier for two families—one now with an additional mouth to feed—to make ends meet on 400 acres of land. So, after the fall harvest, Kahl packed up his family and moved them to Los Angeles County.

Gordon had become enamored of California during the time he worked there as a picker in the fruit orchards. He liked the warm weather, especially when it was below zero back in North Dakota. And there was plenty of work there for someone who was as good as Gordon at fixing carburetors and doing tune-ups on automobiles. Everyone in California owned a car and they drove them everywhere. All those cars and all that driving meant repair work and a job.

But each spring, Gordon and his family would return to Heaton. He and his father would clear the fields of the rocks and boulders which gradually surfaced, having been planted some ten thousand years earlier by a retreating glacier. Then father and son would plant the small grains, spring wheat, and durum wheat. That was all they planted. It was all any farmer in east-central North Dakota would plant: wheat and cattle silage. In that hardscrabble land, thousands of piles of stones circled the fields and stood in silent testimony to the farmers' labor; and the rolling uplands were pock-marked with holes.

But even more limiting to crop production than the condition of the land was the uncertainty of rain from year to year. On the average, the area received about seventeen inches a year. It was enough rain, should it come at the appropriate time, to water the small grain seeds and help them grow into golden shafts of wheat. It was not enough, however, to allow for planting thirsty cash crops, such as beets, soybeans, and corn, crops that were found 100 miles east in the Red River valley.

Not that the land couldn't provide a living; there were excellent plots which, once cleared of rocks, produced fine harvests. North Dakota provided the world with more than four-fifths of the durum wheat, which was then turned into spaghetti, macaroni, and a host of other pasta products. But it was a tough area to farm. An area where farming was more of a gamble than in the valley. So, to hedge his bets and see to it that his family was provided for, Gordon, after each harvest, would return to California.

During one of those winter trips, Gordon was introduced to the teachings of the Christian Identity movement, an apocalyptic religion that divides the world into two distinct camps, good and evil, preaches Holy War in which any means can be used to destroy evil (evil being incarnate in nonbelievers, who are Satan's soldiers on earth), and sees conspiracies everywhere. It's a church that believes the second coming of Jesus Christ is at hand, and that it will follow a nuclear war between the United States and the Soviet Union; that only its members will survive the war and be called upon by God to build the New Israel in America. Christian Identity ministers preach the inherent superiority of the white Aryan race, and maintain that Jews, blacks and other nonwhites, like animals, have no soul. It's a church that counts among its saints Adolf Hitler, and supplements Bible readings with racist and anti-Semitic literature such as *Billions for the Bankers, Debts for the People, The Negro: Serpent, Beast and Devil,* and *The Holy Book of Adolf Hitler.*

The Identity religion was far removed from the Congregationalist faith in which Gordon was raised. But shortly after the war, Gordon came to agree with his father's views and quit the Congregationalist church. Gordon and Joan, who had been raised a Catholic, turned to the Mormon church for spiritual guidance. This was the 1950s, when Senator Joseph McCarthy was waging his war against communism. Gordon believed McCarthy's claims that communists were infiltrating the government and other segments of society and he found comfort in the hard-line anti-communist stance of the Mormon church. But that comfort was short-lived. Gordon soon came to believe that the religious ceremonies of the church were a carbon copy of the rituals practiced by the Bavarian Illuminati and the Masons,* whom he believed to be pawns of the Jews and children

---

* Kahl and other members of the far right believe that secret societies such as the Illuminati and Masons are front organizations used by the Jews to undermine Christianity. The Illuminati, which was formed in 1776 in Bavaria, Germany, and included among its stated goals replacing an individual's dependence upon religion and superstition with philosophy and reason, was outlawed by authorities ten years after it was created and ordered to disband. The far right, however, maintain that the Illuminati's membership simply infiltrated the Masons and continued its un-Godly work. Kahl frequently pointed to the back of a one-dollar bill and the symbol of the pyramid with an eye at the top. That symbol, Kahl contended, actually represented the Illuminati slogan—Liberty, Equality, Fraternity—and was proof that the Jews, through their control of the Illuminati and now the Masons, controlled the country's monetary system.

of Satan; therefore he and Joan quit the church in the latter part of the 1950s.

By this time, the couple's family had grown to include three daughters; Lorna was born in June of 1951, and Lonnie in June of 1958. In August of 1959, the couple had their first son, a boy they named Yorie Von Kahl. It was Yorie who would become his father's favorite. A child who grew to idolize his father, Yorie accepted Gordon's views of the world without question, adopting them as his own.

A second son, Frederick, was born in 1960, and three years later, Loreen, the couple's last child, was born.

As his family started to come of age in the 1960s, Gordon became more concerned with the direction in which the government was taking his country. About the time Loreen was born, the government removed the silver certificate dollar bill from circulation and replaced it with what Gordon saw as the "federal fraud," known by most people as the Federal Reserve note. That action suggested to Kahl that another piece of the conspiracy puzzle had been put into place. The bankers in control of the Federal Reserve System now had the power to create money out of air, a power which allowed them to manipulate the marketplace. Now those questions which were planted in Gordon's mind during World War II nagged at him. He needed answers, and set out to find them.

He flirted with the John Birch Society, joined for a brief time, but decided it wasn't true enough to the principles he held. He quit and joined the Constitutional party, which had been established in North Dakota by Dr. Clarence Martin of Medina. The party believed the government to be an extension of the Christian church, and that the Constitution was a biblically derived document which should be strictly interpreted. The reforms that the party sought were to do away with the federal income tax, dismantle all social welfare programs and agencies, repeal the Federal Reserve Act, and return the country to the gold and silver standards.

The summer after President John F. Kennedy was assassinated, Gordon attended a Constitutional party meeting in Fessenden,

North Dakota, where the guest speaker was Aaron Flett, a spokesman for the tax protest movement.

At that meeting, Gordon heard how the Sixteenth Amendment
to the Constitution was illegal because it hadn't been formally ratified by three-fourths of the states. He heard that since the Sixteenth Amendment conferred no rights, imposed no duties, created
no office, and had not bestowed power or authority on anyone, it
was an unconstitutional law that no one was bound to obey and no
court was bound to enforce.

Gordon heard how the Internal Revenue Service collected taxes
for the Federal Reserve System, a private corporation controlled by
the Jewish owners of eight international banks, and not for the
government. He heard that the goal of those bankers was to destroy
Christianity and establish a one-world government run by communists and socialists. For proof of that, Gordon was told, all a
person had to do was look as far as the Communist Manifesto,
which was written by the freemason Karl Marx. There, in the second plank of Marx's blueprint for controlling the world, a person
would find the call for a heavy progressive income tax. So, Kahl
heard that by paying income taxes, a person was unwittingly fi-
nancing the eventual overthrow of the Christian Republic of the
United States of America.

Gordon also heard that President Kennedy was killed because he
learned of the conspiracy, refused to become a part of it, and, instead, planned to expose the plot to the American public.

Kahl took the information and returned to his Heaton, North
Dakota, farm. There, he turned to his three favorite documents—
the King James version of the Bible, the U.S. Constitution, and the
Articles of Confederation—for guidance. At night he studied the
matter, sometimes well into the early morning hours, and long after
the rest of the family had retired to bed. During the day, while
doing his chores, he reflected on what he had read and discovered.
Finally, in 1967, it became clear to him what he must do. Gordon
wrote a letter to the Internal Revenue Service and informed the
bureau that he would no longer "pay tithes to the Synagogue of

Satan under the second plank of the Communist Manifesto" to finance his country's destruction. "Never again will I give aid and comfort to the enemies of Christ," he wrote.

The IRS responded with a letter requesting Gordon's appearance before a federal tax court. Gordon ignored the letter and all other letters that followed it. As far as Gordon was concerned, there was nothing further to discuss. He had studied and researched the issue and made his decision. The matter was closed.

He could be stubborn, almost to the point of arrogance, once he had decided that his way was the right way. There would be no wavering from the chosen path.

It wasn't that Gordon Kahl was an unpleasant man. Despite his stubborn streak, friends and neighbors said that if you avoided discussing politics and religion—which wasn't difficult in that such subjects were regarded as personal and thus were out-of-bounds in most conversations among these private farmers—there was a great deal to like about Gordon Kahl.

Although quiet, Gordon was personable, got along easily with children, and had a strong sense of loyalty to both family and friends. He didn't drink alcohol, smoke tobacco, or use foul language. He was viewed as honest and hardworking, a man who had a knack for making over any rough-sounding truck, tractor, or automobile into a smooth-running machine.

Anyway, argued his friends, hadn't Kahl fought for the right to hold his beliefs, no matter how idiosyncratic they seemed to others? Some even saw Gordon as a real-life war hero.

About the same time that he decided to stop paying his taxes, Gordon also decided to stop taking his family to California.

The state had lost its appeal. There were too many people there, strange-looking people who wore long hair, dirty clothes, and held strange views about love, peace, and property. Gordon decided the family should spend its winters in west Texas, one of the most conservative enclaves in America.

During the day, he worked on a steaming operation in the oil fields outside of Odessa. At night, he attended various political meetings, seeking an outlet for his beliefs. As Gordon saw it, the United States had become a "conquered and occupied nation," said Joan. "Conquered and occupied by the Jews and their hundreds or maybe thousands of front organizations doing their un-Godly work."

There were many of these front organizations which worked to enslave white, Christian Americans, Gordon told his wife. And he wasn't alone in his opinion. His wife remembered that "there were a lot of people down there who were beginning to see it as Gordon saw it."

In 1973, Gordon found some of those kindred spirits in the Posse Comitatus, a group that embraced much of what was preached by Christian Identity and endorsed many of the Constitutional party's aspirations for governmental changes but one which also offered its own distinct ideology.

Gordon reclaimed his "individual sovereignty" by operating his trucks and automobiles without a driver's license and flying his small airplane without a pilot's license. The Bible, and a true Christian Republic, according to Gordon, didn't allow such infringements on a man's freedom.

A year later, in 1974, Gordon was named the group's state co-ordinator in Texas. At first, his activities were limited to soapbox recruitment speeches to workers in the oil fields and repeated disputes with law enforcement officials over his insistence on driving without a license. But, by 1976, Gordon was prepared to take his message to a larger audience. He and five of his fellow Posse members appeared on a half-hour television program in Texas, and exhorted citizens to stop paying their income taxes.

"All a Christian has to know is that the income tax is the second plank of the Communist Manifesto. You can't support Satan and call yourself a Christian," Gordon told the viewers. "When you become a Christian, you put yourself on the opposite side of the government." Gordon told his viewers how he had stopped paying his taxes nine years earlier.

This time the IRS did not send him a letter. Instead, they sent a U.S. marshal with a summons for Gordon to appear in federal court in Midland, Texas. He was charged with willful failure to pay his income taxes for the years of 1973 and 1974.

Gordon, who listed as his occupations laborer, preacher, farmer, and pilot, welcomed the court fight. It was an opportunity for him and his followers to unmask the fraudulent nature of the tax system and warn an unsuspecting public of the dangers it faced. Each day Gordon arrived at the courtroom wearing a gold hangman's noose, the symbol of the Posse, on his coat lapel. And on the opening day of the trial he defiantly told the presiding judge, "I didn't fail to file my taxes. I refused to file my taxes."

He also refused to enter a plea of guilty or not guilty, contending that the court did not have jurisdiction over him as an individual.

"I understand God's laws, but I don't understand Satan's laws," he told the court.

Gordon's enthusiasm for the court battle soon faded, however, when his religious and First Amendment arguments were repeatedly disallowed. This was a tax case, Gordon was reminded.

Gordon's attorney argued that Gordon and his supporters were being punished, not because they didn't pay their taxes, but because they dared go on television and admit they weren't paying taxes. "This man has such a strong commitment that his actions were totally governed by his religion. He was a man without choice on it," said Gordon's attorney.

"I would show . . . it was not his activities in breaking the law that brought him before this court," his lawyer continued. "He, as records show, didn't pay income taxes from 1969 forward. He wrote the Internal Revenue Service and said 'I am not paying them. I can't pay them. It is sinful to pay them.' He is not here for that. He is here because in 1974 he appeared on television for thirty minutes."

It was a contention not disputed by IRS officials who testified at the trial.

Nonetheless, Gordon was convicted on June 22, 1977. Before sentence was passed, Gordon was asked if he had anything he wished to state before the court.

"I felt I had a choice to make. I realized I could be cast into prison here or I could spend an eternity in the Lake of Fire. It seems to me that the choice of the two would have to be whatever punishment I have to receive here. That's all I have to say," responded Gordon.

Gordon was sentenced to one year in jail and placed on five years' probation. He also was ordered to disassociate himself from the Posse and any other group that advocated a willful disobedience of state and federal laws, and to start paying his income taxes. Still defiant, Gordon said he would rather spend six years in prison than finance the "work of Satan."

Following his sentence, Gordon was ordered to undergo a psychiatric examination at the federal prison hospital in Springfield, Missouri. He was found to be fanatically religious, with schizophrenic characteristics, but not psychotic. After three months, Kahl was allowed to return to Heaton to await the outcome of his appeal.

When he arrived home, Gordon promptly went to the Wells County registrar of deeds and transferred the ownership of his four-hundred-acre farm, which was left to him after his parents died, from his name and Joan's to that of the "Gospel Doctrine Church of Jesus Christ, Alter Ego of Gordon Kahl." This was part of a new tactic by the Posse and Identity Church to circumvent the dreaded income tax. The groups figured that if "Christian misleaders"—a term applied to ministers of mainstream religions—could be exempt from the tax, so could the ministers of the true Christian churches.

In 1978, the appeals court upheld Gordon's conviction and, on January 2, 1979, Gordon entered the prison camp at Leavenworth, Kansas, where he served eight months and four days of his one-year sentence.

Shortly after his release, Gordon heard that his friend, William W. Rhinehart, had died of a heart attack at a federal prison in Arizona. Rhinehart was a fellow Posse member who had appeared with Gordon on the television broadcast in Texas and had been tried on the same tax charges as Gordon. Gordon was told that despite repeated pleas from prisoners, the authorities delayed giving

Rhinehart medical help. Gordon was convinced that the government in order to silence Rhinehart had poisoned him with a drug
that induced a fatal heart attack. And he believed that a similar
fate awaited him should he be returned to prison.

"I am satisfied that they [the government] consider me enough
of an enemy that if I ever went back to prison, I would never come
out alive," said Gordon. "I can give up my religion or I can stand
and fight. I don't see any other alternative."

The words sounded ominous, but the threat was toothless. No
one wanted Gordon. He signed his monthly probation reports as
required. He violated no laws. At least not until April 15 when he
again failed to file an income tax return.

In August of 1980, Gordon received a criminal summons ordering
him to appear before a federal judge in Texas and show cause for
failing to comply with the dictates of his probation. The summons
was subsequently set aside, but Kahl saw it as another attempt to
silence him. He reasoned that if the government was going to harass
him for not filing his income tax returns, there was no need to
continue submitting his monthly probation reports. When they
would arrive in the mail for his signature, he simply tossed them
in the garbage.

Kahl hadn't heard the final words from the IRS. In November,
a lien was filed against eighty acres of his land. Unless he paid the
back taxes—a bill which had mushroomed from $7,074 to nearly
$35,000—he would lose nearly a quarter of his land.

Finally, Joan Kahl, who had for eighteen years quietly feared
something like this would happen, broke her silence. She pleaded
with Gordon to pay the money and save the farm. Her brother, a
successful farmer, and several of their neighbors had agreed to help
finance the repayment. Gordon refused. If anyone bought the land
and tried to farm it, Gordon told Joan, he'd ask them to leave. Those
eighty acres were his, no matter what the Internal Revenue Service
ruled.

Shortly after the beginning of the year, the IRS seized the land.
It would put it up for auction later to recover its money. And on
March 31, 1981, a federal warrant from Texas arrived at the U.S.

marshal's office in Fargo, North Dakota, and directed that Gordon Wendell Kahl—federal taxpayer 501-14-2682—be arrested for violating the conditions of his probation. As a matter of routine, the warrant was sent to the office closest to the individual to be arrested. In this case it was sent to Minot, which had two deputy marshals. Several days later, both deputy marshals, along with a county sheriff's deputy, drove to the Bowdon, North Dakota, farm of Herman Widicker. They had information that Gordon worked there off and on as a farm laborer. When the officers arrived, they were met by Widicker and three other men. They were told Kahl had already left for home. The officers also were told that it would not be in their best interests to try and arrest Kahl at his farm, unless they were looking for trouble.

The officers accepted the advice at face value. They had heard about Gordon's vow that he would not go willingly with any police officers who tried to arrest him. Gordon's farm was rumored to be an arsenal with "guns in every corner, in every room, and behind every door," said one officer.

The deputies called their Fargo headquarters for instructions. "Back off until we've had an opportunity to review the situation," responded U.S. Marshal Harold "Bud" Warren.

Warren didn't look like the type to avoid a confrontation. He was a large man, thickly built, who seemed even more imposing because of his ramrod-straight carriage. He wore a stern, sometimes even harsh look and combined a knuckle-crushing handshake with a deep baritone voice that seemed to have only one volume setting—loud. But Warren was a cautious man. He didn't like to take unnecessary risks or place himself in untenable positions. And his personal caution spilled over into his relationships with those he worked with in the marshals service. Warren made it a habit to tape nearly all conversations he had with his superiors in order to protect himself should he do something that his superiors might later try to reprimand him for doing. Warren didn't trust people or institutions.

Bud Warren had been in law enforcement for almost thirty years, nearly twenty years with the marshals service, at one time assigned to the witness protection program where he served as guardian to mafia-types who wished to tell all about the underworld and stay alive at the same time. For the last four years he'd been the U.S. marshal for the state of North Dakota. But with the election of President Reagan, Warren's tenure as marshal—a political appointment—was drawing to a close. He wasn't going to have any violence occur during the last couple of months on his watch. Not if he could help it, and not over someone's failure to put a signed monthly probation report into the mail. There had to be another way.

Warren called Texas for information about Gordon. The man is one crazy son-of-a-bitch, Warren was told by the sheriff. But aside from spending a few nights in jail for repeatedly driving without a license, he wasn't a violent man. Warren received a different appraisal when he called the sheriff of Wells County, where Heaton is located.

"Try to take him and you'll be in a world of hurt. The man will kill you. No two ways about it. He'll shoot you dead. He's a crack shot with a high-powered rifle. The man just takes great pride in shooting," said Sheriff Curtis Pellet, who had had more than one run-in with Gordon.

"After acquiring information from Texas, from the people up and around Heaton, it satisfied me that we would have to work out a situation to afford a peaceful surrender of Gordon Kahl or we were going to have problems," Warren remarked later.

Warren telephoned Gordon to see if a man-to-man meeting couldn't be arranged.

Kahl saw little point in a meeting.

"I have no intention of going down there [to Texas]. I was tried illegally, I was sentenced illegally . . . I don't see any reason why I should go through that again," said Kahl.

"I have an obligation to fulfill," said Warren. "And I intend to see it completed."

Gordon agreed. "You got that job you've got to do. If you want to work for the communists that is your choice," he said. "But I'm not going to give up my religion. I've got nothing to lose. I am satisfied you will be coming to take me away or kill me, one of the two. I haven't shot anybody since World War II, but I haven't forgotten how."

Warren persisted. "At least we should try to find a peaceful solution," he pleaded.

After nearly an hour, Gordon agreed to a meeting if two conditions were met: Warren wouldn't try to arrest Gordon, and several of Gordon's friends would be allowed to attend. "You can have a hundred people there if you want. I don't care," said Warren, accepting the conditions.

The meeting was set for a Thursday night—Wednesday night was church night and no one would be available—at the farm home of Kahl's neighbor, Bud Brakel. Attending with Brakel would be the Reverend Peter Dyck, a Baptist minister who ran a small Christian school in Harvey and who pastored the church outside of Heaton that Gordon occasionally attended, and Herman Widicker, Gordon's friend and sometime employer. No guns would be allowed.

On April 11, just days before the meeting, an interview with Gordon appeared in the *Harvey Herald,* the local newspaper. In it, Gordon reiterated his position that the income tax is one of the commandments of Satan. Warren also was quoted as saying he didn't think Kahl was a physical threat to society. Yet, despite his public pronouncements, and his assurances to Kahl that he didn't care who else was in attendance, Warren was nervous. He didn't know Kahl, he didn't even know what he looked like. Nor did he know any of the individuals who would be at the meeting. Were they like Kahl? Did they hold the same beliefs? Was he walking into a trap? Warren called Sheriff Pellet for some answers.

The presence of Dyck, Brakel, and Widicker—who were solid church-going, community-oriented people—should deter any violent response by Kahl, said Pellet. He added, however, that if Yorie Kahl and Scott Faul, a fellow Posse member and friend of Gordon's, attended the meeting, Warren would have all the ingredients needed for an explosive situation.

More than once Pellet had been lectured by Yorie about his constitutional right to carry a gun without a weapons permit. A permit, said Yorie, was a man-made law that wasn't legitimate in the eyes of God. Yorie also told Pellet that any sheriff who insisted on enforcing such man-made laws was working for Satan and could be killed. "I could shoot you and it would not be held against me in the eyes of the Bible," said Yorie during one heated discussion in Pellet's office.

Like Gordon, Scott Faul had had his share of run-ins with authorities over taxes. The twenty-nine-year-old Faul had been convicted in Burleigh County Court on charges of failing to file proper state income tax returns, in both 1977 and 1978, on earnings of $140,000. Pellet also had firsthand, gun-point experience with Faul, who operated a chemical-free, thousand-acre farm about six miles south of Harvey. It occurred shortly after the twenty-nine-year-old Faul clashed with the local school board over the issue of sex education being taught in the classroom, and he pulled his two children from the public school. The school started legal action, and Pellet went to the farm to serve Faul with a summons that ordered him to appear in court. Pellet was met at the front door by Faul, who carried a semiautomatic rifle.

"There is no need for that. I'm not here to arrest you," said Pellet.

Faul pointed the rifle at Pellet's chest. "Nobody is ever going to arrest me," he said. "Get off my property or I'll shoot you."

"I'm leaving," said Pellet as he backed down the steps. As Faul closed the door, Pellet stuck the warrant in the door and left.

Those two are nothing but trouble, Pellet told Warren. "Call me when you get out of the meeting," said Pellet. "If I don't hear from you, I'll assume something happened and prepare for the worst."

It wasn't exactly a ringing endorsement for Warren's plan.

Wednesday, the day before the scheduled meeting, Warren left his Fargo office, climbed into his unmarked car, and drove the 120 miles to Heaton. He wanted to get a look at Gordon Kahl; if he spotted him alone and unarmed perhaps Warren could arrest him. The marshal planned to arrive before church ended and station himself outside of it and act as inconspicuous as possible. But he was fooling only himself in thinking he would go unnoticed. In any small town in rural America, strangers are sighted quickly and, just as quickly, fall under the suspecting eyes of the community's inhabitants. The watcher becomes the watched.

At one time, Heaton was a thriving, if small, farming community. It boasted three grain elevators, two banks, a lumberyard that served the region, several churches and taverns, a post office, clothing store, general store, butcher shop, billiards hall, cafés, and a blacksmith shop. But now, the town Warren traveled to was in every way, but name, a ghost town. All that remained was a combination gas station–general store that was open on a part-time basis and offered little in the way of selection. Its owner even stopped stocking cigarettes because he didn't want to give thieves a reason to break into the ramshackle building. And there was the Heaton Bible Church that was housed in what was once a tavern.

When he arrived in Heaton, Warren drove past the church, where he saw an unarmed, elderly man leaning against the building, a smile on his face and his cap pulled over one eye, like a Dead-End Kid.

Warren drove to the end of the street, made a U-turn and again passed the church. The man was now sitting in an older model, Chrysler station wagon. If that was Kahl, Warren had missed his chance to arrest him. Reportedly, Kahl carried several weapons at all times in his vehicle.

Warren pulled across from the church, parked his car and watched as the people filed out of the church. No one else matched Kahl's description. Warren returned to Fargo.

The next morning he telephoned Kahl to see if the meeting was still on. "You were here last night, weren't you?" asked Gordon.

"I was. But I was only there to see what you looked like," said Warren.

"All I've asked for is to be left alone. I won't bother you as long as you don't bother me," said Gordon. "If you had tried to take me, I would have had to protect myself. If you had tried to take me, you'd have to out-talk that mini-14.

"Nothing personal, you understand," he added.

Warren assured Kahl there would be no arrest attempt at, during, or following the meeting. Just to be safe, Warren then called Rev. Peter Dyck and asked him to ride with Warren to the meeting.

Despite Warren's concerns, the meeting had a congenial, if at times tense, atmosphere.

"We aren't going to have any violence for a probation violation," Warren told Gordon and the half-dozen other men gathered around the table in the spacious dining room of the Brakels' well-kept, two-story home. But, he added, a no-action course would take from him any flexibility he might have in seeing the situation resolved. "We have to do something," he stated.

Gordon was unmoved. "The IRS so much as admitted at my trial that the actions against me and my fellow patriots were a 'matter of getting us out of circulation,' " said Gordon. "If I go back to jail, the government will see to it that I'm permanently put out of circulation. I won't return."

"Gordon feels he has been pushed over the brink," said Mr. Dyck. "He has only one thing left to do. None of us cherish that. None of us want to see that. But something needs to be done to protect Gordon's religious beliefs."

Others at the table wondered aloud why the government, and the IRS in particular, insisted on prosecuting Gordon, a man who rarely earned more than $10,000 a year.

"The whole thing is so ridiculous because Gordon's never had any money. He's never made any money," said Mr. Dyck. "You are pushing something so out of proportion."

Warren responded, "If Gordon's correct, and there was serious misconduct in the government's handling of his case, he should get a good tax attorney and fight the matter in court, not outside the courtroom."

"I don't need a tax attorney," said Gordon. "I need a religious attorney. I need a Christian attorney. Somebody that will get down to Satanism and Christianity. I don't think such an attorney exists."

Finally, after nearly five hours of discussion, Warren offered a compromise. "Let's have somewhat of a moratorium here for, say, thirty days. You contact some people and satisfy yourself whether or not you got a fair shake from the government. You can talk to an attorney and make arrangements for an appearance in court.

"In the meantime, I will contact the people that I work with, including your probation officer, the U.S. attorney, the people in Texas, and I'll endeavor to have this case transferred from Texas to North Dakota."

The agreement seemed satisfactory to everyone involved, including Gordon. The meeting ended with a feeling that there was a reasonable chance for everything to end peacefully.

On June 15, 1981, nearly eight months after President Jimmy Carter was defeated for re-election, Warren resigned from the political patronage position of U.S. marshal and accepted a new assignment as deputy marshal in the state's Grand Forks office. He turned over his office and the unresolved Kahl matter to a man who had once been his deputy, Kenneth Muir.

Kahl, technically a fugitive, openly walked the streets of Heaton, Carrington, Harvey, Minot, Medina, and other North Dakota towns near his farm. Oh, he heard out what a tax attorney had to say about his case. But the man only talked about the government's laws, not God's laws, which further convinced Gordon that he would never return to a courtroom, not in Texas, not in North Dakota. His next battle would be fought on the site he chose. "If World War III is going to start, it is going to start right here [his farm]. I have got nothing to lose," he told Warren.

Despite the tough talk, Kahl didn't seem anxious to confront the authorities. Winter was approaching, and it was again time to head south. Texas was no longer a place Kahl felt welcome, but there were other places where fellow patriots and Christians lived. In October, Kahl and Joan quietly slipped away to a small farm outside of Mena, Arkansas. They didn't arrive as Mr. and Mrs. Gordon Kahl. Convinced he was marked for execution by the government, Gordon left their true identities in North Dakota. In Mena, they would be Mr. and Mrs. Sam Louden.

While in Arkansas, Gordon attended meetings of the Association for Constitutional Enforcement, a group, like the Posse, that opposed personal income taxes and was steeped in the religious teachings of the Identity movement. Gordon was a welcomed guest at the ACE meetings. In their midst, he was one of the most respected leaders of the fight against the anti-American forces at work in the United States. He was a man the government couldn't break. He was a man harassed, hounded, and sent to prison by the anti-American forces. Yet, he remained unbowed and true to his beliefs. Unafraid to continue the fight for both the farmers and the country.

Among Gordon's most ardent admirers in ACE was Leonard Ginter, a sixty-one-year-old retired carpenter. Ginter considered Gordon both a true patriot and a true Christian. The two men also shared a common interest in the Posse Comitatus: Ginter had been a member of the Posse when he lived in Wisconsin. After one ACE meeting, Ginter shook hands with Gordon and told him if there was ever anything Gordon needed, all he had to do was ask. Gordon thanked him.

Aside from ACE meetings, Gordon traveled to the Covenant, Sword and Arm of the Lord compound, located near the Missouri-Arkansas border; there he participated in some survivalist training exercises. He also hosted his own meetings, which sometimes lasted for days as patriots discussed and debated the solutions needed to right the country. Gordon drew strength from his stay in Arkansas. He was in his element, among fellow Christians and true believers who honored him, and he even broached the idea to Joan that the couple should make Arkansas their permanent home.

Arkansas was not, however, Joan's idea of home. She didn't like all the strangers for whom she found herself cooking meals and whose stays grew longer and longer. "They were good people. They were patriots, but I didn't want to be bothered," said Joan.

She had hoped that when Gordon was released from prison his attitudes would have changed, or at least he would tone down his political rhetoric, but he did neither. And Joan was concerned about the influence Gordon exerted on their oldest son, Yorie. "Yorie had so much respect for his father that I don't think he'd dispute his word for anything," said Joan, who felt such idolation on Yorie's part could only lead to trouble. Keep your political thoughts to yourself, and let Yorie lead his own life, she told her husband.

But Joan's concern came years too late. Gordon's and Yorie's lives were already tightly interwoven, their philosophical and ideological beliefs in lockstep with each other's.

As a child, Yorie had been inculcated with the philosophy that a Jewish-Masonic conspiracy was attempting to destroy the true Christian government of the United States. The philosophy contended that conspirators could give a secret hand signal and loans were readily available, or enemies quickly dispatched. Yorie's beliefs weren't based upon any real-life experiences; he accepted whatever his father told him as truth, and was intolerant of conflicting opinions.

When Yorie's junior class civics teacher disputed some of Gordon's philosophies, which Yorie had parroted in the classroom, he quit school and joined his father in the oil fields in Texas. At seventeen, Yorie watched his father forced into prison by the conspirators. Like his father, he was humiliated by the government's treatment of the Posse members at the trial. When Gordon came home from prison and said a return to prison would end in his death, Yorie believed and vowed: "I will not let my father be taken." When Gordon formed his own church, Yorie was made bishop in it. When Yorie married, and his wife, Janice, gave birth to a son, the couple named the child Gordon Wendell. When Yorie spoke, friends and family heard Gordon. The voice was pitched a bit higher and was less assured, but the words were Gordon's.

Joan attempted to communicate with her son, especially on the tax issue. "The value of the land far exceeds the taxes, but if we don't pay the taxes we'll lose the land forever," she told Yorie.

But her protests were useless. Each time she raised the subject, Yorie became more enraged. How could she even consider paying money to Satan's servants, said Yorie.

Joan's face showed the strain. The lines grew harder and deeper. Her cheeks became more sunken and her eyes hollowed. She looked older than her fifty-five years.

Then, "the light bill came and on it was a name other than mine," recalled Joan. She rebelled. "You can have your beliefs and do what you want with them, but I don't want to be part of it," Joan told Gordon. She wanted her name back. She wanted her home back. She decided to return to Heaton, where the couple's youngest daughter was going to graduate from high school in May. She gave that excuse to Gordon for her return.

But Joan had other plans in mind, too. She was going to borrow money from her brother and pay off the tax lien owed to the IRS and get the farm back, and she was plotting, for the first time in her thirty-seven years of marriage, to leave her husband, at least for a while. She was going to take a job, save her money, and move to Texas to live with her oldest daughter.

Yorie returned to Heaton with Joan. Now married, he took up residence at the farm with his wife, and their two children. Joan took an apartment in Carrington with her daughter Lonnie and got a job as a housekeeper with the hospital in town. And, without either Yorie's or Gordon's knowledge, she got her brother to pay off the back taxes on the farm. Her brother now owned the land, but agreed to return it to Joan and Gordon once their tax situation reached some kind of settlement.

Joan began saving her money; each month she sent some to her daughter Linda, in Texas, with the instructions to send it back, when Joan told her, along with a request that Joan help care for Linda's family. She needed that request so Gordon wouldn't be suspicious.

It wasn't long before Gordon returned to Heaton, and when he found out about Joan's subterfuge, both he and Yorie exploded. Paying off the lien was akin to giving aid and comfort to the enemy, said Gordon. She had betrayed him.

Nor could such a betrayal go unpunished. On August 27, 1982, Joan was notified by letter that she had been excommunicated from the Gospel Doctrine Church of Jesus Christ, Alter Ego Gordon Kahl. The notification came from Yorie, who acted in his capacity as bishop of the church. "You usurped authority which you did not have and have attempted to negotiate and compromise by paying tithes and other blackmail payments to the tithing collectors of the Jewish-Masonic Synogogue [sic] of Satan . . . for the purpose of securing a more favorable treatment by Satan's servants in regard to certain church property," wrote Yorie.

"Should you see the errors of your ways, repent of your unscriptural and unChristian actions, and conform your future days of probation to be in accord with the Laws and Commandments of God as revealed by Jesus Christ and recorded in the Scriptures, we will be most happy to return you to full fellowship with the Saints who make up the body of Christ.

"It is with the most profound regret that I find it necessary to take such drastic action, but it is with the hope that it might prevent worse mistakes in the future," concluded Yorie.

Within a few months, Gordon's and Yorie's outrage passed, and they accepted Joan back into the family. But she wasn't so readily accepted back into the church. She still had to prove she was on the side of the saints. Until then the excommunication order stood.

Meanwhile, during the fall and winter of 1982, having returned to North Dakota from Arkansas, Gordon resumed his efforts to awaken farmers to the conspiracy that threatened to enslave them. Farm rallies, attracting up to a hundred people and featuring patriot speakers from Utah, South Dakota, and Montana, were held in Jamestown, Zeeland, and Ashley. At those rallies, farmers were told how they could use do-it-yourself lawsuits to save their farms, or Public Office Money Certificates to repay their debts. (The POMC was nothing more than a piece of paper that stated the person would pay his debts once the government returned to either the gold or silver standard.) Gordon also warned the small farmers against joining the various farm aid programs, which he said were just another trap to make them dependent upon the government.

In November, Gordon traveled to Halstead, Kansas, where he met with Keith Shive, the founder of the Farmer's Liberation Army, and discussed the possibilities of some cooperative efforts between the patriots in the two states. Gordon was so impressed with Shive that he invited him to North Dakota to address a series of farm rallies in late February of 1983. And almost immediately after he returned from Kansas, Gordon, along with Yorie and Scott Faul, crisscrossed North Dakota to drum up interest in Shive's visit.

Gordon also resumed his efforts to organize a Posse-style township. Monthly meetings were held at Dr. Clarence Martin's clinic in Medina, or at James Coleman's veterinary clinic in Ashley, where plans for the township were discussed and outlined. Strength was in numbers, argued Gordon, and the township would give them the strength needed to carry the fight against the conspirators. Without the township, Wells County would punish Scott Faul for removing his children from public schools, where such evils as sex education were being taught. The state would close Len Martin's small Christian school in Ashley, North Dakota, because it wasn't accredited. And, of course, the bankers would take away the family farms.

It seemed to Gordon that each day another farmer lost his land to the bankers and the government; that each day more children were brainwashed by the humanistic textbooks used in the public schools. The power of Satan's servants was growing. They were taking control of the land. They were taking control of the children. And they had already manipulated his wife into paying tithes to the Satanic IRS.

But they wouldn't get him. Gordon refused to file his income taxes. He refused to sign his probation reports. And still wanted as a parole violater, he refused to go into hiding. Gordon had a message to deliver, and he delivered it openly to the people in Ashley and in Springfield, Colorado, and in Medina. The time had come, said Gordon, to "engage in a struggle to the death between the people of the Kingdom of God and the Kingdom of Satan."

4

A Call to Duty

That Sunday, the thirteenth of February 1983, Ken Muir and his wife, Lois, returned home at about two o'clock in the afternoon. Home was a large, unpretentious, two-story stucco duplex, which sat along a placid south Fargo street that in the summer revealed broad, green lawns, shaded by tall, leafy elm trees. They had purchased it in 1961, after Lois's bad bout with the flu turned out to be Laurie, the couple's third, and final, child.

It had been a pleasant day so far. As usual, the two of them attended services at the First Methodist Church. Then, they and a dozen friends drove north of the city out to Tom and Joan Humphrey's farm where Sunday school class was followed by a hearty brunch of pancakes with raspberry syrup, scrambled eggs, sausage, and bowls of mixed fruit. The conversation had been spirited and amiable, if, at one point, a bit uncomfortable for Ken.

Rather uncharacteristically, Lois had boasted about how good Ken was at his job as U.S. marshal. It embarrassed him and Ken didn't like to be embarrassed, or to reveal any type of emotion. He felt it was a sign of weakness for a man to readily show his feelings. While he had an easy smile, about the only time someone could tell if he was angry or upset was when the corner of his mouth started to quiver.

Despite his embarrassment, he wasn't angry about Lois's remarks. Actually, they made him feel good. Certainly they had had their differences during their thirty-five years of marriage, differences that had been punctuated with more than one threat of divorce.

And Ken had reason to be proud of his twenty years in the marshals service. His career started in Oxford, Mississippi, where he was assigned to protect James Meredith in his attempt to integrate Ole Miss University. Struck with a rock and bleeding severely from a head wound, Ken had held his position, and his actions were commended by both President John F. Kennedy and his younger brother, Attorney General Robert Kennedy. "You prevented a serious and tragic incident from becoming a disaster. Had you failed, our country would have suffered irreparable damage," President Kennedy wrote in his letter to Ken.

Ken believed his career would culminate with his retirement as the U.S. marshal for the District of North Dakota. "After twenty-one years in the marshals service, it [becoming marshal] is really something to finish your career with," Ken said at his swearing-in ceremony.

After they arrived home that Sunday afternoon, Ken went upstairs to change out of his suit. He was going to shovel the sidewalk. Not that he really needed to; the sun and warm temperatures had already completed most of the work. But it would give him an excuse to get outside and sneak a cigarette or two. He had been trying to quit, just like he had been trying to lose those extra thirty to thirty-five pounds that were starting to settle around his midsection. He didn't look obese, but at fifty-three years old, and only slightly above average in height—five feet eleven inches—the 235 pounds he was carrying around was too much. His graying hair was going, his eyesight needed to be corrected with glasses, and now both Ken and his doctor agreed that he would have to shed some of himself and quit smoking if he wanted to stay in good health.

As he savored the springlike weather, occasionally putting his shovel to work, Lois came to the door. "Telephone," she said.

Ken entered the house and picked up the receiver. It was a deputy from the Bismarck office. "We've located Gordon Kahl," he said.

Gordon Wendell Kahl. The name was familiar to Ken. Too familiar. Kahl was like an open sore that wouldn't heal, growing uglier the longer it went untended.

In law enforcement, minor warrants were overlooked regularly; sometimes the paperwork and the man-hours needed to serve them outweighed the offense. A misdemeanor could be overlooked; even the failure to file an income tax form could be ignored. In their testimony at Kahl's first trial in Texas, IRS agents acknowledged that it wasn't common practice to take legal action against someone who made less than $10,000 annually. That explained why, for five years, the IRS had left Kahl alone. He wasn't a big fish. He wasn't even small fry, and what the government could have squeezed from Kahl wouldn't have covered the court costs. But all that was changed when Kahl went on television and flaunted his nonpayment and urged others to follow suit. That couldn't be tolerated. And now here Kahl was again, doing the same damn thing. In newspaper interviews and at farm rallies, Kahl talked openly about not paying his taxes. He even directed threats toward his probation officer, as well as a former U.S. marshal and anyone else in a uniform. Should they try to arrest him, Kahl said, he would kill them, and a person could threaten to kill law enforcement officers only so often before action had to be taken.

Arrest attempts were tried. A lot of service time had been wasted trying to serve Kahl a warrant for a misdemeanor probation violation. In the latter part of June 1981, they borrowed state Bureau of Reclamation vehicles and posed as surveyors along a road Kahl was known to frequently travel when going to work. But Kahl didn't use it that day. They got a second chance to execute the warrant in September, when the marshals service was notified that Kahl was in the Carrington hospital being treated for injuries he sustained when he crashed his son's Cessna 172 aircraft after it ran out of gas on take-off from his farm. But when marshal deputies arrived the next morning, all they found was an empty bed. Sometime during the night or early evening hours, Kahl had removed the intravenous tubes from his arms and fled the hospital. After that he dropped out of sight, but perhaps this time they had him.

The telephone call had come from Robert Cheshire, a deputy in the Bismarck office. Minutes earlier Cheshire had received a telephone call from state radio and was told that Deputy Sheriff Bradley Kapp of Stutsman County had spotted Kahl's vehicle in the parking lot of a clinic in Medina. Kapp had wanted to know if the warrant for Kahl was still outstanding. Cheshire called Kapp, informed him the warrant was still outstanding, and asked him to maintain surveillance on the clinic until the marshals arrived. Kapp agreed. Now Cheshire and Jim Hopson—a fellow Bismarck deputy—were prepared to leave for Medina immediately to make the arrest. Could Ken send a backup unit?

Ken agreed to meet Cheshire and Hopson outside of Medina.

After he hung up the telephone, Ken went back upstairs to change clothes again. He told Lois, "We're going out to try and get someone we have a warrant for." A tax protestor, he told Lois without mentioning a name.

"What time will you be home?"

"I'm hoping to be back in time to watch the last segment of 'Winds of War.'"

"Be careful. Don't try to be a hero," Lois remarked, only half-jokingly, as Ken went out the front door and down the porch steps.

She didn't give him a kiss good-bye; after all, he'd be home again before she had a chance to miss him. It was one of those taken-for-granted things that often come back to haunt people.

Ken arrived at his office on the second floor of the Old Federal Building shortly before three o'clock and set about locating a deputy to accompany him to Medina. He first called his chief deputy, Ron Evans. Evans had transferred to Fargo two weeks earlier from Miami, and was still living out of a motel as he searched for a house for his family. Evans wasn't in his room. Ken called Harold Warren next. Warren was one of the last people Ken wanted as company in the closed quarters of a car on a 125-mile drive. There was a lot of bad blood between the two strong-willed men. Ken felt that Warren, while marshal, had been unfairly critical of Ken's work and that Warren's performance evaluations had cost him a promotion to chief deputy. Ken didn't help the relationship when, after his appointment as marshal, he let Warren stew for several days before he granted Warren's request to be reassigned as a deputy marshal to North Dakota. The two men had also clashed over how to take Gordon Kahl into custody.

Warren had been a member of the detachment that impersonated highway surveyors while waiting for Kahl to drive past. At that time he told Ken that it was a stupid idea, that if he thought Gordon Kahl would "fall for that kind of Keystone Kops, Tinkertoy setup, then you, Marshal Muir, must have your head up your ass."

It was Warren's view that a safer way to arrest Kahl would be to wait until he took his wife grocery shopping. The grocery store was about the only place he knew that Kahl didn't carry a weapon with him. While Kahl and his wife were pushing their shopping cart down the aisle, two or three deputies could come up behind him, grab him, and the arrest would be completed without incident, said Warren.

Ken's response was to tell Warren that "as marshal you did it your way, now I'm marshal and I'll do it my way." Still, Warren knew Kahl by sight and he was one of Ken's deputies. When he called, Warren was home.

"Gordon Kahl has been spotted, and two deputies are coming out of Bismarck and we're going to drive out and pick him up," said Ken. "I'm calling to see if you want to ride along."

"Is that an order?" Warren asked.

It wasn't, Ken responded.

In that case, Warren replied, he did not necessarily want to ride along.

"So that's the way it is?" asked Ken.

"I guess so," answered Warren.

Ken hung up and called Carl Wigglesworth, a deputy and the

district's acting warrants inspector. Wigglesworth would meet him at the office and the two of them would drive out to Medina to arrest Gordon Kahl. Carl left his wife and reported to the office.

After Ken had hung up the telephone on him, Bud Warren stood holding the receiver in his hand. "What's wrong?" his wife asked him.

"Someone will be dead before the day is over," Warren replied.

5

No Place to Hide

Medina rests in a small valley off Interstate 94, about 125 miles west of Fargo. A large billboard, with a pelican on it, stands just before the exit ramp, announcing the town's existence to all passersby. There is little to distinguish Medina from the many other small, quiet, farming villages and towns that dot the rural Midwest. In February, many of the town's 520 residents turn their attention to the high school's basketball team, which made its first appearance in the state tournament just two years earlier and finished in sixth place. The town did gain national attention in 1949 when it changed the pronunciation of its name, from mah-DI-na to mah-DEE-na, the way federal judge Harold R. Medina pronounced his name. The city council enacted the change into law following the trial of eleven communists in New York at which Medina had presided.

Pickup trucks, with gun racks in the back window, are familiar sights along the two blocks of Water Street, the town's business district. There are the drug store, grocery store, and post office. The Coffee Cup Café serves home-cooked meals followed by homemade desserts; and Gil's Bar is the place to go for cold beer, a place where locals hang out and where a stranger might overhear conversation in German. At the east end of Water Street, on the edge of town, sits a plain-looking, one-story building. Its official name is the Medina Medical Center. But to anyone who had lived in these parts for the past twenty years, it was better known as Doc Martin's Clinic.

Dr. Clarence Martin moved to North Dakota in 1948. He had graduated from the University of Pennsylvania's School of Medicine in 1943, and then entered the United States Army, where he served, at the rank of captain, as a battalion surgeon in the Pacific theater. Following the war, Martin attended a six-months medical refresher course at Harvard University and he then returned to Pennsylvania for one year before packing his medical bag and moving west to North Dakota, where he set up a practice as a country doctor.

It was a practice that flourished; a seven-days-a-week practice that was appreciated by the rural residents. To his patients and those who knew him, Martin, who looked the part of a country doctor with snow-white hair and a white beard, was a kind, gentle, and peace-loving man, who, with the wave of a hand, would assure someone that money wasn't important. What was important, he would tell them, was their health. "If you get some money some time, stop by and pay," Martin told more than one person who was short of cash. In 1982, the community honored his many years of service with a Doc Martin Day. Among the hundreds of people in attendance were many who had been delivered as babies by Martin and whose own children were now cared for by him.

Martin didn't limit his activities to medicine. Politics was an addiction whose cravings he filled by being active for more than twenty years in the conservative movement in North Dakota. His views were strongly held, and they were principles on which he patterned his life. Once, in 1962, he offered to treat poor people for free so they wouldn't have to accept government welfare payments. Too much government interference was not healthy for the individual, he believed.

Martin was the founder of the North Dakota chapter of the Constitutional party and in that capacity met Gordon Kahl in 1969. The two men became fast friends. They traveled together to Martin's cabin in Montana, where they would spend long evenings debating each other's views on the Bible. Martin served as the Kahl family's physician, and sometimes as their banker, lending Gordon money when a mortgage payment was coming due. Like many friends, however, the two strong-willed men had their differences. Martin was a conservative, yes, but not an extremist like Kahl. He didn't share his friend's belief in British Israelism; nor did he accept racist and anti-Semitic views. On more than one occasion Martin, citing passages of Scripture, attempted to change Kahl's position. This Sunday would be one of those times.

Gordon arrived at the clinic in his 1970, brown, two-tone station wagon at about 2 P.M. He was accompanied by Joan, who came along to visit some women friends who would be at the meeting, Yorie, and Scott Faul. The three men carried mini-14 rifles, with banana clips. Yorie also wore a shoulder holster that held a .45-caliber pistol. Martin greeted them at the back door of the clinic. He had to talk with Kahl. A week earlier at a similar meeting in Ashley, Martin, Kahl, and another man, David Broer, had been chosen as a steering committee to draft a charter for the formation of the Continental Township. Martin wanted Gordon to withdraw his support for the charter plank that banned the membership of blacks. The purpose of the township, said Martin, was to prepare the community for when the banks failed, the established government collapsed, and anarchy and outside invaders threatened to destroy their way of life. Their township, said Martin, would be ready with the nucleus for an independent government that would assume the responsibility of providing for the welfare and protection of the people. All people, argued Martin. Blacks and Jews included. The Bible demanded such an open-arms type of government. Even though the total number of blacks in North Dakota comprised less than one-half of one percent of the population, Martin was adamant.

Gordon was equally adamant. No blacks would be allowed. Blacks are children of Satan, not God, said Kahl, and they are used by the Jews to weaken this country through intermarriage. On that point, said Gordon, he shared the beliefs of his Idaho contacts, which included the Reverend Richard G. Butler, founder of the white-supremacist Ayran Nations in Hayden Lake and pastor of the Christian Identity–steeped Church of Jesus Christ, Christian. A man's race was his nation, preached Butler, and neither should be polluted by contact with inferior individuals.

As their argument intensified and their voices rose, some of the group's members started to arrive at the clinic. David Broer and Vernon Wegner, who drove together from Streeter, a town twenty miles south of Medina, came in and seated themselves on the east side of the room, next to Yorie and Scott.

With the exception of Martin, David Broer was easily the most well-read member of the group. Since high school, the forty-three-year-old Broer, a self-employed carpenter, had amassed 225 college credits without earning a degree. Although he stood six feet two inches tall, with a medium build, he was not a physically imposing person. He wore glasses over sad, tired-looking hazel eyes and had his brown hair cut in a conservative fashion. He had a scholarly air about him, which was enhanced by the soft-spoken, articulate way he presented ideas and proposals to the group. He seemed to weigh carefully each word he used.

Rarely did he take one side over another. He spent his energies attempting to find common denominators among conflicting political and religious beliefs that threatened to rend the new township government unworkable, and he relished his role as peacekeeper. Broer considered himself a self-taught legal expert, especially in areas that involved government. It was to Broer that the farmers in the group turned for advice on how to fight government efforts to foreclose on their land, advice he offered readily. Everyone thought he was bright, but some wondered if, like the absent-minded professor, he lacked common sense. Instead of a pointer in his hand, Broer carried with him a 12-gauge shotgun that had a pistol grip and folding stock. He placed it under his seat when he sat down in the clinic's meeting room.

Vernon Wegner sat next to Broer. Had the weather been less mild, Wegner would have stayed at home to chop wood for his home-made stove. As it was, the need for extra wood wasn't as pressing as his interest in this new government. A slightly built man, who stood an inch over six feet tall and weighed 175 pounds, Wegner had brown hair and, despite a scraggly beard and mustache, looked younger than his age of twenty-six. Up until a week ago, he had been the police chief in Streeter, earning $1,000 a month. Now, however, he was looking for a new job as a farm laborer. Until he found a job, or at least some part-time work, Wegner, his wife, Sherry, and their son would have to get by on the $10 to $15 a month Sherry earned from her Sunday paper route. Wegner had been fired by the Streeter city council on the basis of his poor job performance, including an unauthorized purchase of four dozen cans of mace and fifteen tear gas grenades. Wegner had been encouraged by several members of the township group to use his position as police chief to acquire the grenades. They were going to ship them down to the Farmer's Liberation Army in Kansas so its members could respond in kind when the police attacked them with tear gas.

Len Martin bustled into the room and took a seat along the north wall. Len, no relation to Dr. Martin, was the township's scribe. A North Dakota native, he had worked as a reporter in Washington, D.C., for *The Spotlight*, the weekly newspaper and chief voice for the anti-Semitic Liberty Lobby. In May of 1982, after he returned to North Dakota, the fifty-eight-year-old Martin walked across the state with a stuffed toy monkey on his back. The monkey represented the IRS and bore the legend: "Get this monkey off my back." The publicity stunt made him the subject of feature stories in newspapers and on television programs throughout North Dakota and he was featured as a "bright" segment on the network news.

Following this success, he established a small, erratically published newsletter called *Monkey Business* that warned its readers of the allegedly illegal nature of Federal Reserve System, as well as focusing on issues of Christian education and farm foreclosure. Schoolmaster for the American Christian School, an alternative to the public schools, in Ashley, North Dakota, Len had urged Dr. Martin to host these meetings, and had accompanied Kahl and

Faul to Halstead, Kansas, in November of 1982 to meet with Keith Shive, leader of the FLA, and encourage him to bring his message to the state in a series of speaking engagements.

Other members arrived—eighteen in all, not a bad turnout given how nice a day it was outside. One person, however, was conspicuously absent: Darrell Graf, police chief for the town of Medina. Graf had attended many of the earlier meetings and had even gotten sufficiently into the spirit of the group to bring his guitar case to one meeting; inside was a rifle.

As people seated themselves, Dr. Martin and Gordon moved to join the group. The debate was beginning to wear on both men. Gordon took a seat near Yorie, Faul, Broer, and Wegner. He held his rifle between his legs, the stock resting on the floor. Yorie did the same.

Dr. Martin stood at the podium—a free-standing instrument tray—in the center of the room. On the tray was a small American flag. Normally, the group began each meeting with the Pledge of Allegiance and a reading from the Bible. But today Dr. Martin wasted no time getting to the heart of the issue he felt the group had to resolve. "Anyone who is a racist raise your hand," Martin demanded of the group.

Gordon, Yorie, and Scott raised their hands. Although he didn't raise his hand, Wegner told Gordon privately that if four or five blacks had been in attendance at the meeting, Wegner wouldn't have come. Nor would he join an organization that allowed blacks as members.

Dr. Martin pressed his case. "All men are created equal, and racist views run counter to the teachings of the Bible and to the religious nature of the independent township," he said. Martin quoted from 1 Corinthians, chapter 13, which reads in part, "Love is patient, love is kind, love is not jealous . . . is not provoked, does not take into account a wrong suffered, does not rejoice in unrighteousness, but rejoices with the truth."

Dr. Martin also reminded his audience that the decisions made today would have to be justified to Jesus Christ with the arrival of the millennium, the time Christ would return to earth to establish a thousand-year reign.

Gordon refused to accede. No man other than a white freeman can be admitted to the township, he said. Drawing upon his Identity teachings, Gordon argued that the God who created the races commanded the segregation of the races. The very definition of nation is race. The Bible demands segregation, said Gordon. You can't be a Christian and mix with Negroes.

Several blocks away from the clinic, Bradley Kapp patted his filled stomach and excused himself from the dining room table in his mother-in-law's house. It was time to go on patrol, said the Stutsman County deputy sheriff. Kapp left the house, climbed in his pickup truck and drove past the clinic. He knew a Posse meeting was scheduled for that Sunday afternoon, and he wondered if Gordon Kahl might not be in town for it. Kapp knew there had been a federal arrest warrant out on Kahl. And just last Thursday, lawmen throughout the state had been alerted by an all-points bulletin to be on the lookout for him. At the time, Kahl was believed to be heavily-armed and on his way to disrupt an auction sale outside of Minot. But, as he had done time and time before, Kahl eluded the lawmen's net.

Kapp slowed his pickup truck to a crawl as he passed the clinic, and saw a car he thought was Kahl's. He called the state radio dispatcher, who verified the license. Kapp telephoned his boss in Jamestown, Chief Deputy Sheriff Jack Miller. "Kahl's in Medina," said Kapp. "Is that warrant still out on him?"

Miller, a fourteen-year veteran with the sheriff's department, said he didn't have a copy of the warrant, nor did he know the substance of the warrant. "Leave it alone. We'll get a copy on Monday and then we can take action," Miller told his deputy.

Rather than leave it alone, Kapp made one more telephone call to the state radio. "Is that federal warrant on Gordon Kahl still out?" he asked.

The dispatcher didn't know, but she would check with the marshals service in Bismarck. A few minutes later a deputy marshal called and said they would be out immediately to arrest Kahl. Kapp agreed to the marshal's request to keep an eye on Kahl and help them with the arrest.

If he was going to conduct a stakeout, Kapp needed a portable, two-way radio so that from his pickup he could communicate with the deputy marshals driving in from Bismarck, some eighty miles west of Medina. Kapp went to Darrell Graf and asked if he could borrow Graf's radio.

"You're out of your fucking gourd. Call them back and tell them not to come. Call it off," said Graf after Kapp told him why he wanted the radio.

"This is a misdemeanor deal. It's no big thing and it's not worth really creating a problem over." The twenty-seven-year-old Graf had been in law enforcement for about five years, the last two years as full-time police chief for Medina. He was familiar with Kahl.

"Do you remember what we talked about on Thursday when the APB was issued?" asked Graf. "I told you then how I could just see dead highway patrolmen and local police all over the fucking place. Dead and they wouldn't know why. I know what Kahl is like. If you're going to take him, you'd better have a thirty-man SWAT team."

Graf had attended meetings at the clinic. "Gordon was a hell of a nice guy," he remembered, "well-mannered, kind, honest. But I believed him when he said he wouldn't be taken alive in any arrest attempt. Gordon meant business. You could tell in his eyes and the way he talked, he was tired of it all and wasn't going to take any more. He didn't talk in a wild, crazy way. He was very cool, calm."

When it became clear he couldn't change Kapp's mind, Graf gave him the radio and said, "I'm not getting involved. I don't think I could shoot somebody I know if it comes to that."

Kapp responded, "You don't have to, we'll take care of it."

Inside the clinic, the tension in the small room grew as the debate on racism continued. It was broken momentarily when Martin was called into the clinic to tend to a patient. The rest of the group took a break and went outside to enjoy some of the pleasant weather. Gordon approached David Broer and asked for his thoughts on the possibility of organizing a township government without Martin's involvement. Gordon was tired of the steady stream of argument he heard coming from Martin, but Broer didn't think the proposed township could be successful without him. Martin had too large a following to ignore. Broer asked Gordon for time to draw up a possible compromise that would be acceptable to both men.

When the meeting resumed, Broer proposed that anyone wanting to gain membership to the township would have to be sponsored by at least two township members. Martin grudgingly agreed to the membership plan. Gordon vehemently opposed it, in that there would still exist the possibility for black membership. Having heard enough for the day, Gordon angrily announced, "I'm leaving. Anyone coming with me?" and stalked out the north door.

Joan ended her conversation with her friends, rose from her chair, put on her coat, and followed. On her way out she stopped to tell Martin that she agreed with him and that she wished Gordon would eventually come around to Martin's view. She was followed out the door by Yorie. After a couple of minutes, Scott rose from his chair. "I better get going if I want a ride," he told the group. It was a few minutes before five o'clock. The sun was setting and chill had returned to the air.

Minutes later Scott returned to the room. "We're being watched," he said.

It was a standing concern among members of the township group that their meetings might be under police surveillance. Every member knew—thanks to Gordon's extensive research—that the CIA, the U.S. Marshals Service, the FBI, the Secret Service, and all but the smallest sheriff and police departments were under the influence of the Mossad, Israel's worldwide secret police force. Gordon also had cautioned them that in each community—no matter how small—there was a Mossad informant, whose duty was to report on activity that posed a threat to the Jewish-led conspiracy. On occasion, members even joked about who might be the informant in their area. But no one laughed this time. It made sense to them, in that they viewed themselves not as a trivial burr under the government's saddle but as a legitimate threat to the people and groups that ran the country. And here they were, about to organize into a township that would stand up to Satan's servants.

They were being watched.

For nearly two hours Bradley Kapp had been sitting in his 1982 green Ford pickup watching through a pair of binoculars for any activity in the clinic parking lot a block and a half south of his position. As is usually the case, it had been a pretty dull stakeout, made more uncomfortable by the bulletproof vest he wore. That was about to change. People started to mill around the cars. Some of the people even pointed fingers in his direction. Kapp wished the deputy marshals would arrive. He had no intention of trying to arrest Kahl on his own. And he certainly couldn't count on Darrell Graf for any help.

A voice crackled over Kapp's two-way radio.

"We're here. Is everything a ten-four?"

The voice was Deputy U.S. Marshal Robert Cheshire's.

With his partner, James Hopson, Cheshire had just arrived on the outskirts of Medina. He was driving the marshals service's four-wheel drive 1980 Dodge Ram Charger.

The two lawmen, dressed casually in jeans and boots, were waiting in the parking lot of a state highway maintenance garage, some three hundred yards off the Medina exit ramp. Ken Muir and Carl Wigglesworth were due to arrive from Fargo. Hopson and Cheshire donned their bulletproof vests. This was fifty-seven-year-old Hopson's third arrest attempt since being transferred to North Dakota in November of 1981. Prior to coming to the state, the twelve-year veteran of the marshals service had been stationed in Tucson and Milwaukee. Before that Hopson had been a police officer in a town north of Milwaukee.

The thirty-two-year-old Cheshire, a five-year veteran in the marshals service, had tried to take Kahl in before. One and a half years earlier, he had requested permission from Muir to change his schedule so he could spend several days trying to bring Kahl into custody. His request was granted, but the attempt proved futile. But this time they were going to get him. Shortly after arriving at the parking lot, Cheshire contacted state radio and requested that the operator call the sheriffs in Wells and Foster counties and have them stand by with some marked units. That order was quickly countermanded by Muir, who monitored the conversation on his car radio. "Cancel that. We don't want to go any further than what we're going," Muir told Cheshire.

A few minutes later, Muir and Wigglesworth arrived in their maroon, unmarked car. Muir got out and went to talk with Cheshire, and Wigglesworth started to fasten the straps of his bulletproof vest. But before he had done them up, Muir returned and said, "Let's go." Wigglesworth left the straps, threw on his jacket, and climbed into the car.

"We're going to contact the Medina police chief, and set up a roadblock just past the railroad tracks near the grain elevator on the north edge of town," Muir told Wigglesworth. "Cheshire and Hopson will pick up the Stutsman County deputy and serve as the trail vehicle."

Dr. Martin joined the rest of the people who were outside the clinic and who had their attention focused on the green pickup north of them. "That's just Bradley watching. He's always watching things," said Martin, who recognized that the pickup belonged to Kapp, whose daughter Martin had delivered. "Shall I go out and see what he's up to?" asked Martin.

"Don't bother," replied Kahl.

Instead, it was decided David Broer would call Darrell Graf to find out what was going on. Broer and Graf were friends. In fact, Graf had recently sought Broer's advice on what he should do about a dispute he was having with the air force over the security contract he had with its radar and communications facility at Concrete. And it was Graf who had called Broer on Friday, the day after the all-points bulletin on Gordon Kahl was issued, to say that because of the nature of the APB, Broer shouldn't spend time with Kahl. Graf had called Dr. Martin also and asked that he contact Kahl and have him take care of the warrant before something happened.

"Why didn't you come to the meeting?" Broer asked when Graf picked up the telephone at this home.

"I didn't know there was one," Graf lied. He knew very well that a meeting had been scheduled. "I wasn't going to be caught in a room with a federally sought person. One I should be arresting. And I wasn't going to arrest him," Graf said later.

Broer then asked if the APB was still in effect. It was, replied Graf. When Broer hung up the telephone, Yorie and Scott asked if he had gotten the license number of the car that Gordon and the other man were allegedly driving at this time. He hadn't. Broer called Graf back and asked for the license number. North Dakota plate 1906, said Graf. Scott, who was listening to the conversation on an extension, blanched. That was his car. Shauna had used it on Thursday to do laundry in town. What did the police want with him?

Scott, confused about why his car was cited in the APB, allowed his imagination to get the best of him. He remembered a story he had read of John Singer, a Utah farmer who, like Scott, had pulled his children out of the public schools and taught them at home. When Singer defied the state's orders to return the children to school, recalled Scott, the state ordered Singer arrested. But instead, the lawmen waited in ambush and shot Singer down as he walked, unarmed, to his mailbox. Was that going to happen to him? thought Scott.

While Scott wrestled with his imagination, Gordon decided to move his car from the north parking lot to the south parking lot to see if the person watching them would give chase. Gordon, Joan, Yorie, and Scott climbed into the car, and Gordon drove it around the corner. Kapp didn't follow. He was hurriedly trying to give the two deputy marshals—who were lost—directions to his position. Christ, how the hell could anyone get lost in Medina. We're going to lose them, thought Kapp.

Once out of the sight of Kapp, Gordon stopped the car. Joan was nervous. "What's going on?" she asked Gordon. "If there's going to be any trouble, I'll just stay here and have my neighbors come and get me."

Gordon tried to reassure her. "There isn't going to be any trouble. Just stay where you are at," he said. "There isn't going to be any trouble," he repeated.

Gordon, Yorie, and Scott, their rifles slung across their backs, re-entered the clinic. They huddled with Broer and Len Martin in a room off the reception area, discussing the reason for the surveillance and what action they should take. Yorie was overheard to say, "There must be a reason why Graf is not here."

Yorie was particularly concerned about his father's safety. Gordon repeatedly had told Yorie that someday the government would send its agents out to get him. Maybe that day was today. Yorie didn't want to take any chances. He urged his father to change coats with him in order to confuse anyone who might be looking for Gordon. Gordon refused. It wouldn't be necessary, he said. Necessary or not, Yorie insisted and his father relented. Yorie gave his brown coat to Gordon and put on his father's royal blue jacket. "Now all you need is to quick grow some hair," Yorie joked to Gordon.

But the next best thing to hair, said Yorie, would be Len Martin's brown stocking cap with which they replaced the bright blue baseball cap Gordon had been wearing. They would leave the clinic in two vehicles, one of which would be Broer's 1973 brown AMC Hornet. Two farmers at the meeting overheard Broer say he would go along to act as legal counsel to see that everyone was treated correctly should they be stopped and anyone arrested.

The group left the clinic, Broer driving the Hornet with Gordon in the passenger seat. Wegner sat in the backseat of the Kahl station wagon, next to Scott. Joan was in the front with Yorie at the wheel. Broer backed his car out of the parking lot and pulled in front of the Kahl station wagon, and the two vehicles started to leave the clinic.

Just as Gordon and his group were pulling out, Cheshire drove up alongside Kapp's pickup. Kapp gave them a quick rundown of events. "I saw Gordon, he's wearing a royal blue jacket and a blue baseball cap. He moved his car to the south side of the clinic, but I don't think he's left yet."

Let's go, Cheshire said. He told Kapp he was excited at the prospect of taking care of something that had been a thorn in their sides for some time. Kapp got out of the pickup, climbed over Hopson in the passenger's seat, and into the backseat of the Ram Charger. "Just remember," he said, "those people at the clinic are well armed and crazy enough to do something."

Nevertheless, Kapp felt comfortable with these two fellow officers. They seemed to him very professional and businesslike, giving the impression they were ready to take care of any kind of trouble that might arise. As Kapp settled into the backseat with his shotgun, Broer's car, followed by the Kahl station wagon, left the clinic's south parking lot. The Ram Charger fell in behind them. Based on the description Kapp had given him, Cheshire thought he spotted Gordon in the station wagon.

Graf arrived at the fire station at approximately 5:15 P.M. After he had talked with Broer on the telephone, Graf started to make some telephone calls of his own. He didn't like what was starting to take shape, and felt that something bad was about to happen. He called members of Medina's ambulance and rescue crews and asked that they meet him at the fire station.

As the ambulance crew and rescue squad members gathered, Graf told them he thought there was going to be a shootout. "The U.S. marshals are in town to arrest someone who isn't going give up without a real fight," said Graf.

In the background, Graf heard Ken Muir trying to reach him on the radio. "He was calling for me to help, but I just played dumb," Graf said later. "I couldn't see any way to win. Either we were the killers or the killed. It didn't take ESP to see how this was going to end."

Graf's deputy, Steve Schnabel, also heard the call for assistance and asked Graf's permission to answer it. Schnabel, twenty-three years old, had just returned to Medina from weekend duty with the National Guard and was still dressed in his camouflage fatigues.

"I'm not going to stop you," said Graf. "But I don't accept responsibility for sending anyone into a situation where people are going to get hurt, and this is one of those situations."

"I understand," said Schnabel. "But I want to go."

Before Schnabel left, Graf gave him a bulletproof vest.

Minutes later, Graf heard on his radio that the marshals were setting up their roadblock near the grain elevator. The location, well within the town, was unacceptable to him. He got on the radio. It was 5:39 P.M. "You don't have intentions of making a stop there, do you?"

"That's a ten-four," came the response.

"You can't, you've to go out of town a ways. Like . . . a half a mile north on that hill or something," Graf said.

Wigglesworth answered, "There's a couple of avenues of escape up that way. We just thought we'd cut them off here at the railroad tracks . . . cut off their avenues of escape."

Graf persisted. "No, there aren't any avenues of escape. If you go north about one mile to the top of that hill there's a vacant farm. There's turnoffs . . . there's lakes on both sides of the road. If you get them up there, there'll be nobody in town injured."

Wigglesworth concurred. "Okay. There's a ten-four. We'll go."

It was 5:40 P.M.

Graf stood at the door of the fire station. He watched as Broer's brown AMC Hornet drove by, followed by the Kahl station wagon. The vehicles were headed north. Moments later, the marshal's vehicle, driven by Cheshire, passed the station, also headed north. The chase had begun. He looked at his watch. It read 5:43 P.M.

Less than two minutes later, Graf saw a fourth vehicle, a green Oldsmobile Starfire, with a young couple in it, zip by the fire hall. They were heading north, and he had to stop them. Graf jumped into his police cruiser, turned on its red light, and pursued them to the top of Cheese Plant Hill. He pulled next to them, rolled down his passenger window and yelled, "Get the hell out of here. There is going to be a shootout."

The driver backed his car down the hill and pulled off onto the shoulder of the road. Graf looked down the hill, saw that the other three vehicles were stopped at the Reardon place, and panicked. What the hell were they doing? They should be up the road a half mile farther. Wayne and Susan could be in danger. Graf got on his radio and called the fire station. Call the Reardon farm and tell them to take cover, that there could be a shootout, Graf told the dispatcher. And send the ambulance and rescue units to the elevator and have them wait for me.

6

Murder at Twilight

Susan Reardon was busy getting supper prepared in the kitchen of the two-bedroom trailer home she had shared for the past seven years with her husband and, more recently, their two sons, who were four years old and eight months old. They had company tonight. Her younger brother and his girlfriend would be staying for supper. As she worked at the counter, Susan glanced out the east window in the kitchen and saw two cars—a sedan and a station wagon—pull into their driveway. That wasn't an uncommon occurrence. People frequently used their driveway to turn around and return to Medina, which was less than one-half mile to the south. It was a nuisance, but what was a person to do to stop it? These folks, however, didn't seem in too much of a hurry to leave. "It looks like they are using our driveway for visiting now," Susan, in a somewhat disgusted tone, said to her husband.

Wayne got up from his chair in the living room and walked across the room to the picture window to have a look. The sedan, the smaller of the two cars, had returned to the road and appeared to be headed back to Medina. It stopped. Wayne looked to his right and saw a Ram Charger, a red light flashing, come down the hill and pull across the road, stopping within feet of the sedan. Wayne looked to his left. Through the branches of the leafless trees in the shelterbelt, he could see two other cars—a red light flashing on one of them—blocking the north end of the road. The cars were about one-half mile away. One of the vehicles belonged to Medina police officer Steve Schnabel. Wayne returned his attention to his driveway. People were getting out of the vehicles, with rifles.

Wayne and Susan, who continued to watch the events from the kitchen window, were mesmerized by what they saw happening. It was something they'd seen hundreds of times before. But this was different. It wasn't a scene on television. It was real life, and it was in their driveway.

Someone was approaching the front door of the trailer.

The telephone rang. Wayne quickly answered it. "Lock the doors and go to the back of the house," the dispatcher from the fire station told Wayne. "There might be a shootout."

Might be, thought Wayne. As the other three adults scrambled to lock the doors, pull the drapes, and retreat to the back bedroom, Wayne went to his gun cabinet in the enclosed front entrance of the trailer. He took down his 12-gauge shotgun, a box of shells, and returned to the living room. He locked the door behind him.

Wayne fumbled with the shells as he tried to load his shotgun. He was nervous. Scared. Christ, if only the floor were made of dirt he could dig a hole, all the way to China. Wayne, his gun loaded, positioned himself on the sofa directly in front of the door. He didn't know who those people were or what the fight was about. But he would protect his family. If someone came into his trailer with a gun, he would shoot him, Wayne vowed. God, he prayed, don't let anyone come through that front door.

Out on the road, Gordon Kahl, his son, and his allies were hemmed in by the U.S. marshalls. It was Gordon who had first seen the flashing red light in the car parked about one-half mile up the road. "It's a roadblock, turn around," he ordered Dave Broer, and Broer wheeled his car into the driveway. Yorie followed and pulled the station wagon abreast with Broer's car. Yorie rolled down his window and hollered at his father. "I think somebody is following us. Let's get out of here."

Broer threw his car into reverse, backed onto the highway and started to drive back to Medina. He had traveled less than ten feet when Cheshire swung the Ram Charger across the southbound lane, fifteen feet in front of the Hornet. Broer was blocked.

"What in the hell is this?" asked Scott.

"I don't know," replied Yorie, "but I'm getting my gun."

Both men jumped out of the station wagon, fully armed. "Get your head down," Yorie yelled at his mother. Joan slid down the front seat and tried to curl herself into a ball on the floor of the car. Vernon Wegner, in the backseat of the station wagon, laid himself across the floor.

Yorie, his mini-14 rifle aimed at the driver of the Charger, side-stepped along the ridge of the ditch to a telephone pole twenty feet away. Scott ran around the front of the station wagon to the north side of the vehicle. He placed his mini-14 on the roof of the car and aimed it at the men in the Charger.

At the same instant, Gordon got out of the Hornet, crouched behind the passenger door and leveled his sights on the Charger. Broer, his hands frozen to the steering wheel, didn't move. He couldn't. He was scared. Just fifteen yards away were two men pointing guns at him.

The two men were Cheshire and Hopson, who had leaped out of the Charger. Cheshire was armed with an AR-15 rifle, Hopson had a 12-gauge shotgun. Both men used the V formed by the windshield and the open doors to brace their weapons. "U.S. marshals. Put down your guns or we'll blow your fucking heads off," Cheshire yelled. Cheshire, his rifle at the ready, followed Yorie's walk to the telephone pole. "It ain't like I'm going to miss," he told Yorie.

"Put your guns down. It's not worth getting killed over," Hopson hollered.

Kahl responded. "Put your guns down and back off. There is no reason for anybody to get hurt over this."

It was a western-style standoff, and Cheshire didn't like the odds. He got on the radio to Ken Muir, who, along with Schnabel, had driven their vehicles from the north to within 150 yards of the scene. "They got three carbines, Ken. Let's call in more units," said Cheshire.

"Tell them to drop 'em," replied Ken.

"We have. They're not doing it. Let's call in more units," responded Cheshire. It was 5:45 P.M.

Kapp, who had remained seated in the back of the Charger, his shotgun cradled in his arms, was stunned by what he saw unfolding before him. "Why don't we back out of here while we've got the time," he asked himself. But when Cheshire requested additional backup, he understood suddenly that "they were going to settle this once and for all. Here."

If that's the case, thought Kapp, he had better get the hell out of the backseat. All he was doing there was providing a target. Kapp pushed the front seat of the Charger forward and, with his 12-gauge shotgun in his hand, eased past Hopson. He took his position at the back of the vehicle.

At Cheshire's request, Ken Muir was radioing for help. "We have got an emergency. We have, ah, we have three individuals with carbines at Medina, North Dakota. We need Highway Patrol . . . anything you can get. They're standing by their cars. We have them covered," Ken told the state operator.

Radio operator Mary Jane Huber ordered all law enforcement officers to clear the Cleveland Tower channel. "We have an emergency in Medina. The U.S. marshals have a subject under cover. They need assistance. Any units, any units in the Medina area . . . Fifty-two hundred [Ken's call numbers] requests ten–seventy-eight [assistance]," she relayed.

Highway patrolman Dal Yanke was forty miles to the south on routine patrol when he heard the request. "I'm headed that way now," he radioed Huber. It was 5:47 P.M.

Scott fidgeted behind the station wagon. "What do you want?" he called.

"I want him," replied Cheshire from his position behind the Charger's open door. He emphasized his response by pointing his rifle at Gordon.

Scott backed away from the station wagon and started, slowly at first, heading toward the mobile home that was some forty yards behind him. He held his rifle at his waist, aimed toward the Charger. He quickened his pace. Faster. Soon he was moving as fast as he could backwards, while still being able to maintain his balance. He was going to die. He was sure of it.

Wigglesworth saw Scott back toward the trailer and the shelter-belt. "Ken, we've got one running into the woods. I'm going to cut him off," he said.

Armed with an AR-15 rifle, Wigglesworth ran in a crouch fifty yards back up the highway. He cut into the ditch, climbed over a barbed wire fence and began fighting his way through chest-high cattails and reeds. He had moved no more than twenty-five feet, when he broke through the ice and found himself up to his knees in freezing water. Wigglesworth retreated to the fence and ran fifteen feet farther north until he found a patch of dry land. As he turned to cross over, Wigglesworth looked to his left and, about eighty-five yards away, saw Scott standing behind a tree, directly in back of the trailer. Scott had his rifle pointed at him.

Wigglesworth dropped to one knee. "United States marshal. Lay down your rifle, put your hands on top of your head and walk back to the highway," he yelled. Scott moved to a tree that offered more cover. Wigglesworth repeated his order. Again, Scott ignored it. He moved closer to the corner of the trailer. Wigglesworth lost sight of him.

Cheshire, who had not heard Ken's call for assistance, repeated his request. "Permission to call in more units. Ken? Ken, can I call in more units? Come on."

Hopson told Cheshire, "We need them closer. Pull them in closer. We're looking right in the face of these guys. Let's go."

Cheshire again radioed his superior. "Ken, can we call some more units in? Ken, you there? Carl, you want to give me Ken, please. Ken?" There was a hint of panic in Cheshire's voice.

Hopson grabbed the radio mike from Cheshire.

"Hey, you guys, bring yourselves up here. We're standing up here looking these guys right in the face. Come up behind them.

Get in the damn car and move this way. There's somebody almost
in the God damn house."

There was no response. It was 5:48.

Hopson left the Charger, entered the ditch on the east side of
the vehicle and worked his way toward the Hornet. Broer was still
in the driver's seat, and his door was open. "What do you want this
man for?" Broer asked Hopson as he approached.

"We have a warrant for his arrest."

Hopson ordered Broer to "get over here with me in the ditch and
lay down." Broer swung his feet, placed them on the pavement and
then started to shake his head back and forth. He remained seated
in the car.

Kapp took Hopson's vacated position at the passenger door. He
could hear Cheshire on the radio, calling Muir.

"Ken, you on the air? Ken, you on the air? Ken? Ken, you on the
air? Ken? Ken, are you on the air?"

"Okay," came a response.

"Ken, is that you?" asked Cheshire. "I asked you to call in some
more units so we'd at least have the units and the backup here.
Now it's a standoff."

"Yeah. Ten-four. They called for more units," Ken replied.

"Thanks. Thought we lost you there. They got that one unit going
through the trees just near the trailer. He's looking for Carl. Is
that . . . was Carl going out?" asked Cheshire.

"Ten-four. Carl's over there someplace," came the response. It
was 5:50.

Hopson gave up on his attempt to talk Broer out of the Hornet.
He waved to Ken and Schnabel, who held their position 150 yards
to the north, to move in closer. They didn't acknowledge him. Hopson worked his way through the ditch. He crossed the highway
and came up to the rear of the station wagon.

The station wagon had been left idling in the driveway by Yorie.
It was about twenty feet northwest of the Hornet. Inside the station
wagon, Wegner urged Joan Kahl to back up the car. He didn't know
where they would go, but any place would be better than where
they were now. Joan refused. "I'm not going to get my head shot

off," she told Wegner. Wegner slipped out of the backseat and climbed behind the steering wheel. He put the car in reverse and started to back up when he heard Yorie yell, "Look out behind you." Wegner turned around and saw a marshal standing with a shotgun. Wegner slammed the car into park and tried to crawl underneath the steering wheel, making himself as small as he could in the process.

Yorie's warning actually was directed toward his father, who spun around when Hopson slammed the butt of his shotgun on the top of the station wagon. "Put it down. It's not worth dying for," Hopson told Gordon.

"What do you guys want?" asked Gordon.

"All we want is you," Hopson replied. "Put the guns down, we'll talk about it."

As Hopson talked with Gordon, Ken was on the radio with Cheshire. "Can we talk to these people at all?" he asked.

"I don't know. It might help if you guys would get a little closer. We're right down the barrel with these guys," Cheshire replied.

"Yeah, we'll move in," said Ken.

As Ken and Schnabel eased their cars to within twenty-five feet of the Hornet, Ken continued to quiz Cheshire. "What . . . what's with this guy? Who's the guy with the gun? What's he saying? I mean, is he saying anything? What's his problem?" Fear had entered his voice.

"They're not saying anything, Ken. The only one we're talking to is the passenger in this small sedan right here," replied Cheshire. It was 5:52.

After they drew closer, both Schnabel and Ken got out of their vehicles. Schnabel was armed with his service revolver, a .357 magnum, and a 12-gauge shotgun Wigglesworth had given to him. Muir, armed only with his .38-caliber pistol and not wearing a bulletproof vest, moved around to the front of his car. "This isn't worth a life," he pleaded.

The standoff continued. The antagonists stood twenty feet apart. No more words were uttered.

A shot exploded the tense silence.

"Who fired? Anyone hit?" Hopson screamed several times.

Cheshire slumped into the Charger. "I'm hit," he said. Kapp turned and looked across the seat. He saw Cheshire's shirt staining red—it looked like a serious chest wound. Cheshire grabbed frantically for the radio microphone. "Officers hit. Officers hit," he repeated. "Let's go guys. I'm hit bad," he pleaded. It was 5:55.

There was a momentary lull. Then, recalled Wayne Reardon, it sounded like the start of deer-hunting season.

Kapp, who had had his gun sights trained on Gordon, swung his shotgun around toward his son. "Yorie had a ghostly look about him at the time. Then he stepped away from the pole and fired a second time," recalled Kapp.

The shot hissed past Kapp. Kapp, who had never before used his weapon in the line of duty, returned fire. He missed. Kapp pumped another shell into the chamber. He fired again. The shot caught Yorie full in the stomach and drove him to the ground. Kapp fired twice more.

Then, his shotgun still at the ready against his shoulder, Kapp turned back toward Gordon. As he did so, Gordon fired a shot at Kapp that pierced the windshield. Glass fragments were scattered around the passenger side of the Charger. A shard of glass cut deep into Kapp's forehead. He dropped behind the passenger door, and the shooting continued. Bullets hit the door, shattered the windows and ricocheted inside the Charger. "They're trying to kill me," Kapp thought. Blood poured from the wound in his head. His shotgun was empty, and he retreated to the ditch. He looked down and saw that his finger had been blown nearly clean off.

With Kapp down, Gordon turned his attention northward. He fired two shots. One shot ricocheted and hit Steve Schnabel in the back of the leg. He ran, limping, to the cover of the ditch. The second shot struck Ken Muir in the chest, and he dropped to the pavement.

The shooting was over within thirty seconds.

Gordon stepped to the edge of the road, looked at Kapp briefly, then turned away. He walked north toward the two police cars. Gordon passed the body of Jim Hopson that was lying face up behind the station wagon. When the shooting started, Hopson had dropped to the ground. A piece of asphalt, kicked up by a ricocheting bullet, entered his brain through the ear and lodged there.

Gordon walked past the body of Ken Muir that was lying in front of his car, face down on the highway, his head pointed north. He was dead. Schnabel was curled into a ball in the ditch nearby. When he saw Gordon, he pleaded for his life. He raised his arms and said, "Don't shoot. I quit."

"Give me your gun," said Gordon.

Schnabel handed Gordon his service revolver. Gordon took the gun, turned and walked to Schnabel's police cruiser. Gordon climbed into the police cruiser and drove it toward the driveway where Scott was attending to Yorie.

Scott, who had positioned himself near the corner of the trailer home, had fired seven shots in the direction of the Charger. When the shooting stopped, he raced to Yorie, who was lying face down near the telephone pole. "I'm going to die," Yorie told Scott.

"Hang on," Scott told him. "I'm going to take you to Dr. Martin's."

Scott turned Yorie over on his back. Yorie clutched his .45-caliber pistol in his hand. "I think they shot it," he said. "You take it. I won't need it."

Scott saw that a bullet had hit the pistol's hand grip. The bullet had come from Ken's gun. Ken, a marksman, had made it a true shot. If Yorie hadn't had the pistol in his shoulder holster, Ken's shot would have hit him in the heart.

Scott half carried, half dragged Yorie toward the driveway. "Oh, God, Yorie's hit," wailed Joan, who had crawled out from under the dashboard. "It wasn't supposed to be this way."

Gordon pulled up to the driveway in Schnabel's car and got out. "How is Yorie?" he asked.

"He's all right," replied Scott, who didn't want to further alarm Joan.

"Who's that," yelled Scott, pointing toward the fleeing Kapp. Twice Gordon and Scott raised their rifles as if to shoot. They didn't fire.

Instead, Gordon walked toward the Ram Charger. Cheshire, who had been able to get off three rounds in the firefight, was slumped halfway inside the vehicle. His rifle was on the seat. The bullet he took had slipped through the seam of his bulletproof vest. A physician would testify later that Cheshire would have died from that wound alone if he didn't receive medical treatment within minutes. But that wasn't to be.

Gordon looked at the wounded Cheshire, raised his rifle, and fired point-blank into the young deputy's head. Cheshire's legs jumped. A piece of his skull flew twenty feet and landed directly in front of Broer's car. Gordon pulled the trigger a second time. Cheshire's body fell to the ground.

Gordon turned away from the Charger and went to help Scott carry Yorie to the driveway. They placed Yorie in the front seat of the police cruiser. Scott got behind the steering wheel and started for Medina and Doc Martin's clinic.

"Vern, let's get out of here," yelled Broer. As Wegner climbed into the Hornet, Broer handed him a heavy, military ammunition belt and told him to give it to Gordon. Gordon took the bag, threw it into the station wagon, and got behind the steering wheel. Joan, who was in the passenger seat, was nearly hysterical. Gordon took off after Scott. Broer and Wegner followed in the Hornet.

Graf watched Schnabel's car, its red light flashing, approach at a speed nearing seventy miles per hour. He waved it through. The station wagon and Hornet also passed him at high rates of speed. The ambulance that carried Kapp followed the three other vehicles.

Deputy U.S. Marshal Carl Wigglesworth cautiously raised his head and scanned the trees for the man he had chased toward the trailer house. The leafless limbs were stirred by gusts of wind, and he couldn't see anyone.

Wigglesworth had lost sight of Scott Faul when the shooting started. Now it was quiet, deathly quiet. There was no sound and no one in sight. Wigglesworth waited, collected his courage and then started to crawl on his hands and knees back to the highway. He crossed the barbed wire fence and looked up on to the road. He crawled across the highway, into the east ditch and started working his way toward Ken's car. His eyes seemed to play tricks on him in the twilight. About twenty-five yards in front of him, Wigglesworth saw something curled up in a ball. It looked like a dog.

"Ken," Wigglesworth yelled. The dog rolled over. It was Schnabel. "You all right?" Wigglesworth asked.

"I'm wounded," came the response.

"Stay low. I think there is still a guy in the woods. I'm going to check Ken out," said Wigglesworth.

Wigglesworth edged his large body on to the highway and inched toward Ken. When he reached his boss, Wigglesworth placed his finger underneath Ken's left ear. There was no pulse. Over to his left Jim Hopson was lying in the middle of the driveway. Hopson was bleeding from his ear, and rocking his legs back and forth. "Lay still, Jim. There's still someone in the woods," hollered Wigglesworth, who didn't know whether Hopson understood him.

At that moment Darrell Graf and the rescue squad arrived. Graf ran to Wigglesworth. The rescue crew raced toward Hopson. "Get back to cover," Wigglesworth yelled at the rescue crew. "There is still a shooter in the woods."

Wigglesworth ordered Graf to drive the marshal's car up in front of Hopson to offer him and the rescue workers some protection. While Graf drove the car, Wigglesworth sprawled himself across the trunk of the car, his rifle aimed toward the woods. When the car was pulled in front of Hopson, the rescue workers prepared Hopson for the ambulance ride to the clinic.

Wigglesworth gave his rifle to Graf, picked up the shotgun lying next to the wounded deputy, and ran in a crouch toward the Ram Charger. He reached the passenger side and looked into the vehicle. There was blood and gore all over the inside. The window in the passenger door had a single bullet hole in it that had spider-webbed across it. Wigglesworth closed the door in order to move to the rear of the vehicle. The window shattered. Wigglesworth walked around the back of the vehicle. As he turned the corner and looked north, he saw the body of his fellow deputy lying on the ground, his legs pointed north. There was no need to check his pulse. The whole top of his head was gone. Wigglesworth backed around the corner of the Ram Charger. He felt sick. Tears welled in the big man's eyes.

He composed himself and walked toward the ambulance crew, who were ready to take Hopson into town. "He's in bad shape," a crew member told Wigglesworth.

Highway patrolman Dal Yanke and Stutsman County sheriff David Orr arrived. They started to secure the scene and to collect evidence. Orr chalked the positions of the dead men's bodies.

Wigglesworth walked slowly to his car, reached in it and took hold of the radio microphone. "Five-two-oh-six [Robert Cheshire] is DOA. Five-two-oh-oh [Ken Muir] is DOA. Five-two-oh-seven [Jim Hopson] is badly injured," he told the state radio operator.

He then asked the operator, "Would you call my residence. Talk to my wife. Let her know I'm all right."

"Ten-four," came the reply. It was 6:06 P.M.

Dr. Martin and his wife, Dora, arrived at the clinic just as Scott pulled up with Yorie in Schnabel's police car. Martin knew he was needed. He had heard reports over his car's police scanner that there had been a shootout and the wounded were being transported to the clinic.

Martin rushed into the clinic. He turned on the lights to the surgical room, removed the flag that was still on the instrument tray and replaced it with his instruments. He went into the hallway of the clinic and saw Scott struggle to get Yorie inside the clinic. Joan followed close behind.

Yorie was white and sweating. His clothes were soaked in blood. He started to stagger, despite Scott's attempts to steady him. He appeared ready to faint. Martin grabbed at him. "Yorie, Yorie, what happened?" he asked.

Yorie was too weak to answer. Then the pain bolted through him. He screamed. "Ma, it hurts. Ma, it hurts," he said over and over. "Ma. I got a lot of pain." Martin and Scott carried him into the surgical room and placed him on the operating table.

Yorie was in hemorrhagic shock caused by the severe internal bleeding from the two most critical wounds: one to the abdomen that threatened the right kidney and one that threatened Yorie's liver and lungs. He is dying, thought Martin. I've got to stop the bleeding.

Martin had treated Yorie since he was ten years old for an assortment of scrapes, bruises, and childhood ailments. Now, he was fighting to save the life of his best friend's son. Martin administered two cc's of adrenazane salicylate to try to stop the bleeding. He gave Yorie two shots of Stadol, a morphine-based painkiller, and started an IV to replace blood loss, stabilize the pressure, and prevent vascular collapse. Yorie drifted in and out of consciousness. He asked his mother to take off his clothes. Joan took off his shoes and pants and opened his shirt. Yorie said he knew he was going to die. He asked his mother to take care of Janice and the babies. Joan tried to assure him everything would be all right.

After he helped Yorie onto the operating table, Scott left the room and headed out the door of the clinic. He was confused. He didn't know what he should do next. He needed to think, clear his head. As Scott left the clinic he was met by Bradley Kapp, who had just arrived in the ambulance. Kapp looked directly into Scott's eyes; he was angry. Kapp poked Scott hard in the chest and said, "You're in real trouble now." Scott said nothing. He turned away and let Kapp pass.

Yorie's screams, coupled with Joan's mournful wails, gave Kapp the impression he had walked into the middle of a madhouse. He took a seat ten feet from the operating room where Yorie was lying. He cradled his hand, which was hurting like hell. Martin scurried over and gave Kapp a shot for the pain and started to examine the hand. "Why did this have to happen?" Martin asked. He didn't expect an answer to his question and Kapp made no response. The ambulance crew returned and carried Jim Hopson in on a stretcher. Kapp waved Martin off. "Bother with the ones going out," he said.

Martin hurried over to Hopson. He was conscious. No, he didn't feel any pain, he said. But he was nauseated and he was cold, his feet were cold, he said. Martin took Hopson's pulse. It was steady. Martin looked around his clinic. There was little more he could do for these people. They had to get to a hospital that had better equipment and more staff. Martin told the ambulance crew to prepare to take both Yorie and Hopson to the Jamestown Hospital, twenty miles to the east of Medina. He would call ahead and let the hospital staff know they were coming. During the ambulance ride to the hospital, Yorie, during a brief moment of consciousness, would tell Martin, "Doc, I did what I had to do."

Kapp sat back in the chair and waited for the painkiller to take effect. Just in front of him, the clinic door opened. Through it walked Gordon Kahl. He had a rifle in each hand and a smile on his face. He looked directly at Kapp. For a brief second, Kapp considered reaching for his pistol that was in the holster at his side, but he thought better of it. It would be suicide. Anyway, what the hell would he pull the trigger with. His finger was gone.

Gordon walked toward Kapp. "We could have talked this over instead of shooting," said Kapp. Gordon said nothing. He just smiled. A member of the ambulance crew turned toward Gordon. "That's a heck of a thing to do, shooting people over income tax," he said.

"It's more than just a little income tax," responded Gordon.

"Was it worth it?" asked the crew member.

"It was worth it to me," Gordon responded in a steely voice.

Gordon walked past Kapp and into the room where his son lay on the operating table. Dora Martin, up to her elbows in Yorie's blood, saw Gordon, and then saw the weapons. "You're not coming in here with those guns. Get those guns out of here," she screamed.

"Okay. Okay," said Gordon as he backed quickly out of the room and left the clinic.

Gordon joined Scott outside. It was getting dark and it was cold. Their breath hung in the air. The ground fog wrapped around their legs. Soon, the fog would drape the countryside and visibility would be near zero. Gordon went to his station wagon and started unloading guns and ammunition. He placed them in Schnabel's police car. Gordon got into the driver's seat and Scott got into the passenger's side. They drove off.

———

The Reardons waited anxiously for Darrell Graf to pull his police cruiser into the driveway. The dispatcher had called and said the police chief would evacuate them from the scene. There was a possibility a gunman was still in the woods near their home, and it was believed they would be safer if they spent the evening at the motel in town, said the dispatcher. The Reardons agreed. When Graf pulled into the driveway, Wayne, Susan, their two children, and Susan's brother and his girlfriend quickly left the trailer home and piled into the police cruiser. Graf took them to the Medina Motel, which was owned by Wayne's father.

A few blocks away from the motel was the clinic. Graf decided to pay a visit to it. Dora Martin was the only person there. Her husband had left for the Jamestown Hospital with the ambulance to tend to Yorie and Jim Hopson. Joan Kahl had accompanied him. Shelly Kapp came for her husband and took him to the hospital. Dora Martin said she didn't know where everyone else had gone.

7

Broken Lives

Lois Muir awoke from her nap shortly before 6 P.M., and started to think about what she should make for supper. Ken should be home soon. As she busied herself in the kitchen, the telephone rang. It was Rodney Webb, the United States attorney.

"Is Kenny home?" he asked.

No, said Lois. Had she heard about something happening to some marshals, Webb queried. No, she responded, trying to keep the worry out of her voice. "If anyone calls, don't tell them anything," Webb said.

Lois thought that was a strange request. "It's tough to tell some-one anything when you don't know anything."

She was alarmed.

Early on in their marriage, Lois would worry each time Ken went out on assignment. Eventually, she learned to control her concerns about the inherent dangers of Ken's job. Anyway, this was North Dakota, not Chicago, or Detroit or New York. Bad things don't happen in North Dakota. But maybe they do, she thought.

Lois started to pace back and forth between the kitchen and the living room. Her heart was pounding. "What is going on here," she asked herself. She was alone. She needed to talk with someone. Lois tried to call her brother Gordie. He wasn't home. She resisted calling any of her children, not wanting to cause them unnecessary worry. On her second attempt, she got hold of Gordie, who came right over. "What is happening?" she asked repeatedly.

They soon had an answer to her question.

Webb, accompanied by his wife, Betty, and assistant U.S. attorney Gary Annear, came to the door. Webb was a reluctant messenger. When he had accepted his appointment as United States attorney nearly three years before, Webb never dreamed this would be one of the duties that went along with the job. He was glad his wife had come along. Webb didn't try to sugarcoat the news he was bearing. How else could he say it? Kenny has been killed, said Webb. Lois had thought she was prepared for the worst. Since the first telephone call she had braced herself for the possibility that Ken was dead. But Webb's words hit her with such force that her defenses crumbled. "No, this can't be," she said over and over. She felt faint. Her brother held her. She started to cry.

Then, as if someone inside her flipped a switch, she reined-in her emotions. She composed herself. She worried about making coffee and seeing that everyone's cup was filled. The house began to fill up with people. Friends and neighbors came over, their arms, in true midwestern fashion, laden with food. Her parents arrived and then her children: Laurie, who was still in college, and Roxanne, and Richard, who were both married and had children of their own. Richard, the tears racing from his eyes, wanted to go after the people who killed his father. But his grandfather pulled him up short and ordered him to stop crying. "You have to be strong for your mother," he said.

The telephone on the kitchen wall wouldn't stop ringing. Gordie screened the calls. Those from reporters were given to Webb. Those from family and friends were given to Lois. Jim Hopson's son called. Bob Cheshire's wife, Lynn, called. A young boy who had been in Ken's Junior Rifle Club called. Finally, it was too much, and Lois retreated to the quiet of her second-floor bedroom. Her mind spun. There was so much that had to be done. She had to be strong, for Kenny's sake. She forced herself to think about the days ahead. Which cemetery? The funeral arrangements. She thought about how sharp a dresser Ken was. "What clothes would he wear?" she asked herself.

Shauna Faul was in the cramped quarters of her tiny kitchen fixing a batch of doughnuts when the news bulletin flashed on the family's television set. She ignored it. She had more important things to do than stop and listen to a news report that didn't concern either her or her family. She had to finish making the doughnuts and then get started on supper.

The doughnuts and the hot meal would serve as peace offerings to her husband when he returned home from his meeting in Medina. The meeting had been the source of a spat between the two earlier in the day. Shauna, who had awoken that morning feeling ill, wanted Scott to stay home from the meeting. Not only could she use the help in caring for the couple's five children, several of whom also complained of being sick, but Scott had been out with the boys the night before and should now spend a little time with his family. But Scott was determined to go. The meeting wasn't social, it was business, and it was important that he attend. At noon, he got into his car to make the thirty-mile drive to the Kahl farm. The couple parted in stony silence and avoided the customary kiss good-bye.

Shauna smiled as she thought about the fight. Some food and a short nap had improved her disposition. Shauna knew the meeting was important to Scott, and while she wasn't sure about everything the group hoped to accomplish—the men talked politics, the women talked kids—Shauna knew they were trying to do right for people by getting to the root of the problems facing the farmers who were losing their land, and the mothers who didn't want their children taught sex education before they even knew their ABCs. There were times when Shauna wondered if the energy Scott committed to the group's efforts was worth it. Nobody else seemed concerned. She would hear Scott tell people of the dangers facing the country— the IRS, the Federal Reserve, the sex education in the schools— and people would just shrug their shoulders and respond, "What can you do? It's the law." Yet, rather than discourage Scott, those responses seemed to harden his resolve to continue the fight.

His concern for the people around him was what attracted Shauna to Scott more than twelve years before, when Shauna was a sixteen-year-old sophomore and Scott an eighteen-year-old senior in high school. That, along with his masculine good looks. One week into their relationship, Shauna knew Scott was the man she would marry. Theirs had been a small-town courtship: high school basketball games, movies, and, when there was nothing else special to do, drives up and down Main Street. They were rarely out of each other's company.

On her eighteenth birthday, Scott asked Shauna to marry him. His proposal was followed immediately by the question: "Do you want to milk cows?" Shauna answered yes to both questions, and they were married nearly one year later on April 19, 1974. Within a few months, the couple's first child, Scott Jr., was born. The next year, they had Sheila, who was soon followed by Shannon, then Shane, and finally Shantel.

Scott hadn't been joking when he asked if Shauna wanted to milk cows. Almost immediately after the birth of their first child, Scott taught Shauna, a city girl, the ways of the farm. Not only did she milk cows but she also learned how to drive, as well as maintain and repair, the tractors, combine, and other pieces of farm machinery. Just as they had been in high school, they were always side by side on the farm. It wasn't long before Shauna would enter the house after completing the chores and wonder aloud to herself, "Why would anyone want to do this for a living?" But she grew to love the farm, the land, and the satisfaction she derived from such a life, and she adopted it as her own.

The jangle of the telephone stirred Shauna from her thoughts.

"Yorie has been shot and he might die. Dad and Scott are gone," said Janice, Yorie's nineteen-year-old wife.

Shauna was stunned. "What happened?" she stammered.

"I don't know. But whatever it was, it was bad," said Janice, who then hung up the telephone.

Shauna stood silently in the kitchen, the receiver still in her hand. "Where is Scott?" she asked. Shauna started to weep. The children, she thought; she couldn't frighten the children. Shauna wiped away her tears, hung up the telephone, and returned to the kitchen counter. She finished the doughnuts, washed all the dishes, and started to clean the house. "Scott didn't do anything wrong. He's going to come home," she kept telling herself.

Despite her efforts, anxiety overwhelmed her. She threw down the dust rag and called Bud Brakel, a friend of both Scott and Gordon. "Where is the car? Where is Scott?" she asked. "I don't know what is happening," Brakel replied.

Shauna put the children to bed. They sensed something was amiss—usually such an early bedtime was administered as punishment, but they had done nothing wrong, and were anxious in their confusion. Shauna paced through the house, and finally turned off all the lights and climbed into bed. She started to pray. You have got to help me, you have got to take my hand, she pleaded with God.

As she prayed, Shauna was joined in bed by four of her children— two on each side of her—and she willed herself not to cry. The children mustn't be further upset. Shortly after midnight, as the children slept, Shauna slipped out of bed, unplugged the radio, and carried it into the adjoining room. She plugged in the radio, turned it on, and her heart stopped. "Scott Faul, twenty-nine, Harvey, is being sought by authorities in connection with a shooting in Medina that left two U.S. marshals dead," said the newscaster. The tears that she had contained burst forth. "Oh my God, what is going to happen?" sobbed Shauna.

Just before 11 P.M., U.S. marshals, FBI agents, deputy sheriffs, and North Dakota Bureau of Criminal Investigation agents entered the waiting room at the Jamestown Hospital, where Joan Kahl was expecting word on her son's condition. "You'll have to come with us. We want to ask you some questions," one of the lawmen told Joan.

Joan protested. "I've got to see how Yorie is. He's dying," she said. That didn't matter, she was told. She had to come with them. She was under arrest. "But I didn't do anything wrong," she said.

A court would decide that, an officer told her. Joan was led away, and guards were placed at the door of Yorie's hospital room.

The lawmen took Joan to the Stutsman County sheriff's office, where she was questioned by chief deputy Jack Miller, and three other law enforcement officers. "Where were you today?" asked Miller.

"We were at a meeting at the Medina Clinic with several other people. My husband, myself, my son—who's up in the hospital— and Scott Faul. We were there along with many others," said Joan, and added that the only reason she accompanied her husband was to see two lady friends from Gackle who were going to attend. "I don't get a chance to [visit] very often and that was meeting them halfway. So consequently, during the meeting we did our visiting," said Joan.

Miller asked what the meeting was about. The IRS mostly, said Joan, and the corruption in our public schools. "There's just a little bit of everything, like what's going on in the world that is not very pleasant," she said.

"Could you give me the names of some of the other people at that meeting so we could possibly talk to them?" asked Miller.

"I know only Dr. Martin and Len Martin by first and last names," said Joan. "The others I don't know. I've never even seen some of them before. They come from various parts of the state."

Miller asked Joan if she ever expected trouble at any of the meetings she attended.

"Well, yes," she replied. "I knew years ago, after my husband found out the income tax law was never passed, that someday there would be trouble. It's Satan's work is what it is."

Finally, Miller asked if Joan knew where her husband was now.

"No, I . . . No. I sure don't know. I was gonna say I wish I knew, but maybe it's good that I don't," said Joan. "I don't know. I just don't."

After twenty minutes, the interview ended and Joan Kahl was taken into custody. She was charged with murder.

Vernon Wegner was awakened by a tapping at his window. As he went to answer the door, Wegner looked at the clock on the microwave oven. It read 2:11 A.M. Jack Miller was at the door. "The FBI has some more questions they want to ask you. Will you come with me to Jamestown?" he asked. Okay, said Wegner. At about the same time, two other officers were making a similar request to Dave Broer.

After the shootout, Wegner and Broer had returned to Streeter by way of the grid of farm roads; ten miles south, where they were passed by a highway patrol car heading north, two miles east, a mile south, a mile west, a mile south, a mile west, a mile south, a mile west until they reached the outskirts of town. Both men knew they were in trouble. "I might just as well go home and say goodbye to my family," Broer told Wegner. They decided to call Jack Miller, the chief deputy sheriff in Stutsman County whom Wegner knew from his days as police chief. They had to tell somebody what happened out on that road.

Broer dropped Wegner off at home. Wegner had to knock on the door because his wife had locked it. When Sherry opened the door, Wegner brushed past her. "What's wrong?" asked Sherry. "All hell broke loose," Wegner replied. "There was a gunfight and I think one or two guys are dead."

"Why? What happened?" asked Sherry. Before he could respond, the telephone rang. It was Dave Broer. Had Wegner called Jack Miller yet, he asked. Immediately after Broer hung up, Wegner called Miller's residence, but he was out, on duty. Wegner telephoned the sheriff's office, but he wasn't there either, so Wegner identified himself to the dispatcher and asked that Jack call him because he had some information about the shootout near Medina. Wegner called Broer back and urged him to call Miller as well. Two minutes later, Miller returned Wegner's call and said he'd be stopping by to talk with him.

Shortly before 8 P.M., Broer, his wife, Joanie, and several others who had been at the Medina meeting, arrived at Wegner's house to watch the news accounts of the incident on television.

As they took their places around the television, the phone again rang. Wegner answered. It was the sheriff's dispatcher. "Meet Jack Miller outside your house," she said.

"Boy, I don't know if I want to do that. I'd just as soon have him come in," said Wegner.

"Don't argue with me," she told Wegner. "Just meet him outside."

Wegner hung up the telephone and peered out his window. Miller was already there, waiting. Wegner slipped on a pair of boots, an army jacket, and turned on the porch light before stepping outside. When he walked out in the yard, he could see Miller had his pistol drawn. Behind Miller, another man held a shotgun. "Are you being held hostage?" Miller asked Wegner. The question surprised Wegner. No, he replied. "Is Broer armed?" No, said Wegner.

Miller returned his pistol to the holster and the man behind him ran back to the patrol car and put his shotgun away. The two lawmen entered Wegner's home.

For the next two hours, Wegner and Broer were grilled about what happened on the road. They were asked to draw maps of the scene. At 10 P.M., the questioning was over. Miller thanked them for their cooperation, and the two officers left.

Evidently, Miller hadn't asked all the right questions, and now the FBI needed some answers. It wasn't until early morning when the two men were delivered to the Stutsman County jail in Jamestown—where they were frisked and ordered to change into some jail house coveralls—that they found out the government wanted more than information from them. They were arrested and charged with murder.

Just three miles from Scott Faul's farm, Gordon Kahl pulled his car into an abandoned shed. Both men were tired, cold, and hungry. Deeply engrossed in his own thoughts neither spoke.

When they left the clinic, Scott and Gordon had taken turns driving over the fog-shrouded back roads in the stolen police cruiser. On the car's scanner they heard that an all-points bulletin had been issued for them and their vehicle. When they drew within a half mile of Gordon's farm, they abandoned the car in a shelterbelt and walked to Gordon's home, where Gordon changed clothes and picked up additional ammunition. Then they left in Gordon's green, 1966 Rambler. Just the day before, Gordon had replaced the timing chain, gears, and gaskets on the car. He had borrowed a quarter-inch drill to complete the repairs and had joked with the mechanic that he would return the tool on Monday "if they don't shoot me first."

Again the two men took the less frequently traveled back roads, where they encountered no traffic. When they arrived at the shed, they pulled the car into it, and tried to rest. Finally, Scott broke the grim silence. "What are we going to do?" he asked.

"I don't know, Scotty," Gordon replied.

8

Innocence Betrayed

The Fargo-Moorhead *Forum* ran an editorial following the shooting: "Two lawmen are dead and others in the Medina, N.D., shootout lie in hospitals, some seriously wounded. The region and the nation are in shock over what happened last Sunday, and there are chapters still to be written before the tragic story is finished.

"Who would have thought that an attempt to serve a warrant on a man wanted for probation violation in a federal tax case could result in such havoc."

Who indeed. In North Dakota, whose inhabitants warmly referred to it as the Peace Garden State, violent crime was almost nonexistent. The crime rate was by far the lowest in the nation, nearly sixty times less than the national average, and residents were blessed with a certain security. They could share a smile with strangers, walk the streets unafraid after dark, leave their children alone to play, and discover a neighborhood composed of well-kept houses and well-manicured lawns. North Dakotans didn't lock their doors, whether they were home, in the backyard, or down the street visiting with a neighbor. Often, during the winter, they left their automobiles empty, the motor running, while they ran inside a store to complete some last-minute errands.

But, as news of the shootout reached into homes across the state, people rose from their chairs and walked quietly to the doors to check the locks. Some people went to their gun cabinets and took down a shotgun, a deer rifle, any weapon that offered a sense of security, and loaded it. People picked up their telephones and called family, friends, and neighbors: Did you hear? Can you believe it, here in North Dakota? Sure, people were frustrated with the low farm prices and high interest rates. Foreclosures, auction sales, bankers, and government all got them down, and sure, they talked tough and threatened to do something about it. But people said crazy things when they were frustrated. The shooting jolted the people's sense of security, their sense of identity.

"It was a moment," wrote Mike Jacobs, editor of the *Grand Forks Herald,* "that sent shockwaves of sadness and fear through the collective body of the state's residents.

"It is not just that two men are dead, two more critically wounded, two others scarred; nor that families grieve for missing fathers. However crass it sounds to say it, these things happen every day. In the newspaper business, we are inured to them," wrote Jacobs. "What is rare is the terrible realization of the hate and ugliness among us that burst out at Medina. I doubt that many of us appreciate the estrangement some our neighbors feel from the political process that we take for granted. I doubt that many of us realize that some among us are capable of such an act of violence. And I doubt that many of us understand the desperation of some of our fellows or the philosophy that sustains them.

"It is shocking, but all of it is here, among us, nurtured in our quiet streets and open spaces. The announcement of it in Sunday's gunfire shattered the image that we have held of ourselves."

Farmers had rallied before to political groups that used anti-Semitic rhetoric and blamed the economic woes on powerful, distant, and evil conspirators bent upon robbing them of their prosperity and, eventually, their freedom. In the 1890s, Mary Elisabeth Lease, a leading populist from Kansas, warned farmers about the power of the "British Bankers" and the un-Godly influence of the Rothschilds. Even so admired a person in populist folklore as William

Jennings Byran—who pleaded the creationist's cause against Clarence Darrow in the "Monkey Trial"—embraced extremist views. Yet, the efforts of those groups and leaders were largely confined to the political arena, and were nonviolent.

Until the shootout at Medina, activities of these self-proclaimed, latter-day populists were nonviolent. Most of their convocations or protest actions were seen as little more than time-consuming nuisances. The do-it-yourself lawsuits clogged the dockets of the federal courts. The common-law liens filed against the personal property of IRS officials inconvenienced the agents, particularly those who found the sale of their property delayed until the title was cleared. The arrest warrants issued by the Posse Comitatus unnerved those who received them. But in each case, the lawsuits were termed frivolous and dismissed; the liens were called fictitious and lifted; and the arrest warrants were viewed as someone's idea of a sick joke and ignored. No one was hurt and justice prevailed. At least in the eyes of the government.

But to the people who filed the lawsuits, placed the liens, and issued the warrants, the government's response just closed other avenues they believed would right the wrongs they saw, and release the frustrations they felt with the world. Instead of the wrongs being righted, the people who filed the actions were ridiculed and branded as nuts, loonies, and kooks. Denied legal recourse, their frustration mounted until it found its release. After the shootout at Medina, the authorities were gravely concerned that violence would now appear to extremists as their only modus operandi.

If violent action was the only means these people had to fight the system they couldn't accept, it could be a long, hot decade for courts and lawmen throughout the Midwest. The government's own reports projected that by the year 2000, more than 1 million of the country's 2.2 million farmers would be driven off the land. That was a loss of nine farmers an hour, twenty-four hours a day, 365 days a year for the next seventeen years. There were other, equally frightening numbers being reported. The IRS said tax protests had nearly doubled each year since 1978, when the agency first started recording the incidence. In that year, there were 6,700.

That number grew to 9,900 in 1979; 12,823 in 1980; 23,000 in 1981, and 44,500 in 1982. Not large numbers, but the trend was ominous.

Even more disturbing were law enforcement reports that placed members of these independent, and often feuding, organizations together at paramilitary training exercises in Wisconsin, Kansas, California, Illinois, Missouri, Idaho, and Arkansas; and further reports that weapons were being stockpiled: fifty thousand rounds of semiautomatic ammunition at a Posse enclave in Colorado; hand grenades, a thirty-gallon drum of cyanide, and an armored personnel carrier at the CSA's Missouri-Arkansas stronghold; and a virtual arsenal at the Ayran Nations' complex in Hayden Lake.

The shots fired on that prairie road in North Dakota echoed across the flat lands of the Midwest and sent a chill through the state houses, law enforcement centers, and court houses of the region. Authorities didn't want to view Gordon Kahl as a standard-bearer for the depressed farmers, but they also knew Kahl wasn't an anomaly, a lone, crazed gunman gone amok. Rather, he represented a malignancy that was spreading throughout the Heartland. What would surprise authorities was how deep the evil had rooted itself in the dark, rich soil. In 1986, a Lou Harris poll, commissioned by the Anti-Defamation League, revealed that 75 percent of Iowa and Nebraska residents believed the farm crisis was caused by the Reagan administration and international bankers, while 13 percent said the blame rested with religious groups like the Jews. In response to another question, 27 percent of the residents said that farmers had always been exploited by Jewish bankers. The poll also showed that nearly 25 percent of the population was aware of the Posse Comitatus. In another poll, the *Des Moines Register* found that 45 percent of Iowa's bankers characterized their relations with farmers as tense. In that poll, 50 percent of the bankers said they had been verbally abused by farmers within the last year, 13 percent told of physical threats, and 4 percent reported that either they, or one of their employees, had been assaulted.

Again, not large numbers. But terrorists don't need 51 percent of the vote to exercise their will. And now that the tough talk of the past had been punctuated with violence, extremists had become terrorists. And as such their rhetoric and actions were no longer dismissible.

In states throughout the Midwest, authorities moved quickly to close the Pandora's Box they believed had been opened by the Medina shootout. In Kansas, a legislature committee recommended that the legislature authorize the purchase of fifty semiautomatic rifles for the highway patrol in case of confrontations with radical groups. In Missouri, Wisconsin, and eight other states, legislation was introduced that made it illegal to teach or train people in the use of explosives and firearms where the intent was to create civil disorder. In Nebraska, the highway patrol's investigative division was ordered to monitor and collect information on residents affiliated with the Posse Comitatus or any other extremist group.

What they were treating, however, were the symptoms and not the disease. Farmers, small-town businessmen, and others were still being displaced by the farm crisis that gripped the region. The anger and hatred remained, and the killings would continue.

Within the next several years, more people would die at the hands of individuals who embraced this unlikely blend of fundamentalist religion, guns, and white supremacy.

Alan Berg, a Jewish talk show host in Denver who repeatedly spoke out against the militant right was gunned down outside his home by members of The Order on the evening of June 18, 1984. Just twelve days later, Lewis Byrant, a black Arkansas state trooper, was shot eleven times when he stopped a member of the Covenant, Sword and Arm of the Lord for a minor traffic violation. On April 15, 1985, Jim Linegar, a Missouri state trooper, was killed at a roadblock near a CSA stronghold when he stopped a van that belonged to one of the group's members. And on Christmas Eve of that year, Charles and Anna Goldmark, and their two children, were beaten and stabbed to death by a member of the Duck Club, a tax protest group, who considered the family part of the communist-Jewish conspiracy. The Goldmarks, a prominent Seattle family, weren't Jewish.

Some of the true believers died in defense of their cause. On

October 23, 1984, Arthur Kirk, a Nebraska farmer who faced the loss of his land because of a $300,000 debt, was shot and killed during a brief skirmish with a state patrol SWAT team. Kirk, who was a member of the National Agricultural Press Association, felt he was defending himself against the Mossad, Israel's intelligence agency. In that same year, on December 7, Robert Matthews, founder of The Order, was killed on Whidbey Island, off the coast of Washington, at the end of a thirty-six-hour gun battle with federal and state lawmen. The confrontation occurred shortly after Matthews issued a declaration of war against the Zionist Occupational Government, better known as the United States government.

Other, equally disturbing events would occur across the American landscape. In March of 1986, two Lyndon LaRouche supporters won in the Democratic primary race in Illinois.* The victories forced Democratic gubernatorial candidate Adlai E. Stevenson III to form the Solidarity party and run candidates against the LaRouche supporters in the general election. Later that year, Velma, Oklahoma, farmer Larry Humphreys, an Identity adherent who inherited more than $5 million from his father, established the Heritage Library, which became home to more than 100,000 books and documents related to the Christian/patriotic movement.

Then, in February of 1989, David Duke, former Imperial Wizard of the Knights of the Ku Klux Klan, ran as a Republican and won a seat in the Louisiana state senate. Duke claimed that he was no longer a white supremacist. Instead, said Duke, he was a white civil rights activist. A racist by any other name. A year earlier, Duke had run as the Populist party's presidential candidate. A native of Louisiana, Duke got more than 23,000 votes in that state's presidential primary and outpolled two mainstream candidates, former Arizona governor Bruce Babbit and Illinois senator Paul Simon. On Super Tuesday—on the ballot in Arkansas, Missouri, Oklahoma, and Texas—David Duke received more than 41,000 votes. During his presidential run, Duke warned voters against race-mixing and

* LaRouche's National Democratic Policy Committee contends, among other things, that international bankers and the drug cartel controlled by Great Britain's Queen Elizabeth are part of a Zionist plot to control the world.

the power of the Zionist-controlled news media, and referred to alleged biological evidence that blacks are mentally inferior to whites.

Duke's victory in Louisiana was the first fruit born of a new strategy endorsed by the so-called Christian Patriot wing of the extremist movement, said Lynora Williams, executive director for the Center for Democratic Renewal. According to Williams, the new strategy was first proposed in 1987 by, among others, A. Jay Lowry, publisher of the Clinton, Arkansas, based *Justice Times,* a monthly newsletter that claims to be "The Original Voice of the Second American Revolution!!"

"It is true that many are attempting to drop out of the system by getting rid of bank accounts, drivers' licenses, rescinding social security numbers, and denying jurisdiction in the courts," wrote Lowry in the December 1987 issue of the *Justice Times.* "[But] the election process is the game that is played. It is time to unite! Not under a third party banner which has proven so many times to be a failure, but to take over one of the major parties. Some say it should be the Republican Party."

Williams said one reason the Republican party was selected is because of its twenty-year-long "Southern Strategy," which publicly pandered to racism. Another reason, said Williams, is because some of the more conservative members of the party—such as former U.S. congressman George Hansen of Idaho, and state senators Jack Metcalf of Washington and Wayne Stump of Arizona—had openly courted the support of Christian Patriot supporters.

Hansen was a member of the Congress from 1974 to 1985, when he was convicted of failing to make proper financial disclosures and served a six-months prison sentence. Since that time, Hansen has crisscrossed the country promoting his "Free America" and "Operation Joshua" drives, which are designed to bring fringe elements into the Republican party and intended to "bring the walls of bureaucracy down and ring in a new era of freedom and prosperity . . . a real Second American Revolution."

Likewise, said Williams, Metcalf has collaborated with far-right activists in a campaign against the Federal Reserve System, while a letter from Stump has been widely distributed by extremist groups. In the letter, addressed "To Whom It May Concern," Stump attacked the Fourteenth Amendment and claimed that the freed slaves made citizens by it were a different class of citizen than the organic white citizens of the unamended Constitution.

Williams noted that Duke's victory probably ended the debate about whether the major party strategy was the best way to play the political game. Now, she said, the far right is likely to consolidate into a unified approach. And, she added, "should the Christian Patriots, Populists, right wing tax resisters and Kluxers arrive at a common strategy, stumble upon a charismatic and credible candidate, and manage to keep the machine running smoothly, their political organizing might strike paydirt in 1992.

"Continuing economic crisis for farmers and workers will spur others to take the white pride promises of the far right seriously," she warned.

But all that was yet to come. On February 13, 1983, authorities were concerned only with finding and arresting Gordon Kahl. Something they hoped to do without any further bloodshed.

9

The Delicate Thread

Rodney Webb willed away his fatigue.

It was Monday, Valentine's Day, nearly fourteen hours since the shootout, and since he had lost his friend Kenny Muir. After carrying the tragic news to Lois Muir, Webb had returned home and tried to get some sleep, fitful at best. There were a lot of chores ahead of him. He had to name a chief prosecutor, and a lead investigative agency. And the press would have to be managed carefully. This was clearly no ordinary case. The calls he had fielded the night before included those from the *New York Times, Washington Post, Kansas City Star, Baltimore Sun, Los Angeles Times, Chicago Tribune, Des Moines Register, Minneapolis Star and Tribune,* the Canadian Broadcasting Corporation, NBC, CBS, ABC, and nearly every newspaper and television and radio station in the state. An old-fashioned western shootout on the prairie. It was big news. Big enough to be the lead story on each of the three network morning news shows and front-page news in every newspaper in the region, if not the country. All those reporters would be demanding more information and more details. It was only a few minutes after 8 A.M., and the requests for more news had already started. Each of the six extensions on his telephone was lit.

God, if he only knew what had happened. How could Kenny have been the one that got hurt? If Rodney was ever in a tough situation, he would want to be with Kenny Muir. The man knew how to handle a weapon. How could he have finished second in a gunfight?

The trim, handsome, forty-six-year-old Webb, his thick, dark hair flecked with gray, fished in the pocket of his blue pin-striped suit coat and withdrew a pack of low-tar cigarettes. He knew he would have to quit smoking soon—his doctor had made that quite clear—and he would quit. But not today. He lit the cigarette and looked at the presidential appointment that hung on the wall of his large office on the second floor of the Old Federal Building. It was Kenny who had framed the document for him.

At no time during his active pursuit of the job as U.S. attorney, did Webb ever think he would be faced with the kind of case now before him. This type of violent crime just didn't happen in North Dakota. People might disagree with their government, they might protest its tax policies, and even feel ill will toward it because of the farm crisis. But they didn't use violence as a means to accomplish change. They didn't kill law enforcement officers doing their duty. At least they hadn't in the past.

Not that Webb now felt he couldn't handle the job he received in 1981. If there was one thing Webb was absolutely sure about, it was his ability as a lawyer. An expressive man, who gestured freely with his hands and often struck the top of his massive hardwood desk to emphasize a point, Webb exuded self-assurance and confidence in his skills. Although most of his twenty-three years of legal work had been spent in private practice, handling divorce cases, drawing up wills, and reviewing contract agreements, Webb had also served as state's attorney for Walsh County, where Muir had been born and spent most of his childhood, and as municipal judge for the city of Grafton.

The choice of who would lead the prosecution was not an easy one. The case offered a great challenge to anyone who enjoyed trial work, and it was a high-publicity case that would be watched closely not only by the public but by the Justice Department as well. It would be, in all likelihood, a once-in-a-lifetime case for a prosecutor. Webb wanted to experience and face that challenge—he wanted to try the case himself. Then, there was Gary Annear, who was the first assistant and most senior member of the office. Annear had attended law school with Webb at the University of North Dakota in Grand Forks and was one of Webb's closest friends in Fargo. But Webb chose neither himself nor Annear. Following an agonizing self-appraisal and an honest assessment of the strengths and weaknesses of his two most senior assistants, Webb decided to go with Lynn Crooks, arguably the best prosecutor at any level in the state of North Dakota. Crooks would be the lead attorney for the prosecution.

In his corner office, Lynn Crooks strikes a relaxed pose, even while preparing for a case. He leans back in his overstuffed chair, his feet settled firmly on his wooden desk. He can usually be found in shirtsleeves, his tie loosened at the collar and either a pipe or toothpick clenched in his mouth. He is quick to laugh, and even quicker to regale a visitor with lengthy and detailed accounts about his latest fishing trip. A former hunter, his weapons now sit unused in his gun cabinet. Amid the diplomas, family pictures, and commendations that decorate his office walls are his own paintings of ducks, a seashore, a ship at anchor, and, most prominently, a portrait of his wife, Nancy.

After being informed of the shootout Sunday night, Crooks sensed he would be tapped as chief prosecutor and immediately started to prepare the government's case. Scrupulous preparation was one of his trademarks. At the start of each trial, the forty-one-year-old, bespectacled Crooks would enter the courtroom with one, two, three—however many were needed—loose-leaf, ring binders under his right arm. In those binders were all the notes, worksheets, and assorted information pertaining to witnesses, investigative reports, and evidence, all the backup Crooks would ever need to try the case. Each case was meticulously planned and organized so that there were no high points, no low points and, most importantly, no surprises.

In his thirteen years as an assistant U.S. attorney, Crooks had built a reputation for toughness. A short, stocky, solidly built man, with some hair still left on his balding head, Crooks had often been likened—both in looks and demeanor—to a bulldog in the courtroom. His one soft spot was for the victims. He saw himself as their advocate, the redresser of the wrongs against them. To Crooks's mind, the government's overemphasizing of the rights of the defendant as opposed to the rights of the victim was a failure of its promise to society to enforce the laws so the people wouldn't have to do it.

Crooks had tried more than 150 cases during his career, but this was easily the biggest trial he had ever personally handled. A few years back he had assisted a Justice Department attorney in successfully prosecuting the government's case against American Indian Movement leader Leonard Peltier, who had been accused of killing two FBI agents during a gun battle with militant Indian activists on South Dakota's Pine Ridge Indian Reservation in 1975. For his part in that trial, Crooks received a commendation from the Justice Department. But in this trial, he would be making both the legal and the tactical decisions. It would be his case to win. Or lose.

Crooks never doubted he would take the case if it was offered. "If you enjoy trial work you look for cases like this," he said. But there were certain inherent pressures in this case that Crooks had never experienced in all the other criminal cases he had tried. The most compelling of those pressures was the emotional factor. Crooks knew both the officers that had been killed, considered them his friends. "I didn't want to let the families down," he would say later.

And there was pressure from the Justice Department. Two days after the shootout, Rudolph W. Giuliani, the second-highest-ranking official in the U.S. Attorney General's office, arrived in Fargo for a briefing. During the briefing, he stressed—as if his presence alone wasn't emphasis enough—that the matter was of tremendous concern to the Justice Department. They had lost two of their marshals and the department would not look favorably upon any errors or mistakes that would allow their killers to walk away with anything less than the stiffest penalties. This meant no fuck-ups.

Several days later, Giuliani further emphasized that point by sending one of his senior trial lawyers to again assess the situation, with the idea of taking on the responsibility of trying the case. Giuliani's envoy, Lawrence Lippe, was a man short on pleasantries. His first words to Webb, when they met in the lobby of the Town-house Motel in Fargo, were that he, Lippe, had been the man who went down to Texas, fired the attorney general and two of his assistants, and took over as prosecutor in the trial of the Judge John Wood murder case. (Wood, the first federal judge killed since 1900, was slain in 1979 before he was to preside over a drug trial in San Antonio.) If he felt he could best handle the case, Lippe wouldn't hesitate to take over in Fargo, he told Webb. But following Crooks's presentation, Lippe leaned back in his chair, looked at the attorneys gathered around the table and told them, "You people have your act together. You will lead the prosecution."

Webb was relieved. He didn't want the "Man from Lansing" scene replayed in his courtroom. In the movie *Anatomy of a Murder,* Jimmy Stewart, playing the role of a defense attorney in a rural Michigan town, won an acquittal for his client by making a fool of the out-of-town prosecutor, who didn't understand or appreciate the mores of the region.

Crooks had known Muir and Cheshire and was friendly with their families, but he also had ties to the defendants. Like them, his roots were deeply embedded in North Dakota's fertile soil. He, along with two older brothers and a younger brother and sister, had been raised on a small—480-acre—farm near Hankinson in the southeast corner of the state. He had plowed the earth, planted the seeds, and then stood back and watched in awe as the miracle of life took center stage under the hot summer sun. Although now a city denizen, the dirt was still under his fingernails and each year Crooks would till the soil in back of his home, plant a garden, and tend it. He watched with concern how the farm crisis—to Crooks it was a crisis—was tearing apart at the seams the farm structure he had grown up with and had loved. In his eyes, the crisis had killed the small farmer and had secured for the Midwest an unstable economic situation for the next twenty to thirty years.

It was a crisis that also threatened the very fabric of society, which, in Crooks's mind, was held together by the delicate thread of faith in the country's system of laws. Once that faith was lost, the fabric could quickly unravel, leaving society bared to anarchy—or worse. The crisis had spawned a small, but vocal and expanding, segment of the farm community that started to tug at the thread. The extremists considered the government their enemy and believed that its system of justice was used not to help and protect the farmer but to take away his land and his home. And so, rather than obey the laws, they resisted them as a matter of principle.

Shortly after the shootout between Kahl and the marshals, *The Forum,* Fargo's daily newspaper, said in another editorial that the killings brought to the surface the "apparently large number of citizens who are unhappy to one degree or another with our system of taxation.

"Many of them are farmers, farmers who are beset with low prices for their crops and mountains of bills that can't be paid and with the ogre of foreclosure constantly at their door. These are not disciples of Kahl's violence; they are troubled people who feel they have no place to turn.

"This should tell federal and state officials that just perhaps they aren't understanding very well, and not communicating very well with a percentage of our people. Perhaps there should be more explaining from on high about the need for taxes, about how our country operates."

Crooks wondered if there was any satisfactory explanation that could be offered to a person about to lose his land through, really, no fault of his own. It wasn't a civics lesson he needed, but help to keep his farm.

Although he strongly disagreed with the message the extremists offered to the farmers, Crooks understood its appeal. He had grown up in the belief that the American farmer was the last of the rugged, free-spirited individualists and that as long as he didn't bother anyone, he shouldn't be bothered, especially by the government.

"All of us, in a certain sense, are tax protestors at heart. We don't like taxes, we don't enjoy paying taxes," said Crooks. "But as much as we spit, sputter, mutter, complain, and write to our congressman, we pay them, rather than die on the cross. We see a need for them.

"But Gordon Kahl, at some point, separated himself from that logic. He went on strike, so to speak, and zeroed in on an antisocial philosophy that can't be allowed by society," said Crooks.

10

In from the Cold

It was nearing 10 A.M., Monday, when Rodney Webb walked slowly, and sadly, down the hallway to the conference room and the throng of waiting reporters. He was still thinking of Kenny, remembering when the two of them had toured together all the federal facilities in North Dakota. During that time their friendship had blossomed. They had talked about their families, their children, the similarities between their wives, how they enjoyed playing bridge, and their futures.

Webb stopped at the door and put out his cigarette in the ashtray before he entered the room. This press conference was the first of what would become a series of almost daily media briefings held by Webb to recap the government's search efforts of the day before, and to outline its trial preparations. The conferences outraged defense attorneys, who viewed them as a blatant attempt by the government to indoctrinate the state's residents against these evil, aberrant people living in their midst and thereby taint the pool of prospective jurors. Defense attorneys later claimed, that, at best, the briefings violated every tenet of the Fair Trial/Free Press guidelines by commenting on the character and reputation of the defendants. And, that at worst, the practice bordered upon ethical misconduct through the release of materials that increased the sensationalism of the event, inflamed the public opinion, and led people to prejudge the individuals in custody.

Defense attorneys also were angered by what they considered a double standard applied by trial judge Paul Benson on the release of information. Shortly after the shootout, a defense lawyer issued a statement suggesting that the law enforcement officers, because they had an ambulance on call, had planned for the violence that erupted on that prairie road. Immediately after the comments appeared in the press, all the defense attorneys were ordered to appear before Benson in his chambers. Benson issued them a stern warning against making any further statements about the case to the press. Yet, argued the defense attorneys, there was Webb, or some other government official, appearing each day before the news media to issue statements that implied—and in some cases flat out contended—that their clients were cold-blooded killers, extremists, gun-toting religious zealots, executioners, and anti-tax fanatics.

Later, in defense of his actions, Webb said that he had no choice but to hold the press conferences. "If I would have said, 'No comment,' they would have hanged me. They were needing and wanting information," said Webb.

Webb took his position in front of the bank of microphones that were set up on a table in the back of the large conference room. The room was ablaze from the bright television lights. "This is a sad day for law enforcement in North Dakota," Webb told the assembled journalists. "I don't know how it could happen. Ken Muir was a conservative, experienced law enforcement officer. He was completely surprised or overwhelmed."

Webb speculated that because of the political and religious fanaticism of the suspects, they "may have been psyched up or on a psychological high after the meeting," but added that the reaction by the suspects to the service of a misdemeanor-type warrant was virtually incredible. "The officers certainly did not expect the suspects to be as heavily armed or offer the resistance they did."

Joan Kahl, David Broer, and Vernon Wegner—Yorie was in serious condition at the hospital—are in custody and will be charged with murder at a hearing that afternoon, said Webb.

During that hearing—as the murder charges were read to the defendants by U.S. Magistrate William Hill—David Broer fainted, and fell to the floor on his back. At the same moment, Joan Kahl, confused by the courtroom surroundings, became hysterical and screamed, "I don't understand this at all. I didn't commit a crime. I was just riding along. I didn't touch a weapon."

Hill quickly ordered aid for Broer and then tried to calm Joan, and cautioned her to remain silent since anything she said could be used against her at later hearings. Hill then ordered Broer, Joan Kahl, and Vernon Wegner held without bail. Three days later, when it became clear that Yorie would survive his wounds, Hill held a similar hearing in Yorie's hospital room, where he, too, was charged with murder.

Webb ended his press conference with a statement that expressed confidence that the intensive, FBI-led search—currently hampered by fog and the fact that Kahl and Faul had a police radio—would soon result in the apprehension of the other two suspects.

Webb's decision to have the FBI lead the investigation was not popular among the U.S. marshals, but he didn't care. Webb didn't believe the U.S. Marshals Service should be investigating its own tragedy. The situation was already emotionally charged and the marshals who had arrived from across the country to aid in the investigation were "big, powerful, angry men."

The biggest and, probably, most angry of them was Chief Inspector Chuck Kupferer. Kupferer presented an imposing figure. He had fiery red hair and looked like someone central casting would send over as a stand-in for Matt Dillon. He presented himself as a man's man, an ass-kicker, someone who wasn't afraid to stir things up a bit if it helped get the job done. He had a reputation for getting the job done and had played a major role in the capture of The Falcon, Timothy Boyce, following his escape from a federal prison after he was convicted of spying for the Soviet Union. Webb admired action-oriented people, but he felt Kupferer's aggressive style was ill-suited for the present situation. There was a potential for still more bloodshed and Webb wanted to do everything within his power to prevent it. He didn't want any posse-type action, but a conservative leader who would keep the lid on by using a slow, deliberate approach. Richard Blay, the agent in charge of the FBI's regional office in Minneapolis, was such a man.

Although Blay, at forty-eight years old, wasn't so aggressive as to push to the center of a crisis, the lean, strikingly handsome ex-Marine had a certain self-confidence that grew from knowing he was good at his job, and that he had the respect of his superiors. After he arrived in North Dakota to assume charge of the investigation, Blay felt confident he would have the two suspected killers in custody within a couple of days. It was a confidence that would be sorely tested, not only by Kahl and Faul, but by the land that offered them aid and comfort.

Singer/songwriter Scott Jones described his native state as being "Miles and miles, of miles and miles." It is, more than seventy thousand square miles of miles. More square miles than all six states that make up the New England region. And crisscrossing each of those square miles were roads, some no more than a cow path, but roads that could be traveled and which led to somewhere. Gordon Kahl and Scott Faul knew many of those roads, and they had the survivalist training to live off the land accessed by them.

Richard Blay was jostled about as he peered through the gun slots of the armored personnel carrier that bounced along the bumpy terrain and circled the twenty-one-by-thirty-six-foot green and white farmhouse. Try as he might to get a glimpse at the interior of the wood-framed, single-story building, he couldn't see a thing. The gun slots of the National Guard vehicle were too damn small. He ordered the driver to return to the road where earlier that afternoon he had established his command post, several hundred yards away from the house.

Blay had waited almost a full day before approaching the Kahl farm. Neither he nor any other lawman was the first on the scene.

Hours earlier, as Webb was conducting his press conference, two young reporters from a television station in Minot had set out to find the Kahl farm with the intention of getting some video of authorities searching it, for the six o'clock newscast. When the two, reporter Rae Schobinger and photographer Peggy Ulrich, spotted the mailbox that had "G. W. Kahl" printed on it, they figured they were in the right place. But the only life they saw was a large black dog inside a green pickup truck that sat in the farmyard. Scared, yet determined to get a story, the two entered the yard and, for the next ten minutes, took video of the pickup truck, which also contained weapons and ammunition, a white station wagon, and the farm home. They left without ever seeing or talking to a law enforcement officer. Later, Schobinger would tell an Associated Press reporter that federal agents had said the farm was the most obvious place for Kahl to go. She had wondered, if the house was the most obvious place for Kahl to go, why wasn't the law there?

The authorities didn't get there earlier, said Blay, because he wanted the crime scene at Medina secured and he was waiting for additional officers to arrive. "You are not going to go out to the farm unless you can do it right," he said.

Now, Blay had the farmstead surrounded by more than a hundred heavily armed federal, state, and local law enforcement officers, including members of four SWAT teams. The tension hung heavy in the brisk, cool air, as the lawmen—some dressed in camouflage uniforms, faces blackened—anxiously awaited word from Blay to begin the assault. But Blay wouldn't command any action, not today. It would be dark soon, and with the darkness would come fog. Intelligence reports suggested that the farmstead was honeycombed with tunnels and booby traps. Blay's tour of the area turned up nothing, yet that didn't mean the dangers didn't exist. Nighttime wouldn't be the time to find out. Instead, Blay would have his people isolate the farmstead tonight and wait until morning to approach the building. If Kahl and Faul were in the house, they couldn't escape with officers stationed every few yards around the farmstead. And if they weren't inside the house—well, Blay would rather lose time than one of his men.

A number of the officers didn't want to wait until morning and suggested just burning the damn house down. That would bring Kahl out if he were in there. Blay understood that many of the men were functioning on too few hours' sleep—if they had gotten any at all—and, beyond their fatigue, they were cold, angry, and frustrated. He would not allow them to goad him into becoming Kahl's judge and jury, into doing something impulsive or dangerous.

He didn't want a repeat of the night before.

As the lawmen battled the feet-numbing cold and waited for morning, some thirty miles to the northwest of their position, a green, beat-up 1966 Rambler pulled to a stop along the side of a gravel road. Inside the car, Scott Faul looked at the elderly man he had come to admire and even idolize during their three-year friendship. Tired and worn out, Scott was overwhelmed by sadness. It was time to say good-bye to Gordon, maybe forever. He knew Gordon could take care of himself, yet Scott could not shake the feeling that he was letting down his friend by not going with him, wherever it was Gordon was going.

But Scott had to see Shauna and his kids. He had to touch them, hold them, let them know he was all right and, most important, tell them that he didn't do those terrible things people said he had done. While he and Gordon sat in the shed and waited for nightfall, Scott had listened to the radio and all day long heard himself described as a murderer. It was a terrible misunderstanding. He hadn't killed anyone. The two marshals who died on that road had assaulted them. It is not a crime to arm yourself and fire your weapon when your own life is endangered, as his had been by the marshals. It was self-defense.

Scott said good-bye and climbed out of the car. His pistol was in a holster strapped around his waist; he carried a shotgun as well. Scott watched as the car's taillights disappeared into the thick fog. One-half mile to the east was his farm, his family and, in all likelihood, the police. It would be too dangerous to go there immediately. Seeing him, the police would probably shoot him before he could give himself up. They'd probably shoot him anyway. He needed help. He needed to let someone know he wanted to surrender. Scott turned to the west and started walking toward the yard light, a half-mile away, that glowed eerily through the fog.

It was about 8:30 P.M., when Arlie Roller finished milking his cows and started feeding his calves. He heard his name called twice. Arlie looked around the barn, his eyes stopping at the outline of a man standing near the door. Arlie moved closer to the door. It was Scott Faul. "Can I see you down by the shop when you have finished your chores?" Scott asked.

Arlie nodded his agreement. Scott retreated from the door and Arlie returned to his cattle. As Scott turned away from the barn door, he met Arlie's wife, Dorothy. "Oh, my god, Scott," she said as she moved to put her arms around him and give him a hug. "Do you know where my wife is?" Scott asked. No, replied Dorothy. Scott said he had come to speak with Arlie. "I didn't want anyone to see me," he added. Scott then turned and started to walk toward the shop. Dorothy went into the house.

Fifteen minutes later, Arlie met Scott in the shadows of the yard light. "I'm in a terrible mess," said Scott. "I didn't shoot nobody," he insisted. "I don't know what to do. I want to give myself up, but I'm afraid to get killed."

Scott's thoughts, concerns, and fears tumbled out of his mouth. He shouldn't have gone to the meeting, he had had a bad feeling about it. How was his wife, his family? He had let down his friends, Shauna, his kids. What should he do? he asked.

Arlie, who had known and liked Scott for most of Scott's life, tried to calm his young neighbor. "If you want to give yourself up, I will help you," said Arlie. They decided to call Ted Seibel, an attorney in Harvey and a friend of Scott's, to help arrange the surrender. Scott left the shotgun and his pistol in the shop and the two men started toward the house. Before they entered, Scott reached into his pocket and pulled out a folded brown piece of paper that looked like it had been torn from a grocery bag. He handed it to Arlie. It was a note from Gordon Kahl, said Scott, and should he be killed, he wanted Arlie to give it either to Seibel or Shauna. Arlie put it into his pocket without looking at it.

Scott made two telephone calls to Seibel, who, after the second telephone conversation, said he would be at the farm within ten minutes. Ten minutes passed and the telephone rang. It was Seibel. He would be driving a white automobile and no one should be alarmed when he pulled into the yard. Scott sat quietly at the kitchen table and waited for Seibel.

When Seibel arrived, the first thing he asked Scott was whether he was armed. Scott held out his arms to indicate he had no weapons. Seibel telephoned the task force headquarters in Jamestown. Scott would turn himself over to deputies at the Wells County sheriff's office in Fessenden, said Seibel, but he did not want Sheriff Curtis Pellet on hand. Scott was afraid of Pellet, afraid he would kill him if given the opportunity. Authorities assured Seibel that Scott would not be harmed and said they would immediately send two agents to Fessenden to assume custody of him. Seibel then called the sheriff's office, repeated the request, and said they would be in town within the next ten minutes.

Before they left, Scott retrieved the note from Arlie and turned it over to Seibel. On both sides of the note were hand-printed statements over the signed signature of Gordon Kahl. On one side it read: "Scott and Yorie had no part in shooting anyone. I don't know if one of the marshals fired first or if it was one of the others who had us surrounded. I heard a shot and Yorie said 'I'm hit.' One of the marshals yelled and looked back over his shoulder, and said 'Who fired'? [*sic*] About that time someone else fired and I saw Yorie fall.

"I realized then that we were all going to be slaughtered, as the marshals pulled down on the rest of us and I fired as fast as I could locate a target. Yorie's .45 in the shoulder holster took a rifle bullet from either the first or second shot—and I believe the other shot came from a shotgun. My wife Joan had no part in it. She only went along to visit with a couple other ladies who were going to be at the meeting."

The other side read: "I realize that being an enemy of the Jewish-Masonic-Communist-Synogogue [*sic*] of Satan is not conducive to a long life, so I am writing this while I still can.

"I am saddened by the fact that my hand had to be the instrument which sent these men to their reward, however they attacked us, and fired first, so I feel I was right, and justified in defending myself and all those who were placed in this extreme danger with me. Had I to do it over again I would have to do the same. I feel that we were in the same kind of danger that I faced while flying in WWII when we were attacked, and had to defend ourselves, and send good men to their death." [signed] Gordon W. Kahl

It wouldn't be the last time Gordon would try to get his side of the story out to the public.

The telephone rang just as Scott left the house. He waved goodbye to Arlie, who left to answer the call. Moments later Scott returned to the house and grabbed Arlie's hand and shook it. "Thank you," he said.

Arlie lowered the telephone and looked at his friend. "Be good now," he said.

The news of Scott's planned surrender charged the atmosphere at the task force's headquarters. The lawmen knew that with each day that passed, chances of apprehending Kahl anytime soon would drop considerably. They didn't want the search to go on indefinitely, and Faul's surrender might provide them with the break they needed. If Faul had been with Kahl all this time, he might know where he was now, or where he was headed or, at the least, the names of people to whom he might turn for help.

Almost immediately after receiving Seibel's telephone call, the FBI's supervisory special agent John E. Shimota and Deputy U.S. Marshal James F. Maji were dispatched to Fessenden to take Faul into custody. The two officers arrived shortly before midnight, read Faul his rights, and then secured him in their car for the 152-mile return trip to Jamestown, where he was booked, fingerprinted, and charged with two counts of first-degree murder. After he was processed, Faul was questioned about Kahl's whereabouts. "You know more about that than I do," he told his interrogators, Kupferer and Shimota.

The officers persisted.

"I'm not saying any more until I've talked with my attorney," Faul responded to each subsequent inquiry.

After nearly one-half hour, the lawmen terminated the interview. They had gotten nothing of value from Faul regarding Kahl's whereabouts. Zilch. The authorities found themselves no closer to finding Kahl than they had been three hours earlier when Faul surrendered.

The morning sun burned away the few remaining wisps of fog that shaded the small farmhouse. It would be still another pleasant winter's day in North Dakota.

Energized by the sun's warmth, the Kahl family's year-old black Labrador raced from the house to the perimeter line established by the officers surrounding the building. There the dog stopped, gave off a bark or two and dashed off. It returned a second and a third time. Sometimes the puppy darted playfully among the officers before it wheeled around and headed back toward the house, where it started the circuit all over again. After it passed several times, lawmen decided the dog's actions were giving away their position. An officer raised his rifle, aimed, and fired at the dog, wounding it in the throat.

"When human life is on the line, you don't worry about a dog," said FBI agent John Shimota.

It wasn't the last shot fired that day.

At approximately 12:45 P.M., Tuesday afternoon, the first tear gas canister smashed through a front window of the Kahl farm home. The canister was fired exactly fifteen minutes after Richard Blay had used a bullhorn and ordered Gordon Kahl to come out of the house with his hands on top of his head and surrender himself. It was followed by twenty-five more canisters and hundreds, thousands, of rounds of weapon fire. A mile to the north, Lonnie Kahl, Gordon's twenty-four-year-old daughter, sat at the kitchen table in a neighbor's home and listened to the crescendo of rifle fire and shotgun blasts. "This is unbelievable. He's not dangerous.

"They're hunting him like a dog," she cried.

Sitting with Lonnie was Janice Kahl, who, along with her two

young children, Katie, three, and Wendy, two, had been turned
back by police when they attempted to return to the farm home
after visiting Yorie in the hospital. A distraught Janice was concerned about the well-being of the eighteen nanny goats and
twenty-eight chickens she and Yorie tended on the farm. "There
is going to be some serious trouble if we can't take care of the
livestock," said Janice, who also revealed she was pregnant with
the couple's third child.

The welfare of livestock was the last concern of the authorities,
who were taking no chances. The shelling lasted for more than an
hour before lawmen, wearing gas masks, stormed and entered the
dwelling. Inside, the air was thick—suffocating—with the pungent
odor of tear gas; frilly window curtains lay shredded on the floor
and shards of glass and spent tear gas canisters were scattered
everywhere—on the sofa, in the piano, on the kitchen counters, on
and around the children's toys. A search of the three-bedroom home
uncovered some fifty weapons—rifles, shotguns, pistols, knives, a
crossbow—fifteen gas masks, thousands of rounds of ammunition
and hundreds of pamphlets and documents about the Posse and
the Identity movement. But no Gordon Kahl.

That came as little surprise to most of the lawmen, who, from
the start, had operated on the theory that Kahl and Faul had stayed
together after the shooting. Faul's surrender, thirty miles away,
strongly suggested that Kahl had slipped any net set for him at the
house. Even before the assault began, Lynn Crooks had told reporters in Fargo, "I think the consensus is, there is the probability
he [Kahl] isn't there." Yet, they couldn't be certain.

"If we had to do it all over again, assuming we know now what
we knew then, we probably would do it the same way," an FBI
agent told reporters later.

Kahl's friends, neighbors, and family, however, were stunned
and angered by the government's actions. The shooting of the dog
and the seemingly senseless destruction of the Kahl home appeared
to them to be motivated by revenge and revealed the government's
true intentions: Kahl's death, not his capture.

Jack Nason, a tax protestor from Helena, Montana, spoke for

many of Kahl's supporters when he told reporters, "The feds came against this farmhouse like an army, and in Satanic fashion riddled it with bullets and in a demonstration of contempt for life, shot the innocent dog."

Six hours after the onslaught began, the lawmen were gone. Only one member of North Dakota's state highway patrol remained on the scene to await the arrival of a carpenter to board up the twenty windows of the house. Before leaving, a marshal told Janice she would have to wait a couple of days for the tear gas to dissipate before moving back into the house. The marshal was off by some five hundred days.

Just about the time the first tear gas canister was fired into the Kahl home, Shauna Faul entered the visitor's room at the Stutsman County jail in Jamestown. She had been informed the night before that Scott had turned himself in to authorities, and that she'd have to wait until morning to see him.

On Tuesday morning, Shauna packed a change of clothes for Scott and arrived at the jail assuming her husband would return to the farm with her. She believed that once Scott talked with the authorities and told them he hadn't done anything wrong, they would allow him to return home.

That hope evaporated as Shauna watched her husband, escorted by sheriff's deputies, shuffle into the room. He was dressed in a black prison jumpsuit and shackled in handcuffs and leg irons. Dark rings circled his eyes, and he looked sick and withdrawn. He didn't look at all like her husband, thought Shauna, who gasped softly at the sight of him. The couple sat across from each other. Shauna fought back the tears and looked hard at Scott. She needed to know the truth.

"What happened out there?" she asked.

Scott's voice trembled as he responded. "It was so bad. It was so terrible."

His voice cracked and Scott started to cry. "I didn't do anything, Shauna. I didn't do anything," he wept. "Shauna, you wouldn't have believed that day. It was almost like they were animals."

Shauna started to cry. She wanted to reach out and touch Scott, but was stopped by the pane of glass that separated them. For the next few minutes the couple cried. No words were spoken.

Then, Scott composed himself. No one was murdered out there, he told Shauna, who continued to weep. Two men died, but no one wished for that to happen, he said. Gordon was forced to take those lives in defense of his family, his friends, and himself, said Scott.

"Don't worry," he told Shauna, "I'll be home soon. I didn't do anything wrong. All I did was defend myself after being shot at, and that isn't a crime."

But until he was released, it was her duty to keep the family and farm together, said Scott. "You have to keep it all together until I get home," he repeated.

Shauna nodded and started to dry her tears. "I will," she said.

"The truth will be known," Scott assured her. "I didn't do anything wrong. It was self-defense."

11

A Message from Kahl

On Wednesday morning, February 16, flags all around North Dakota were raised, and then lowered to half staff, in the memory of Kenneth B. Muir. A few hours later, Muir's family, friends, comrades-in-arms, complete strangers—more than six hundred people—crowded shoulder-to-shoulder in the Methodist church in Fargo and paid their last respects to him. Among the mourners were North Dakota governor Allen Olson and Assistant Attorney General Rudolph W. Giuliani. The next day, a similar gathering would occur in Bismarck to honor Robert Cheshire.

A hundred twenty-four miles west of Fargo, on the road where Kenneth Muir died, members of the Medina Fire Department used soap and water to remove the bloodstains and debris from the section of road where the shootout occurred. They did their task at the request of Wayne Reardon, who, along with his wife, Susan, were finding it not quite so easy to erase from their memories what they had witnessed just a few hundred feet from their mobile home.

Aside from the participants, the Reardons were the only eyewitnesses to the shootout and, as a result, would be called upon by the government to provide valuable testimony in the upcoming trial. But the Reardons did not have a particularly warm feeling toward the government. With each day that passed, Wayne grew more angry and bitter about the way the arrest attempt was handled. He felt it was wrong that his family had been put in such danger, and that the roadblock should not have been set so close to his home. Wayne noted that all three vehicles in the farmyard had sustained damage from gunfire, and that a bullet lodged just four feet from his infant son's crib.

"Miles and miles away from this place, that would have been the thing for me and my family," he said.

Why and where the marshals tried to do what they did would be questions that would haunt the government throughout the search for Gordon Kahl, through the trial and months and years beyond. These were questions raised in letters to the editor, newspaper editorials, and in conversations among private citizens and law enforcement officials. And they were questions to which the government had no answers.

"The full answer to these questions, unfortunately, will elude us forever simply because they died with Marshal Ken Muir . . . and Deputy Marshal Robert Cheshire.

"The answer to the question, therefore, as to why they decided to interrupt that beautiful Sunday afternoon by attempting to arrest Kahl must forever remain in speculation," Lynn Crooks wrote in response to an editorial that appeared in *The Forum*. "It can only be assumed that they went because it was their duty. That was the kind of men they were.

"The question as to why they attempted the arrest on an open road can best be answered with a series of rhetorical questions: What would have been a better location? At the clinic? At a supermarket? At a neighbor's home? Where did Kahl go that he did not take his weapons with him? His wife (said) he even took them to church.

"Where could the arrest have been attempted where the potential did not exist for innocent bystanders being injured if Kahl resisted arrest?" Crooks continued "The Reardon driveway was chosen as a scene of confrontation by Kahl, not the marshals."

James Wickstrom, however, felt he had the answers. The forty-year-old, self-proclaimed director of counterinsurgency for the

Wisconsin-based chapter of the Posse Comitatus, called a press conference two days after the shootout and told reporters that the Wisconsin chapter, along with Posse units in other states, had gone on alert.

"I don't know what is going to happen across this country in the next forty-eight hours. It is the general feeling that the government has declared war on the people of this country," he said.

Wickstrom also directed a threat toward Stutsman County deputy sheriff Bradley Kapp, who, claimed Wickstrom, was used as an infiltrator by the FBI and had instigated the shootout. For his role in the incident, said Wickstrom, Kapp could be punished at any time by the Posse. It was a threat Kapp took seriously.

"If some son-of-a-bitch tries to make a hit on me, I'll shoot him," responded Kapp, who no longer left his home without a weapon.

It wasn't Wickstrom's intention, however, to send a hit squad after Kapp. Nor was his interest in Gordon Kahl motivated by the desire, as he claimed, to "vindicate an innocent man who was forced into shooting two innocent men."

Wickstrom had never met Gordon Kahl. But he saw in the shooting and its aftermath an opportunity to preach the gospel according to the Posse, and he viewed Gordon Kahl as a symbol, the perfect recruitment poster for his own extremist cause.

Wickstrom, who received more than 16,000 votes in a 1980 run for the U.S. Senate and more than 7,700 votes in a 1982 race for the governorship of Wisconsin, already held celebrity status among the true believers. His taped Identity sermons were circulated throughout the country, and he pocketed fees of up to $500 for lectures and talks, at which he pounded the Bible as he delivered his messianic visions of white, Christian America. "Who's who, who's Jew?" Wickstrom asked his audiences in a sing-song cadence that turned into a bombastic roar when—having plucked nerves taut with the fear, desperation, and hopelessness felt by those attempting to cope with the decaying fabric of rural America—he outlined the problems facing the country and offered his solutions to them.

The shootout provided Wickstrom with a national audience for his message. A sturdily built man, Wickstrom marshaled all the skills he had learned from his previous career as a tool company salesman and, later, sales trainer, to sell himself and his cause to the country. Dozens of reporters attended his almost daily press conferences at the Tigerton Dells Tavern, located on the 570-acre compound. He gave tours of the township, which was home to approximately two hundred people, and encouraged reporters to watch and television cameras to roll as he baptized members of his flock in the Embarrass River that winds through the rocky area. Wickstrom appeared on the talk show "Donahue," the Cable Network News, and before the annual meeting of the Wisconsin Broadcasters Association.

He also appeared before hundreds of people who gathered in rented motel conference rooms, like the one at the Holiday Inn in Fargo where he delivered his Posse message on Sunday, May 1, 1983.

"How many people do you think in the United States today, or tomorrow, when the mailman comes again, are going to be served or get a notice that they are being foreclosed upon? Either their car, their truck, their house, their ranch, their farm?" Wickstrom asked more than one hundred people who spent that pleasant spring afternoon hearing him speak.

Wickstrom paused. He let the questions linger over the audience.

"I will lay you odds there is going to be a whole bunch," answered Wickstrom, his voice rising with each word until it reached a roar and filled the room. "And there is going to be a lot of tears in this land."

Many in the audience nodded knowingly. Yes, they knew of people—friends, neighbors, relatives—who had been foreclosed upon, who were about to be foreclosed upon or who would soon face that fate. Most of the audience was in any one of those three categories.

Wickstrom recalled a simpler time, years before, when "people owed nothing to no one and when they had a problem . . . all the neighbors came around.

"If a barn burned down and all the cattle were in the barn, do you know what the neighbors did?" he asked. "They not only came over within the next few days and built that barn, they took a cow out of every herd and they brought them cows to that farmer and that man could still support his family.

"And that's what this nation was all about," said Wickstrom, his voice again reaching a roar, filling the room. "And they didn't need a permit from the DNR [Department of Natural Resources] or the Bureau of Land and Mines to be able to bring the cow from one farm to another.

"But what do we have today?" he asked.

"Some stinking Jew insurance company," Wickstrom said. "And then if your barn does burn down you've got to settle with the kikes, who then tell you because the barn was so old it lost all its value. And, of course, the cattle wasn't worth as much as you thought they were on the market, and you lose all that money.

"And then you got faulty wiring in it, of course. There is always that problem, right? And because there is maybe one-sixteenth of a wall still standing, it's not a total destruction.

"So how much do you get out of the insurance policy you've been paying them damn Jews?" Wickstrom asked. "Not much, do you?"

Then, he continued, where are your neighbors to pick out a cow or something to bring over? What neighbors?

"If one of you had a bankruptcy in here right now that totalled $12,000 or $14,000, I couldn't help you. I don't know of [anyone] sitting in this room who could," he said.

The reason for that, said Wickstrom, is because "our people are working today and getting absolutely nothing out of their work except paying off the banks, which are totally owned by the Jews."

His sermon, which lasted more than three hours, also included a revisionist history of World War II that contended the Holocaust never occurred; that it was a hoax perpetrated by the Jews to win worldwide sympathy and lead to the establishment of Israel. In Israel, claimed Wickstrom, the Jews now have a permanent base from which to fulfill the un-Godly plan set out in the Protocols of the Elders of Zion, the forgery that alleged that Russian Jews, in 1918, devised a plot to control the world.

After Wickstrom completed his diatribe, many of the farmers in the room sat stunned and appalled by what they had heard. This was too much hatred, even for people faced with the loss of their land, their home, and their way of life. As they left the room the farmers waved away reporters who tried to talk with them. And, once out of the sight of the motel, they tossed away the Posse and Identity literature that had been given to them. They didn't want to be associated with all that hatred.

Some in the room, however, were drawn to the foot of the stage and the tables that held taped cassettes of Wickstrom's other sermons, his pamphlet *The American Farmer: 20th Century Slave*, and other Identity-tainted literature, such as Sheldon Emry's *Billions for the Bankers, Debts for the People*, which argued that any interest on a debt was usury and a violation of God's law. All that material was there—for a small fee—to help people better understand the evil that threatened white, Christian America.

Wickstrom was a hot property, even when it became clear that he had no idea of Kahl's whereabouts. The news media would not, could not, let go of its fascination with Wickstrom. Journalists recorded Wickstrom's comments as if each were pearls of wisdom that should be saved for future generations. In a way, they were right in doing so. Wickstrom provided them with a window to a sinister philosophy that was winning support from good, if naive, men and women across America's Heartland.

Wickstrom wasn't the only person to rise to Kahl's defense or invoke Kahl's name when demanding changes in the monetary policy, the tax system, and the Constitution of the United States. The Medina shootout made Gordon Kahl to the extremist movement what John Brown became to the opponents of slavery after his attack on Harpers Ferry—a symbol that time for talk had run out. It was now time for action.

Anna Bourgois, chairwoman of the National Democratic Committee, a tiny, right-wing organization in North Dakota, told journalists that her group, as well as others throughout the country, agreed with Kahl's view that the Federal Reserve System was illegal

INSET: Gordon Kahl's home near Heaton, North Dakota, after lawmen stormed the building.

Vehicles belonging to the United States Marshals Service sit on the road east of Medina, North Dakota, where just hours earlier there had been a shootout between lawmen and Gordon Kahl. In that gun battle, on February 13, 1983, two U.S. marshals were killed and three other law enforcement officers were wounded.

Three days after the shootout, lawmen from across the country line the wall of the First United Methodist Church in Fargo to honor slain U.S. Marshal Kenneth Muir.

Gordon Kahl, upon his 1977 arrest in Midland, Texas, for a failure to file.

An Iowa farmer begs other farmers not to participate in an auction of his farm equipment, which is being sold to satisfy his debts.

ABOVE: A forced sale of farm equipment in Illinois: farmers make their bids on the machinery offered.

Farmers in Kansas take their cause to the city.

An Iowa woman weeps as she watches her family's farm sold at a forced auction. The friend who consoles her wears an adhesive-tape cross that carries the plea "Save Family Farms."

ABOVE: James Wickstrom, Identity minister and self-proclaimed national director of counterinsurgency for the Posse Comitatus, urges others to join his cause.

A member of the Ku Klux Klan paramilitary unit prepares for a guerrilla training exercise at a camp in Alabama in 1980.

ABOVE: Yorie Von Kahl, left, David Broer, center, and Scott Faul are led from the federal courthouse in Fargo after being sentenced for their participation in the shootout.

Leonard Ginter, later convicted on charges of harboring the fugitive Gordon Kahl, is escorted into the Lawrence County Courthouse in Walnut Ridge, Arkansas.

A makeshift honor guard of American Legion veterans fires a salute during the burial of Gordon Kahl.

INSET: Joan Kahl, flanked by her daughter Linda Kahl Holder and son Fred Kahl, weeps during the graveside ceremony for her husband.

A simple wooden cross, adorned with a plastic flower, marks the grave of Gordon Kahl in a prairie cemetery near Heaton, North Dakota.

and that the United States should return to the gold standard. While Bourgois said she didn't condone violence, she did understand how it could occur. "People who are pushed too far may react violently," said Bourgois, who was the U.S. Senate candidate for the state's small independent Conservative party.

In Montana, Red Beckman, an author and leading member of the anti-tax movement, held a press conference and called for a special grand jury from outside of North Dakota to investigate the events leading up to and surrounding the shootout. Beckman, who would run as a third-party candidate for governor of Montana in 1988, contended that such a jury would find that the arrest attempt was intended to "put a show on at tax time so people will bow down and pay the illegal income tax."

Similar press conferences and rallies were held by differently named anti-tax, constitutionalist, and survivalist groups in Kansas, Virginia, South Carolina, Illinois, Texas, Utah, Washington, and Arkansas. The theme was basically the same: Violence wasn't advocated, but the government had chosen the confrontation and Kahl had had every right to defend himself against the unjustified and illegal attack. And, if necessary, members would take up arms to win back the country for the people.

Joan Kahl didn't want any more violence. Shortly before noon on Wednesday, Joan, dwarfed by a phalanx of U.S. marshals, entered a second-floor conference room in the federal courthouse, stood in front of a cadre of reporters and television cameras and appealed that her husband "give yourself up, before anybody else gets hurt."

Hunched over, she looked tired and worn, like someone on the verge of giving up. She broke into tears when she spoke of Yorie. "Our son is in critical condition, two men are dead, and others are going to be hurt. I don't want you dead, too. Please, I can't take it anymore," she pleaded.

"Please, Gordon, please," begged Joan. "They won't hurt you. I've been treated real well here."

Gordon's response came three weeks later in a sixteen-page letter that was sent to friends, supporters, and journalists. The first half of the letter, which bore Texas postmarks, detailed Kahl's side of the shootout. It read:

I, Gordon Kahl, a Christian patriot, and in consideration of the events which have taken place within the last few hours, and knowing to what lengths, the enemies of Christ (who I consider my enemies) will go to separate my spirit from it's [sic] body, wish to put down on paper a record of the events which have just taken place, so that the world will know what happened.

I feel that the awesome power, which will be unleashed, to silence forever my testimony, will, if not checked by the power of my God, who is the God of Abraham, and Isaac and Jacob, will cut short my time to leave to the world, these happenings. While urgency, or human weakness, tells me to run, my spirit goes write, so this I am going to do. And if my God continues to protect me, I shall write first, and flee from the hands of my enemies later.

We had just finished our meeting in Medina, concerning how we could best implement the proceedings of the Third Continental Congress, which was to restore the power and prestige of the U.S. Constitution up to and including the 10 articles of the bill of rights and put our nation back under Christian Common Law, which is another way of saying God's law, as laid down by the inspiration of God, through his prophets and preserved for us in the Scriptures, when word was received from someone whose identity I am not able to give, that we were to be ambushed on our return to our homes. I realize now that we did not take this warning as seriously as we should have. The reason for this was because it has happened so many times before, when nothing happened. I see now that the many false alarms were to cause us to lower our guard. . . .

[Not surprisingly, Gordon's version of the shootout placed all blame upon the marshals.]

During this time there was a lot of screaming and hollering

going on but nothing else, so it appeared to be an impasse. About this time a shot rang out, and the driver of the car who I believe at this time must have been supposedly in command, turned around and stood up so he was looking at his men in the east ditch and toward the cars which had come from the north and yelled "Who fired, who fired?" The other man who was with him, echoed his question. At the time the shot rang out I heard Yorie cry out "I'm hit, I'm hit." . . . I took my eyes off the two men who were yelling "Who fired?" and looked over at Yorie. He was still standing, but I could tell he was in pain from the way he stood. About this time, another shot rang out, and I heard Yorie cry out again. I looked over and saw that he was hit again and laying [sic] on the ground.

I looked back toward the two men and saw the one in the passenger side aim at me and I was sure then that they felt the situation was no longer under their control, and the only thing to do was kill us all.

Gordon also assumed all responsibility for the deaths and the woundings of the lawmen.

Vernon Wagner [sic] was unarmed so I know he didn't shoot at anyone and Dave Bower [sic] didn't shoot at anyone either. My wife had nothing to do with it, other than the fact that she had rode along with us, so she could visit a couple of other ladies who were coming to the meeting.

[And Gordon praised both his son Yorie and friend Scott Faul for having] displayed the qualities of first rate soldiers of Jesus Christ. May God bless all of you.

I want the world to know that I take no pleasure in the death or injury of any of these people, any more than I felt, when I was forced to bring to an end, the fighter pilots [sic] lives who forced the issue during WWII. When you come under attack by anyone, it becomes a matter of survival. I was forced to kill an American P-51 pilot one day over Burma, when he mistook

us for Japs. I let him shoot first, but he missed and I didn't. I
felt bad, but I knew I had no choice.

The claims made by Gordon in the letter ran contrary to evidence
that was presented at the February 22 preliminary hearing for Joan
and Yorie Kahl, David Broer, Scott Faul, and Vernon Wegner. At
that hearing, authorities offered the eyewitness testimony of Wayne
and Susan Reardon, which suggested that Scott Faul had executed
Robert Cheshire. The court also was informed of an admission Yorie
made to lawmen at the hospital that he may have fired the first
shot at Cheshire. If what Gordon claimed occurred and what was
introduced as evidence at the preliminary hearing implied a conflict,
said Rodney Webb, it was an "issue that will be resolved in a trial
by jury, and not on the 'Donahue' show."

The second half of Gordon's letter concerned itself with the battle
between Christian patriots and the Satanic Jewish conspiracy
threatening the United States. It was in essence Gordon's declaration of war against his government.

I would have liked nothing other [than] to be left alone, so I
could enjoy life, liberty and the pursuit of happiness, which
our forefathers willed to us. This was not to be, after I discovered that our nation had fallen into the hands of an alien people,
who are referred to as a nation within the other nations [wrote
Gordon]. As one of our founding fathers stated, "they are vampires, and vampires cannot live on vampires, they must live on
Christians."

These enemies of Christ have taken their Jewish Communist
manifesto, and incorporated it into the Statutory Laws of our
country, and threw our Constitution and our Christian Common Law (which is none other than the Laws of God as set
forth in the Scriptures) into the garbage can.

We are a conquered and occupied nation, conquered and
occupied by the Jews, . . . [who] have two objectives in their
goal of ruling the world. Destroy Christianity and the white

race. Neither can be accomplished by itself. They stand or fall together.

We are engaged in a struggle to the death between the people of the Kingdom of God, and the Kingdom of Satan. It started long ago, and is now best described as a struggle between Jacob and Esau.

I would like to write more but the spirit says this must suffice for now. Should the hand of Elijah's God continue to be over me, and protect me, I shall someday see this once great nation swept clean of Christ's enemies, and restored to it's [sic] former greatness. If it should be the will of our Father, and the father of our Lord Jesus Christ, that this be, there will be no way that Ahab's God, and his people can stand before us. Mystery Babylon with all it's [sic] greatness, will be destroyed. Take heart, my fellow Christian Americans, God has said that there will be a great shaking in the land of Israel. That started this evening. Let each of you who says that the Lord Jesus Christ, is your personal Savior sell his garment and buy a Sword, if you don't already have one, and bring his enemies before him and slay them.

To those of you who were engaged in the ambush and attack on us and were spared, thank God you have a chance to remove your support from the anti-Christs who rule our nation. To those of you who are or have been supporting the edicts and commands of the great whore—stop now and come out of her, as her time is getting short, and when the hour of her judgement comes, that you be not judged with her.

I must cease now, and move on. If it should be the will of the Father that I have more to do for him, he will protect me, and no devise whatever that is used against me shall succeed. To my wife Joan, who has been with me for so long, I know this will be a hard and painful experience. However, remember that prophecy will be fulfilled, and you now been a witness to some of it. Remember that I love you as much today as I did when I first saw you more than 50 yrs. ago. Put your trust in

God, and whether I live or die, He will be with you to the end of your days.

I must now depart. I have no idea where I'm going, but after some more prayer, I will go where the Lord leads me, and either live to carry on the fight, or die if that be the case, and for the present at least, I bid you all good-bye.

[signed] Gordon Kahl

To some, the letter read like a textbook on apocalypticism, the fusion of religion and guns one of whose major tenets is the righteousness of Holy War, much like that espoused by the mullahs of Iran. And, like the judgments of Iranian mullahs, who refer to the United States as the whore of Babylon and its leaders as Satanic demons, Kahl's letter should not be lightly dismissed as the rantings of a kook or crazy man.

"To most of us, apocalypticism, at least in its thoroughgoing manifestations, is so spectacular, so potentially destructive, that it is difficult to look beneath its surface," said John Hegeland, professor of Religious Studies at North Dakota State University in Fargo.

But, added Hegeland, a leading authority on the apocalyptic phenomenon taking root in the Midwest, "As one can see from the history of it, it nearly always arises in times of suppression, chaos, fear, or disadvantage. As such, its first appearances are a register of the degree of social and psychological pain people are suffering.

"We are dealing with frightened people caught in the jaws of history, not kooks."

12

Leads to Nowhere

It was still dark on the morning of Thursday, February 17 when Dick Blay left the command center in Jamestown and walked toward his car. Dawn wouldn't break for another hour and, by then, Blay and the rest of the lawmen might well be on their way to putting an end to the search. All around Blay, the more than sixty heavily armed FBI and state bureau crime agents, U.S. Marshals Service and sheriff's deputies cut shadowy figures as they checked their weapons, adjusted their bulletproof vests and moved toward one of the sixteen vehicles that would carry them to their destination.

When quizzed by reporters, Blay told them the maneuver was none of their business and that they would be briefed later.

Blay's order that the newsmen not follow the convoy was tantamount to waving a red cape in front of a bull. It only aroused the anger and curiosity of reporters who had kept a vigil at the task force's command center since the shootout. Within minutes after the last law enforcement vehicle left Jamestown, they were in hot pursuit. One radio station went airborne with its helicopter and, as North Dakotans readied themselves for work, garnished their breakfasts with live reports of the convoy's movements as it speeded along the two-lane highway that cut through the prairie. The trucks

were heading south, and it was easy to guess that the lawmen were
headed for Ashley.

Ashley—population twelve hundred—on the southern boundary
of McIntosh County, a hilly, rocky, slough-dotted region that abuts
the South Dakota border. Approximately sixty miles southwest of
Medina, Ashley and the towns clustered around it—Lehr, Napo-
leon, Wishek, Linton, and Strasburg—are home to the sons and
daughters of German-Russian immigrants, a proud and independent people. Ashley was home also to three known tax protestors
and to the American Christian School, which offered parents a
fundamentalist alternative to the public school system.

The convoy arrived at the outskirts of the community just as the
morning fog started to burn off. Richard Blay ordered roadblocks
set up at all the main roads running into the town. Residents and
persons with business in Ashley were allowed to pass through
freely. The news media, however, were not allowed access to the
sleepy farming community. The attempted news blackout proved
futile when the radio station's helicopter took other journalists on
board and flew over the blockade. The helicopter landed on the
high school's football field and journalists disembarked from it like
an invasion force.

Town residents watched in fear and fascination—some peered
from the windows of their businesses, others sought a better view
from the sidewalk—as heavily armed lawmen rolled by along their
town's well-kept main street and took up positions outside of three
dwellings.

It was about 9:30 A.M. when Jan Phillips dropped her two children
off at the small American Christian School which doubled as a
veterinary clinic. When she looked out the school's window, she
noticed two men looking at the building through binoculars. She
waved at them. They didn't wave back, and what she saw next
turned her blood cold. A group of men jumped out of several cars—
some crouched behind the vehicles—and started pointing rifles and
shotguns toward the school, while other armed men began to move
toward the back of it. A lone individual walked slowly to the door
of the building and was met by the school's only teacher, Len

Martin. The man identified himself as an FBI agent and said they had reason to believe Gordon Kahl was in the area. In a courteous, but firm and businesslike, voice, the agent ordered Martin to send the six schoolchildren home, "open all the closets, leave the doors open and get out of the house." Martin complied.

Phillips returned home with her children to find lawmen already searching her and her husband Michael's house. At approximately the same time, a similar investigation was being conducted at the home Dr. James Coleman, a local veterinarian and tax protestor, shared with his wife, Candy. It would not be the last time the Phillips and the Colemans attracted the attention of authorities. Just weeks after their homes were searched by lawmen, Michael Phillips, a paralegal worker for civil liberty suits, would be charged with practicing law without a license, and the Colemans would be charged with violating North Dakota's compulsory public school attendance law for sending their child to the American Christian School. Dr. Coleman also would become the subject of an IRS investigation. Neither family kept its court date. Less than a month after the charges were filed against them, the Phillipses and the Colemans moved quietly from Ashley to Canada. Later, Dr. Coleman said the government engaged in a vendetta against everyone remotely connected to the Kahl case and that it became clear neither he nor his family could live safely in the United States.

By 1:30 P.M., the searches had been concluded. Lawmen had confiscated hundreds of documents related to the Posse and the tax system, as well as a .357-caliber pistol, but they did not find what they had hoped. There was no Gordon Kahl and there wasn't a clue as to where he might be.

A short while later, the frustration felt by Blay erupted during an impromptu press conference. "We are looking for the murderer of two law enforcement officers and you are telegraphing what is happening," the stern-faced detective told reporters.

"I think you have to look at what your own motives are," said Blay, who grew more angry as he spoke. "You want to get on the news and tell everybody exactly where we are going and when we're going to get there. I think it's irresponsible, I really do."

Blay accused the news media of having tipped Kahl off to the search by broadcasting the convoy's movements en route to Ashley. But that wasn't really the case. The lawmen had not acted on any firm information or positive sightings of Kahl, but on investigative probabilities, coupled with a hope that the fugitive would be found in one of the three homes. Or that at the least, information would be found that could lead them to where Kahl was hiding. "We were looking for the most logical people who would be harboring him. The families in Ashley were his allies," Blay said later.

Several hours later, Blay held a second press conference at the task force's command center in Jamestown, and recanted his earlier accusations. Kahl had not been scared off, he said, he simply wasn't there. However, he still cautioned the media: "I don't question your motives. The only thing I ask you to do is really stop and think. We're dealing with an avowed killer. He is extremely dangerous."

What Blay didn't mention to the gathered journalists was a conversation he had with Justice Department officials, who said they would support any request from him to impose a news blackout on the story. While he was tempted to ask for a blackout, Blay realized, after his anger had subsided, that such a move would only exacerbate an already tenuous relationship with the press.

Blay was followed to the press table by U.S. Marshal Howard Safir, who told reporters the marshals service was offering a $25,000 reward for information leading to Kahl's capture.

"This is the first time we've offered a reward of this amount," said Safir. "We do this because we feel that this case is so significant and the perpetrator is so dangerous that the sooner we can get him apprehended, the better off the citizens of North Dakota and the country will be."

Rodney Webb quickly added that the reward should not be perceived as an admission that the search for Kahl was at a dead end. "It's another tool that investigators are hoping will be helpful," he said.

To the public, however, the perception lingered that a sixty-three-year-old, balding grandfather, dressed in bib overalls and a seed cap, and driving a beat-up, old Rambler was outfoxing some of the best lawmen, supported with the most sophisticated equipment, in America. As the search for Kahl turned from days into weeks and from weeks into months, the public's faith in its law force only diminished. Headlines in *The Forum,* the *Grand Forks Herald,* and other state newspapers tracked the government's ineffectual efforts: "Search task force reduced," "Kahl search headquarters is moved," "Kahl search leads are dwindling," and "Sympathy for Kahl blamed for lack of leads."

A certain perverse admiration for Kahl started to take hold and, to some people, he achieved legendary status.

Caps that said "Go, Gordie, Go" and T-shirts emblazoned with "Gordon Kahl Is My Tax Consultant" started to appear. Pranksters telephoned taverns and restaurants and requested that Gordon Kahl be paged and that he be asked to call home, a request which, when honored by an unwitting bartender or hostess, was greeted with laughter. Ballads were written that sang the praises of Kahl and his stand against the government. The first surfaced several weeks after the shootout and was written by Harley McLain, a political gadfly in North Dakota, who, at various times and on occasions at the same time, campaigned for the U.S. Senate and the presidency on a platform to save the earthworm. The song, which was sent to a number of radio stations in the region, was entitled "Calling Gordon Kahl," and decried the government's actions at the Kahl home.

> Your house is full of bullet holes
> Your windows ain't no more
> This is just a preview
> of what we have in store

> We're the FBI, the CIA and
> the president of the United States
> We're calling you to come on in
> Or we'll throw around our weight

> Calling Gordon Kahl
> Calling Gordon Kahl
> Gordon, please come home.

Although that song did not reach the airwaves, it didn't deter songwriters. Several weeks later, a recording of a second song— "Freedom Fighter Gordon Kahl"—was received by radio stations throughout the state. The second song, written by an anonymous balladeer, praised Gordon Kahl's actions on the road outside of Medina, as well as his political views.

> U.S. marshalls [sic] with a warrant
> Armed with everything but facts
> Came a-callin' for a rebel
> Who refused to pay his tax
>
> Prairie fog has chilled the trail
> But it's known by one and all
> Just what happens
> when you mess with
> Freedom Fighter Gordon Kahl
>
> Now for Gordon and his family
> Things had gone from good to grief
> Since they'd stood up to the tax man
> Making plain their deep belief
> That a land conceived in freedom
> Shouldn't try to charge us rent
> Let alone send out its marshalls [sic]
> To assault the innocent
>
> You'll be worthy of a statue
> By the time they ever catch you
> Keep on running for our freedom,
> Gordon Kahl.

Of course, not everyone, and certainly not a majority of the people, sang Gordon's praises. Even one of his neighbors acknowledged after the shootout that Gordon was "just a killer now."

Still, there was little doubt that sympathy for the outlaw existed and support that was generated for Gordon hindered the government's investigation, a fact not lost on Richard Blay. At one point during the investigation, Blay asked an acquaintance of Kahl's whether he'd tell authorities where Kahl was hiding if he knew. The man remained silent. "You have trouble with that?" probed Blay.

"Well, he is a friend," the man finally responded.

Later, over pizza and a beer at his home, Blay told a reporter, "I think I can understand that answer. If I was a farmer I'd probably be the leader of the damn group.

"We have a tendency to like the rugged individualist who is willing to take on big government," he said.

And, in a way, said Blay, Kahl was a "patriot" in the true sense of the word. He had very openly opposed taxation.

As they searched for the fugitive, lawmen also found that support for Gordon Kahl wasn't limited to North Dakota. In Benzonia, Michigan, the former pastor of the Heaton Bible Church told investigators that "Gordon always helped his fellow man," and, "No, I wouldn't tell you where he is if I knew."

South Dakota farmer Byron Dale said he would gladly hide Gordon, and he told reporters that the government's offer to forgive his $397,000 farm debt in return for Gordon's location wasn't incentive enough. The government denied it made such an offer to Dale, who was later arrested when he tried to pay off his loans with hay and silage.

In Arlington, Texas, a former coworker of Gordon's lectured lawmen about how the "banking industry is the real enemy of the people, not Gordon Kahl," and that he too would keep his mouth shut if he knew where Gordon was hiding. "Gordon won't get justice from you. You guys will execute him on the spot," he told the agents. "That shootout up there in Medina was a planned assassination attempt by the government to shut Gordon up because of his beliefs."

Those views, that Gordon was set up, that the government tried to use Gordon as an example to others who dared protest the illegality of the income tax, that Gordon was ambushed—were expressed again and again, by people in towns such as St. George, Utah; North Olmsted, Ohio; Halstead, Kansas; Harrison, Arkansas; Pinesdale, Montana; Hayden Lake, Idaho; Timber Lake, South Dakota; Pontiac, Missouri, and Hazen, North Dakota.

Many of the investigators, including Richard Blay, were startled at the breadth of the subculture of people who not only shared Gordon's views but saw him as a hero, a man to be respected and hailed. And they were unnerved by the amount of hatred they heard expressed toward the government and some of its citizens.

A woman outside of Streeter, North Dakota, opened an interview with FBI agents with the declaration that all blacks and Jews should be killed. Near Jamestown, North Dakota, a retired air corps captain and border patrol officer, who shall here be known as Mr. Smith, told FBI Inspector Tony Perez that Kahl was "a good man, who was right in a way in shooting the marshals." Mr. Smith, who was slightly inebriated, then asked Perez where he had been born. Cuba, replied Perez. "You must be on Social Security in this country, you son-of-a-bitch," bellowed Smith. Perez, sure that the situation could only get uglier, tried to end the interview. As he prepared to leave the house, Mr. Smith called Perez a coward and told him the "next time I see you it will be from behind the sights of my rifle and I'll kill you."

And there was a certain fear about what the Posse, or some similar group, might do to anyone who turned in Gordon. At a diner in Medina, a farmer agreed with a reporter that the $25,000 reward could take care of a few debts. But the farmer also doubted that anyone who collected the reward would live long enough to pay those debts personally.

Not that the government hadn't received any tips on Kahl's location. It had, plenty of them. One piece of information led investigators to Blue Springs, Missouri, after members of the Covenant,

Sword and Arm of the Lord were overheard in a diner making plans to smuggle Gordon Kahl into Canada. Another steered authorities to an area outside of Missoula, Montana, where it was believed Gordon was being hidden by members of the Duck Club, a Florida-based tax protest group. Still another lead took lawmen to Benton, Tennessee, where Gordon was believed to have attended a convention of the American Pistol and Rifle Association, a survivalist-style group. And investigators were led to Tuscumbia, Alabama, and the headquarters of the Knights of Ku Klux Klan.

Some of the information that didn't ultimately lead authorities to Gordon still proved valuable to other investigations. A tip that Gordon was in the Denver, Colorado, area introduced lawmen to John Grandbouche, a Posse member who had established the National Commodities and Barter Association, a system of debt-free, interest-free barter banks in Colorado, South Dakota, Minnesota, and Iowa. Members of the NCBA converted all their money into silver bullion and gold South African Krugerrands, which were kept in the association banks. In an attempt to avoid paying income taxes, no receipts of the transactions were recorded and the NCBA paid all of its members' bills. In 1985, acting on information first uncovered in the Kahl search, IRS agents raided the banks and confiscated nearly ten tons of silver bullion. According to authorities, the tax-evasion scheme laundered more than $500,000 a day and was used by more than twenty thousand people. A different lead took investigators to a Posse-related group in Bemidji, Minnesota, and prompted an investigation into the group's activities, which resulted in the 1984 arrest of four of its members on charges of conspiring to rob banks and take hostages, and possession of explosives.

There were other tips, however, which only produced anxious moments for Kahl look-alikes and apologies from lawmen. A man at a motel in Great Falls, Montana, was roused from his sleep by a telephone call and a voice on the other end of the line that ordered him to come out of his room with his hands raised. When he stepped out of the room, he was greeted by eight police officers pointing guns at him. It took the man over an hour to convince authorities he was not Gordon Kahl. In Wisconsin, whose state tourism slogan is "Escape to Wisconsin," a seventy-two-year-old Grand Forks, North Dakota, resident was met at a highway intersection by a bevy of state patrolmen with their weapons drawn and a newspaper photograph of Kahl in their hands. The man from Grand Forks had a gun placed to his cheek as he fumbled for his wallet and license to prove that he wasn't who they thought. Nor were they the only persons stopped for being over sixty years old, balding, and driving older-model vehicles with North Dakota license plates. Several people were pulled over in North Dakota, California, New York, and Ohio.

The lack of progress in the investigation frustrated Blay. Yet, he remained optimistic. "There are certain things you do, and we were doing them. We analyzed every lead we got. We discussed them. There wasn't anything that could be done that already wasn't being done," Blay said later.

All the government needed was one solid lead, a telephone call from someone who had seen Kahl or who knew where he was hiding. And that break would come, Blay insisted. Maybe not in the next couple of days, or weeks, or even in six months, but it would come.

And Blay was frustrated by matters other than the fruitlessness of the search. As the investigation dragged on, interservice jealousies between the FBI and U.S. Marshals Service surfaced and threatened to remove the focus of the investigation from aiding the prosecution of the five defendants in custody and finding Kahl. The marshals felt that Blay assigned them all the worthless follow-up leads. And in truth, Blay didn't have a lot of faith in them as investigators. He had a great deal of respect for individual marshals, and he believed the service was composed of a dedicated group of men and women. But overall, he felt they didn't have the necessary skills or training to handle such a case. Only recently had their duties been expanded to include investigative work. Previously, their roles had been limited to that of guardians of the courthouse, missile escort, prisoner transport, and warrant service.

Blay believed that what happened on the road outside of Medina was an example of that lack of training. Somebody should have told

Cheshire to slow down, that this battle had better be fought another day. Not only did they go ahead with the arrest attempt but they compounded their error in judgment by implementing a plan—if it could be called that—where the lives of innocent people were placed in danger and Kahl and his allies were allowed to deploy in a defensive position that assured the subsequent results. It was an unqualified disaster: two men dead, five more wounded, and the man sought by the marshals on the loose.

"The marshals service came out looking like a bunch of asses. It was a perfect example of how not to conduct an investigation or an arrest," Blay said later.

To quell internal bickering, Blay paired FBI agents with deputy marshals in two-person investigative teams, sometimes led by a marshal, sometimes by the FBI. And, except for the lone outburst directed at the news media early on in the search, Blay never revealed the building frustrations, his own and that of the FBI and the marshals, to the public. Outwardly, he presented the image of a cool, collected professional, a person who, despite the demands of the investigation, found time to address service clubs, farm groups, and business luncheons. And he made time after his talks to sign autographs for the middle-aged women in the audience who were probably as taken by his movie star good looks as they were by his speech.

Blay even warmed toward the news media. He made himself more accessible for interviews, displayed a willingness to discuss the investigation and, on occasions, dropped by newsrooms to chat—on deep background—with news reporters and editors. While Blay is easily likable and seems comfortable around people, there was a reason he made himself available to nearly everyone who wanted to speak with him. He was waging a war for the support of the state's residents who were surprisingly willing to suspend their judgment as to who was right or wrong on that road outside of Medina.

Blay sensed strongly from his exposure not only to the investigative reports but also to letters-to-the-editor, ballads, and pro-Kahl T-shirts, caps, and novelty items, that the people of North Dakota felt a deep alienation from their government. This was a problem that had to be addressed by the government. "We have to have compassion for the problems facing [these farmers], an appreciation for them. The way to do that is to show them we aren't a bunch of gestapo who are out to smash heads or kill people," he said.

Or, thought Blay, the government would lose more than two good men to the likes of Gordon Kahl.

13

A Hero's Welcome

Exactly one month after the shootout in Medina, North Dakota, twenty-eight-year-old Karen Russell Robertson readied her two daughters, Michelle, age eight, and Mary, age four, for church services in nearby Mountain Home, Arkansas. As usual on a Sunday morning, she was running late, so she paid little attention when Leonard Ginter pulled into the driveway in his mustard-on-white pickup truck. Although Ginter lived outside of Smithville, some seventy-five miles to the east, he was a frequent visitor to the Arthur Russell farm. And, like today, he always seemed to have someone with him whom he wanted her father to meet.

Well, Karen didn't want to meet him. She didn't want to meet anyone who was a friend of Leonard Ginter. In spite of all his talk about patriotism, the Constitution, and God, or maybe because of it, Karen felt Ginter was nothing more than a con man who was trying to fleece her all-too-trusting father out of his life savings— five thousand ounces of silver he kept hidden in the house—money, thought Karen, that should rightfully go to her and her daughters.

Karen hurried her children out the door, not bothering to say good-bye. She heard Ginter ask her father where the Udeys were, but was out the door before she could hear his response.

The youngest of ten children and a high school dropout, Karen had moved in with her father in November after she had divorced Michael, her husband of more than seven years. She brought her two little girls with her. Father and daughter had frequent, and sometimes violent, arguments over the way Karen raised her children, over her sloppy housekeeping, and over her inability to hold on to a job. Other family members saw Karen as unreliable and selfish, preying on her father in hopes of getting her hands on the silver. Once, Karen tried to enlist the aid of two of her sisters to have her father committed to an insane asylum and was angrily rebuffed.

Despite all that, Arthur Russell wasn't about to throw his daughter and two granddaughters out of the house. Not without Karen at least having a job or a place to live. They were still part of the family and in need of help.

When they returned from church services, Karen noticed that Ginter's pickup truck was gone. After they entered the house, Karen sent Michelle and Mary to their room to change out of their dresses and into play clothes. Her father, who was in the kitchen making lunch, called to Karen. When she entered the kitchen, he turned from the counter, looked directly into her eyes, and, in a whispered but firm voice, said, "I want you to promise you will not say anything to anyone about who will be staying with us for a time."

Karen gave her father a quizzical look.

"I want you to promise," he repeated, his voice raised slightly.

"I promise," said Karen. He had piqued her curiosity.

Arthur arched his eyes over his glasses, and peered at his daughter. A smile crossed his face. He called through the kitchen door to Curly and asked him to come in to meet his daughter. At the door appeared a balding, bob-nosed older man dressed in blue jeans, a plaid work shirt, and wearing military-style boots.

Curly, Karen discovered, was Gordon Kahl.

No sooner had they shaken hands, when Karen asked, "Did you really kill those two U.S. marshals?"

Kahl nodded, and added, "But not until they had fired first."

Before Karen could ask any further questions, Gordon told her to call him Sam Louden, the same name he had used when he lived in Mena, Arkansas, a year earlier. Seconds later, Michelle and Mary entered the room and were introduced to Sam Louden. He told the children, however, as he broke into a grin, to call him Uncle Sam. He was, Gordon told Michelle and Mary, a very popular man and that "a lot of people wanted to see me."

Gordon then excused himself and retreated upstairs to his bedroom. Later that day, Ed and Irene Udey drove over from Cotter, nine miles west of the Russell home. They wanted to meet Gordon Kahl. When they entered the house, Kahl was standing at the top of the stairs. As Gordon started to descend the stairs, Ed Udey started to climb them, and met Gordon midway. Udey wrapped both his hands around Gordon's hand and started to shake it vigorously. You are a hero, he told Gordon, a real American hero.

Hero or not, for the first few days at least, Karen was not thrilled with Gordon's being at the house. Despite his claim that he acted in self-defense and the fact that he didn't look like a murderer, Kahl had killed two men. But Karen found it hard not to like him, and she was especially impressed with the way he treated her daughters. He seemed to love children, and he knew how to handle them without raising his voice. Often Karen would hear Michelle and Mary giggling in another room and, when she looked in to see what they were doing, would find Gordon telling them a funny story or drawing silly pictures for them on his ever-present, paper-filled clipboard.

And Gordon treated Karen with respect, as an adult and an equal. Many nights, after everyone else had gone to bed, the two of them would sit up and discuss the Bible or the book he was reading, *One Straw Revolution,* which was about building up the soil with natural additives, not chemicals and other foreign substances. The two of them also talked about the shootout. Usually such discussions followed news reports about the ongoing search for Gordon. Karen asked once if he was afraid someone might turn him in for the $25,000 reward. No, he replied. The money was only worthless paper, printed by the servants of Satan. No true Christian would want it. As if to emphasize his point, Kahl took his clipboard and drew a picture of a seven-headed beast he said was the symbol of Satan in Revelation.

Karen also found Gordon—Sam—extremely helpful around the house, willing to do whatever chore needed to be done. One thing he wouldn't do, however, was go grocery shopping. That was Karen's job. When food or other items were needed, he would make a list and hand it to her with a $100 bill he would peel from the large roll he kept stuffed in his pants pocket. Often he told Karen to buy something for herself and the children.

Kahl did leave the house on occasion. Several times he traveled to Cotter to have dinner with the Udeys; and nearly every day he would stroll outside of the Russell home. There was little chance of anyone seeing him. The Russells lived just north of the Ozark National Forest, in the middle of a part of the world that seemed lifted from the panels of Al Capp's comic strip of Dogpatch. The area was heavily wooded, hilly, and surrounded by so many trout-filled freshwater lakes that a person seemed just a fly cast away from one no matter where he stood. In fact, not far away, just outside of Harrison to the west of the Russell place, was Dogpatch, an amusement park complete with hillbilly shacks and walking, talking, breathing Li'l Abners and Daisy Maes.

Exactly how Gordon Kahl got from North Dakota to Texas and then to Arkansas, and the route he took, remains unclear. It is generally agreed that Kahl started his trek south on Tuesday, February 15, the last day he was seen in North Dakota by someone other than Scott Faul. On that day, at about 9:30 A.M., as lawmen waited for the fog to lift and prepared to storm his Heaton farm home, Kahl pulled his car into the driveway of a farmstead located ten miles east of Bismarck. There, he asked a woman, who will be known here as Mrs. Jones, for directions to a surfaced road, but not a major highway. Mrs. Jones said that Kahl spoke quickly and, throughout their five-minute conversation, glanced frequently over his shoulder toward the highway. It wasn't until a day later that she recognized the man she talked to as Kahl from a photograph in a newspaper.

Some authorities believe Gordon made the trip over a period of three or four days, maybe more, that he traveled at night and hid during the day, sometimes on the farmsteads of supporters. Other lawmen feel he used his knowledge of the back roads, gained from his many trips between Texas and North Dakota, and made a non-stop trip. The theories again merge in the Crane, Texas, area, where, it is speculated, Kahl put an acetylene torch to his car, buried the pieces, and was then spirited to Arkansas. Whoever took Gordon to Arkansas from Crane, if anyone, is unknown. None of Gordon's friends or acquaintances admit to having seen him at any time after the shootout. But if Kahl did get to Crane, one acquaintance wryly noted, "There are a lot of pickups in Texas, and when they are pointed north they can find their way to Arkansas."

Gordon's first stop in Arkansas was the home of Leonard Ginter, a man who had belonged to the Posse when he lived in Wisconsin in the 1970s. In fact, because of Ginter's past association with the Posse and his current involvement with the Arkansas Patriots party, neither man felt Ginter's home outside of Smithville, in northeast Arkansas, could remain a safe haven for long. After two days it was decided that Kahl would stay with Arthur Russell, who was seen as a true patriot, but whose affiliation with the movement wasn't documented on any police records.

So it was at the Russell home that Kahl would spend his days, watching television, entertaining the children, reading his Bible, and following the legal battles of his wife, son, and three friends.

14

Religious Rights

Rodney Webb answered the telephone at his home. "Jew lover," said the caller, who hung up before Webb could respond.

Webb shook his head and returned the telephone receiver to its cradle. As the trial date neared, the number of harassing telephone calls had become so frequent that Webb and his wife, Betty, told their children not to answer the telephone. While none of the calls included threats against anyone's life, they were unnerving and expressed more hatred and anger than the couple wanted their children exposed to.

The next morning, a neighbor telephoned and told Webb he had seen a man crawling along the riverbank near their houses. The neighbor said he told his wife they should consider moving away until after the trial. "I don't want a sniper mistaking us for you," he told Webb.

Both men laughed at the attempted joke, a nervous laugh. Webb was bothered, and a bit scared, by the amount of hatred generated by what was now referred to as the "Kahl case." He even considered getting a gun to protect both him and his family, but decided against it.

A lifelong resident of North Dakota, Webb was born, raised, and educated in Grafton, a farming community located in the northeast part of the state. After high school, he attended the University of North Dakota, first as an undergraduate and then as a law student. When he graduated from law school, he returned to Grafton and practiced law. Webb knew North Dakota and its people. At least before the shootout Webb thought he knew them.

"There was such a great anger that we didn't know existed until after the shootings," said Webb. "We were surprised this could happen."

But now, he said, he wouldn't be surprised if it happened again. "I don't think Gordon Kahl is carrying the flag for the woes of the farm community, but there is a lot of sympathy among many, many people who feel the government isn't protecting them in the farm field.

"We have an awful lot of people feeling ill will toward their government because of the farm crisis," said Webb. "Sure it could happen again. We have a terrible problem. We were, we are, in a major depression."

Winter turned into spring, and with the return of warmer weather came the farmers' optimism for a good crop, better prices, and an end to the crisis. The tractors, disks, and farmers—tuned, repaired, and rested during the winter hiatus—reentered the fields to work the long-dormant soil and ready it for planting. The air was clear and fresh, and a sense of rebirth invigorated the land and its people.

It was a feeling not shared by those in law enforcement. The search for Gordon Kahl had reached a dead end. The early optimism for a quick capture had given way to a deep frustration born from the fact that all the manpower and sophisticated equipment they had at their disposal had proved useless in finding one man. And the lawmen's frustration was further aggravated by the constant questions from news reporters about their progress. "If I knew where the hell he was at, I would go get him. Now wouldn't I?" snapped one marshal, who said what many on the diminished task force wanted to say.

One lawman who wasn't frustrated was Lynn Crooks. He had already resigned himself to the fact that the government would

never find Gordon Kahl. In Crooks's mind, Kahl had gone under-
ground and would stay there at least until the fugitive himself
decided it was time to surface. Crooks heard the complaints of the
investigators, and he offered them encouragement but no longer
concerned himself with the search. He had a case to prepare, and
that was his only concern now.

His first legal arguments weren't made before a judge and jury,
however, but before the Department of Justice, the U.S. Marshals
Service, and the FBI.

The three agencies wanted everyone in custody charged with
first-degree murder, which carried a life sentence. Crooks ada-
mantly opposed that strategy and fought an uphill battle to get the
charges reduced against Joan Kahl, Vernon Wegner, and David
Broer. To Crooks, that strategy of going for the greatest charge
against all those indicted was a tactical error on both the public
relations and, more importantly, the courtroom front.

Above all else, Crooks felt that the public wanted and deserved
to see the law enforced fairly and evenhandedly. Evidence supported murder charges against Yorie Kahl and Scott Faul, said
Crooks, but no evidence existed for the same charge against Joan
Kahl, David Broer, and Vernon Wegner. Instead, it appeared that
Joan Kahl, Wegner, and Broer had not fired a weapon and had
actually done everything possible to avoid being drawn into the gun
battle. Those three individuals were guilty of other offenses, said
Crooks, but if the murder charges weren't dropped, the public
would be left with the perception that the government was seeking
revenge over justice, a perception that could have unwanted effects
in the courtroom. Once it became clear that the government hadn't
proved its case against Joan Kahl, Wegner, and Broer, acquittal
fever could sweep through the jury box.

Crooks's arguments proved persuasive, and murder charges
against Joan Kahl, Wegner, and Broer were dropped. Those charges
that remained against the three ranged from assault, to accessories
after the fact of a murder, to conspiracy to interfere with the service
of a federal warrant; all carried prison sentences of four to ten years.
The government also agreed to bail requests from Joan Kahl and

Vernon Wegner. Joan was freed on $50,000 bail put up by her brother. Wegner, however, was unable to make his $100,000 bail and remained in custody, as did Broer, Yorie Kahl, and Scott Faul, all of whom were being held without bail.

As he prepared his case, Crooks worried about the trial being turned into a forum for the defendants' philosophical or ideological views. It seemed that all the ingredients were there for a Chicago Seven–like political trial, something he was anxious to avoid.

At the arraignment of the defendants, David Broer, Scott Faul, and Yorie Kahl refused to enter pleas, contending that they were freemen who adhered only to God's law and Christian principles, and that the federal court didn't have jurisdiction over them. Judge Benson entered innocent pleas on behalf of the three defendants. Crooks's concern was further heightened when Yorie, who repeatedly referred to himself as a political prisoner, wanted as his counsel Charles O'Brien, Sr., a paralegal with the Christian Constitutional Law Center based in Cheyenne, Wyoming, the office of which is considered the legal think tank for the tax protest movement. Broer, whose legal experience was limited to a civil suit he filed against the state of Montana, wanted to be named co-counsel.

"We didn't want a bunch of flaky tax protest attorneys taking over the case," recalled Crooks. Nor, he said, did he "want this to be a trial against the tax protest movement."

Crooks asked the court to ban from the trial all evidence related to allegations or contentions of harassment of tax protestors by the IRS, marshals service, FBI, or any other government agency. He also requested that any allegations as to the unconstitutionality of the federal income tax laws, the Federal Reserve System, the federal monetary law or federal laws in general, and Gordon Kahl's sixteen-page letter be disallowed as evidence. "Kahl appears to be arguing that the death of the two marshals . . . was morally justified by what he perceived to be a perversion of the United States Constitution," argued Crooks. "In effect, his point appears to be that he has a religious right to kill . . . to avoid having the will of the majority . . . forced upon himself.

"If these matters are allowed into evidence and the government is forced to respond to them, the trial focus will clearly be diverted to collateral issues."

Publicly, Crooks said he took the action because he anticipated a self-defense argument based on the contention that the arrest attempt was illegal and, therefore, that the defendants had the right to resist, and he wanted to short-circuit such a defense strategy. Privately, however, Crooks did not want to have to argue against the anti-tax movement at this time and with the prevailing mood of the region. "The public stood back and, to a surprising degree, were willing to give these guys their day in court," said Crooks. "I was very much afraid of getting into the issue of the rightness and wrongness of his cause. That wasn't the issue. Murder was the issue.

"I didn't want to have to prove the income tax was right and proper," said Crooks.

Judge Benson ignored the defendants' requests to either represent themselves or have as counsel an attorney from the tax protest movement. Instead, he appointed experienced and competent defense lawyers to represent each of the four defendants who claimed they had insufficient funds to hire their own legal counsel. Warren Sogard, Robert Ramlo, and Jonathan Garaas, all of Fargo, were named to represent Yorie Kahl, Joan Kahl, and Vernon Wegner, while Ralph Vinje of Bismarck was appointed to represent David Broer.

Only Scott Faul retained a private attorney, forty-seven-year-old Irv Nodland of Bismarck, who, when approached by Faul's family and friends, had made it clear he would not accept a court appointment to defend Scott. If Scott wanted him, he would have to pay for Nodland's services. Scott wanted him.

Articulate, sandy-haired, and, despite his daily two-mile jog, soft around the midsection, Nodland, after his graduation in 1964 from Yale Law School—where he had been a classmate of former senator Gary Hart and former California governor Jerry Brown—had returned to North Dakota and established an enviable reputation as a defense lawyer. Nodland's decision to defend Faul was not popular with his partners. Despite the fact that Faul was a paying client, they felt little could be gained by Nodland's handling the case. Some of Irv Nodland's clients also questioned his decision. Shortly after he accepted the case, Nodland traveled to Minot to meet with a man charged with smuggling. As he stood talking with the client through the prison bars, a news bulletin came over the radio that said Nodland was defending Faul. "That's you?" the man asked.

"Yes," Nodland replied.

"How can you defend somebody like that?" asked the client.

"Because I like you," Nodland told his client.

The man, who was facing a thirty-year prison sentence and a $50,000 fine if convicted, smiled back at Nodland.

After the defendants were arraigned, Judge Benson scheduled the start of the trial for May 9, 1983, and gave attorneys on both sides until April 4 to file pretrial motions.

Nodland wasted little time. The same day as the arraignment, he asked Benson and North Dakota's two other federal judges to disqualify themselves from presiding over the trial. Nodland argued that because the duties of the marshals service included the security of the federal courthouses, there had been almost daily contact between the two dead marshals and the three judges. Such contact, he said, would make it difficult, if not impossible, for the judges to maintain an impartial attitude toward the outcome of this trial.

Actually, Nodland would have gladly defended his client before either Judge Ronald Davies or Judge Bruce Van Sickle. The man he did not want sitting on the bench, however, was the man who had jurisdiction over the case—Paul Benson. A quiet, soft-spoken man who had been raised on a North Dakota farm during the dust bowl years of the Great Depression, Benson saw education as the way to escape the barren land and enjoyed tending his roses. To Nodland, there was little difference between Benson and Gordon Kahl. Both men saw the world in black-and-white terms, were moralistically rigid and judgmental, and refused to recognize the weaknesses and foibles of humankind. "I don't see Benson as an evil man . . . [but] you owe it to your client to do anything possible not to have his case tried before Judge Benson.

"He is always civil and always the gentleman. But he is extremely law-and-order oriented and you can't get him to go along with anything except that which is wanted by Lynn Crooks," said Nodland.

The slings and arrows of criticism flung at him by Nodland and other defense attorneys were nothing new to the sixty-five-year-old Benson, who with his black judicial robes sharply contrasted by his white hair, and his six-foot-two-inch ramrod-straight frame, looked like Hollywood's image of a judge.

Benson was a man used to controversy. Almost immediately after he stepped up to the federal bench in 1971, Benson, who earned his law degree from George Washington University after he had returned from service as an gunnery officer with an anti-submarine unit during World War II, became embroiled in public debate when he ruled that a priest had to testify before the grand jury. The ruling, which was eventually overturned, prompted a nationwide outcry from religious groups and resulted in Benson's quitting his church. Later, religious leaders branded him as anti-Christian for striking down a state law that required the posting of the Ten Commandments in all public school rooms, and anti-abortion activists likened him to Hitler when he repeatedly struck down North Dakota's abortion laws. But probably Benson's most controversial case arose in 1977, when he presided over the trial of American Indian Movement leader Leonard Peltier, prosecuted by Lynn Crooks, who was accused of murdering two FBI agents during a gun battle on the Pine Ridge Indian Reservation in South Dakota in 1975. Many of Benson's rulings on evidence in that case ran counter to rulings made by an Iowa judge in an earlier trial that ended with the acquittal of two of Peltier's codefendants. Because of that, Benson was accused by AIM and its supporters—among them Hollywood celebrities such as Marlon Brando, Washington-based politicians, and advocates in the Soviet Union—of being part of a government conspiracy to silence Peltier and destroy the movement. Peltier's conviction, however, has been upheld through several appeals.

Little did Nodland, or anyone else on either side of the case, know that Benson's doctor also didn't want him on the bench. He wanted Benson on an operating table and then spending the next four months recuperating from open-heart surgery. Just days after the arraignment hearing, Benson started to experience an increased tightening in his chest. He was whisked to a local hospital by U.S. marshals under tight security, which included no record of his admittance, and underwent an angiogram. His main artery was nearly completely closed. Unless they removed the blockage soon, Benson could suffer a heart attack that would be fatal, his doctor told him. But Benson vetoed his doctor's recommendation; there would be no surgery until after the trial was completed.

Nor, ruled Benson, would he remove himself from the case.

Nodland appealed the decision to the U.S. 8th Circuit Court of Appeals in St. Louis. The court denied the appeal. "I felt after I lost the recusal that I didn't have very much chance of winning. I did not believe I could get a fair trial from Judge Benson," said Nodland later.

Judge Benson also denied requests for separate trials, a change of venue, and a trial delay. Nodland and Sogard asked that the trial be moved to Wyoming and, in order to substantiate the need for a new trial site, that the trial be postponed for sixty days to allow an opinion poll to be taken that would "demonstrate the actual level of public prejudice and bias with the area from which the jury pool is to be drawn." The two lawyers also argued a delay would allow time for adverse publicity to wear off, and might even give the FBI and marshals another chance to capture Gordon Kahl.

During this period of legal maneuvering, Wegner's attorney, Jonathan Garaas, maintained a low profile and did not file any motions with the court. The reasons for his inactivity became clear on April 1, when he and Wegner appeared before Benson and entered a plea of guilty to the charge of interfering with federal marshals as they attempted to arrest Gordon Kahl. Under the terms of the bargain struck with the government, Wegner would receive no more than a three-year prison sentence, and in turn agreed to cooperate with authorities and to testify against the other four defendants. Crooks downplayed the importance of the plea bargain and said Wegner wouldn't be the government's star witness. "I question whether his testimony will add very much to what we already know. You are not going to find anything he says very startling. He does not supply some big missing piece to the puzzle," Crooks told reporters after the hearing. "He is a minor player, quite obviously. His culpability is considerably less than the others'." Crooks anticipated that Wegner's testimony would even prove friendly to certain of the defendants.

A similar bargain was extended to Broer, who was encouraged by his attorney to accept it. Broer refused. He would stand and win, or lose, with his friends.

In a letter to his supporters, Broer said, "It appears the powers to be are deliberately attempting to discredit the Constitutional movement by labeling many people who disapprove of the present system of taxation as radicals or tax protestors. I am not a violent person nor do I advocate violence. The only way we can achieve a return to the Law of God and to the U.S. Constitution is by the quiet displacement of our present oppressive and tyrannical government. It is to this ultimate goal I remain dedicated."

Broer urged fundamentalists to scrutinize their lives to "ascertain what values take precedent. In my life, God comes first, the United States Constitution second and my family third. Without the U.S. Constitution, the family unit will face even more destructive forces. If we are unsuccessful in thwarting or altering the present course of this Republic, it will most certainly be destroyed as have many European countries.

"I pray the 'powers to be' have not located the Achilles heel of the patriotic communities in the Upper Midwest. It is time to unite for strength, and support each other in this most necessary of causes and activities."

When he accepted the court appointment, forty-one-year-old Ralph Vinje—a Vietnam veteran, small-plane pilot, horse breeder, bronc-buster, and former aviation law professor at the University of North Dakota—told Broer that he was a defense attorney, not a political advocate. Nor, said Vinje, did he want to become an advocate for their cause.

Initially, Vinje thought his admonishment had been too hasty and unnecessary. He found Broer to be a soft-spoken, mild-mannered, and, for the most part, rational man. Except when his client contended that prosecutor Lynn Crooks was a thirty-second-degree Mason, a level that could be reached only after participation in human sacrifice, Vinje heard very little out of Broer that could be considered radical. But as the trial neared, Vinje helplessly watched Broer become more and more suspicious of those who wanted to help him, and more and more willing to listen to the people who wanted to use him and the other defendants as symbols for a cause. Vinje was frustrated by Broer's unwillingness to accept either the plea bargain, or a defense strategy that put him at arm's length to Scott and Yorie. "Dave had illusions the fundamentalists were going to band together, get a large war chest, and help him slay the government. It just didn't happen," said Vinje.

Broer did believe that the patriots would ultimately triumph, and he believed that the truth, their truth, would win in a true Christian court of law. He would strike no bargains with the Satanic-controlled government.

And there was Broer's wife, Joan, who held a press briefing almost daily to rail against the government and sing the praises of the patriots movement. While Vinje admired her loyalty to her husband and understood that she was trying to help, he told both of them her actions could only hurt the case. But again, neither would listen to his advice.

Vinje's frustration with the Broers was brought to a head when, on May 2, just seven days before the start of the trial, Broer filed a motion that demanded he be released from prison on the grounds that the court did not have jurisdiction over him. Caught off-guard by his client's action, Vinje was furious. "How can you be so incredibly stupid?" he asked, and he immediately requested that the court remove him as Broer's attorney.

That same day, Yorie Kahl asked that his attorney, Warren Sogard, be replaced with someone from the patriots movement. In his motion, Kahl referred to his attorney as a "Satan-serving Masonic persecutor." Soon after he accepted the court appointment

to represent Yorie Kahl, the thirty-two-year-old Warren Sogard became convinced his client wasn't a killer. Sogard saw Yorie Kahl
as a poorly educated, unworldly farm boy who had been deeply
influenced by his father and by a philosophy steeped in the paranoid
lore of a conspiracy that could, without fear of legal retribution,
eliminate its opponents through murder and other means. Sogard
felt he understood the danger that Yorie and the others perceived
they were in on that road outside of Medina, and he would incorporate that into his defense, as well as calling into question the
reasonableness of the government's actions on that road. There was
certainly evidence that more reasonable, and safer, ways to arrest
Gordon Kahl had been suggested, but ignored within the marshals
service.

But before he could begin working with Yorie on a defense strategy, Sogard had to convince his client that he was committed to
his defense. To Yorie Kahl, Warren Sogard was one of the enemy,
an officer of the same court that six years earlier had belittled Yorie's
father and demeaned what Gordon Kahl believed to be holy and
good, the same court that sent his father to prison.

In an attempt to alleviate Yorie's fears and appease members of
the tax protest movement who were exerting a tremendous influence on Yorie in regard to his defense, Sogard agreed to take a
"Christian" test that would determine whether he was a suitable
attorney. Administered by members of the movement, the test included questions about the Bible, the U.S. Constitution, the federal
income tax, the Masonic-Jewish link to a conspiracy to destroy the
Christian United States, as well as questions about Sogard's background. Was he a Mason? Was he Jewish? There was much about
the test Sogard found offensive, and he expressed his feelings can-
didly to his questioners. Yet, once the test was completed, Sogard—
to his surprise—was deemed fit to represent Yorie. Over that hurdle,
Sogard believed he was well on his way to winning his client's trust
and confidence, and in the weeks and months leading up to the
trial, Yorie became less argumentative about their differences and
less insistent that religious and ideological arguments be included
in the defense. He seemed to accept Sogard's contention that no

benefit could be derived from a Chicago Seven–like political trial. Not with Benson on the bench.

But Yorie hadn't accepted any of it.

A day after Yorie filed his motion to replace Sogard, Joan Kahl requested—in a motion filed by her lawyer, Robert Ramlo—that the trial be delayed so her son could undergo psychiatric evaluation. She argued that Yorie had slipped further and further into the obsession which he shared with his father and that her son's most recent actions showed him to be "mentally and emotionally unbalanced and unable to rationally participate in the trial process."

And, because of Yorie's mental state, said Joan, she should be tried separately. She told the court that the "foolishness asserted in his motion . . . will reflect adversely on all the rest of the defendants and, in particular, me, since I am his mother."

Benson, however, was not about to have the start of the trial delayed by actions he saw as frivolous and procedurally deficient. Within a day, he had issued a terse one-page order that denied the requests made by all three defendants, and had strongly urged Vinje to remain as Broer's attorney. Following a brief meeting, in which Broer apologized for his motion, Vinje agreed to stay on the case. The stage was now set for the start of the most publicized trial in North Dakota history.

15

On Trial

The line outside the southeast door of the Old Federal Building started to form around seven o'clock on the brisk, chilly morning of May 9, 1983. The line included federal employees, prospective jurors, hopeful spectators, and members of the news media. With one exception, everyone—the federal bankruptcy and administrative law judges, the prosecution and defense teams, the witnesses, the jury panel members, the news media, the general public—had to enter the large, gray-stone, three-story building through that one door, pass through an airport-like metal detector and have their handbags and packages checked by security officers. Only Judge Paul Benson entered through a separate, closely guarded door at the rear of the building. Once inside the building, persons who arrived on the third floor where the courtroom is located were required to pass through a second metal detector, and individuals found wandering the halls on the other two floors were subject to random searches.

Security was extremely tight everywhere in and around the building. A psychological profile worked up by the FBI suggested that Gordon Kahl was suicidal, but that in all likelihood he would commit suicide in a very public manner. And what could offer a more public suicide than an attack on the courthouse where his wife, son, and friends were being tried in connection with the murders of two U.S. marshals.

On the roof of the building, marshals, armed with semiautomatic rifles, watched the line form below on the street. Similarly armed marshals stood guard at the locked entrances to the building, and still other security personnel patrolled the alley and perimeter of the building. A rented, black Lincoln Continental slowly cruised around the outside of the building. In the back seat sat Gus, a bomb-sniffing dog reassigned from Miami to the security force. Street parking next to the building was banned day and night.

Among those standing in line were eighty-one-year-old Nell Stock and her friend Marie Bittner. Both women hoped to get spectator seats and intended to sit through the whole trial. They were so excited about attending the trial that neither got much sleep the night before because they feared they wouldn't get up in time to get a seat. It wouldn't have mattered how early the two women got up that morning, or the next or, for that matter, the next morning. There would be no room for spectators during the jury selection. On that first day, there were few open seats for either the news media or family members of both the victims and defendants.

Instead, the darkly varnished spectator benches, which seat approximately 125 people, were almost filled by the 114 prospective jurors drawn from throughout eastern North Dakota. Before he started the selection process, Judge Benson asked if it would be an undue hardship for anyone to serve as a sequestered juror for the five weeks the trial was expected to last. Thirty-four people raised their hands and sought to be excused immediately.

After he granted the hardship requests, Benson started the voir dire examination, which he conducted himself with questions from both the prosecution and defense teams. Benson asked the prospective jurors if they knew any of the victims or defendants; if they ever had tax problems, were a member of a tax protest group, owned a gun, advocated or opposed gun control, were a member of a Masonic organization, had friends or acquaintances in the Medina area, had been a victim of a crime or if they ever had been convicted of a crime. He quizzed them on what they had read or heard about the case and whether the information they had received would make it difficult for them to be fair and impartial. It was a long painfully slow process.

The defendants observed the proceedings with varying degrees of interest. Joan Kahl seemed preoccupied during the selection. She rarely took her eyes from her hands which she kept clasped in her lap. Seated in a large, overstuffed chair that seemed to engulf her behind the wide, hardwood defense table, Joan Kahl appeared frail and out of place. Yorie appeared unaffected by the process and struck a disinterested pose and paid little, if any, attention to the persons being questioned. His eyes wandered throughout the courtroom, and at times rested on the portraits of past federal judges that hung on the back wall of the courtroom. He doodled on a legal pad provided by his attorney and, occasionally, like a person remembering a good joke, he broke into a smile. Only Scott Faul and David Broer assumed the roles of active participants. They listened intently to the answers given by the prospective jurors to Judge Benson's questions, and took extensive notes. They conferred often in whispered tones with their attorneys. Only during a break in the questioning would they search the courtroom for their wives, who took their seats after the first wave of jurors were excused.

Days passed in the selection of the jury. By the end of the third day it appeared the voir dire was completed, but during a second round of questioning one of the prospective jurors told Benson he thought he was too sympathetic toward the defendants to be fair. An objector to both the IRS and the government's taxing of lower income people, he told Benson he did not want the responsibility of making a decision that would have an adverse effect on another person's life. Benson excused him. He questioned one more person and was told she had already formed an opinion in the case and it would be difficult for her to set it aside. Benson excused her and recessed for the day.

It was midmorning of the fourth day that the jury selection was completed. Of the 114 people who started the process, 29 were excused for hardship causes, 39 were rejected because they said they could not be impartial, 16 were excused following preemptory challenge by the defense, and 9 others were rejected by the prosecution. Seven were not interviewed.

The fourteen people selected—twelve jurors and two alternates—included nine women and five men, who ranged in age from twenty to seventy-one. The panel comprised three secretaries, two farmers, two housewives, two farm wives, a retired teacher, a factory worker, a truck driver, a farm worker, and a retired railroad telegrapher. Seven of them were gun owners, ten were married, two were single, one was divorced, and one was a widow. Two had college degrees, eleven graduated from high school, and one quit school after the ninth grade. There were eleven Lutherans, two Baptists, and one Catholic.

That afternoon, Thursday, May 12, at 1:45 P.M., with the jury impaneled and the spectator gallery filled, the actual trial began.

16

In Cold Blood

"Mr. Crooks, are you ready to proceed?" asked Judge Paul Benson.

Lynn Crooks raised himself from the green leather overstuffed chair. In his right hand he held a yellow legal pad, his left hand was stuffed into his pants pocket. "Yes, I am, Your Honor," he replied.

Crooks circled the broad, hardwood prosecutor's table and approached the podium that stood in front of the jury box. He placed the legal pad on the podium and slowly searched the faces of the fourteen individuals seated before him. His opening statement began with a narrative of the events leading up to and beyond the shooting, and likened the case to a jigsaw puzzle, each piece of evidence a piece to the puzzle. When all the evidence was put together, it would give the jury a picture of what happened that Sunday in February. But, Crooks cautioned, not a complete picture.

"In any criminal case there are going to be holes, and there are holes in this case," he acknowledged. "Two of the key participants are dead and cannot testify."

Some missing pieces are those that provide "proof certain which gun fired which shots that hit a man," said Crooks. "Such evidence does not exist.

"Witnesses will suggest to you who fired some shots, but with regards to others we really don't know who fired them," he said.

Yet, continued Crooks, "Just because a speck of sky is missing or a speck of sea is missing doesn't mean you can't see the whole picture."

Crooks stopped, and again gazed at each of the faces in front of him. Only after he had made eye contact with one juror did he move on to the next. He wanted their full attention for what he was about to tell them, that they could trust him to give them the truth of what happened on that Sunday afternoon, even if that truth damaged the government's case. Of course, Crooks's revelation was a classic courtroom tactic: if there is damaging information to your case bring it out yourself and downplay its importance.

Crooks told the jurors that the government's witnesses may have erred in fingering Scott Faul as the man who walked over to a government vehicle and fired two shots into the skull of Deputy U.S. Marshal Robert Cheshire as he lay in the vehicle with a chest wound. The physical evidence contradicts what the government's witnesses said they saw, continued Crooks, without a pause. The shell casings found near Cheshire's body didn't match the rifle shell casings found at the spot where Faul was seen, he said. Instead, the casings match those found at the location where Gordon Kahl was seen. Crooks turned from the jurors and, in an almost offhand way, also added that Faul had passed a lie detector test regarding the execution-style killing.

Crooks paused, looked at each of the jurors and shrugged his shoulders as if to say so what. He then leaned forward, rested his left elbow on the top of the podium, and brought his thumb and forefinger together. The fact that the government witnesses may have made a mistake does not mean Scott Faul didn't shoot somebody on that road, said Crooks. The government would establish beyond any doubt that Cheshire was actually murdered three times, that the young deputy took three potentially fatal shots, one in the chest that severed a main artery, one in the neck, and one in the head. And the government would show that Cheshire was fired upon from three different locations, and that each of the shooters—

Gordon and Yorie Kahl and Scott Faul—could each have hit Cheshire once. Crooks also said that while the government didn't know who fired the one shot that struck Marshal Kenneth Muir in the chest and killed him instantly, it could have been either Gordon Kahl or Scott Faul.

Although he was not seated at a defense table in the courtroom, Gordon Kahl would be tried in absentia because his case was so intertwined with those of the four defendants. However, Crooks added, this is a murder trial. The political, religious, and philosophical views of the defendants wouldn't be of concern to the government, neither would the trial address why the marshals picked the time and place they did to try to arrest Gordon Kahl on a parole violation.

"The marshals didn't do anything wrong," emphasized Crooks. "Their only fault was in the area of tactics and not understanding what they were going up against."

What Crooks considered, but decided against, telling the jury was that the marshals would have been within their legal rights to have opened fire as soon as Faul and the Kahls had gotten out of their cars with guns in their hands. The marshals wouldn't have been the ones killed on that road. Crooks didn't tell that to the jury because he didn't believe people would have accepted such a course of action, one with which he himself had trouble.

Sixty-six minutes after he started, Crooks picked up his legal pad and returned to his seat. He was followed to the podium by the four defense attorneys, each of whom painted a picture of a person backed into a corner on that Sunday afternoon in February, someone who thought he or she was going to die and who responded accordingly.

Irv Nodland took the podium immediately after Crooks, and he tried to reclaim the advantage of the false accusation that had been made against his client. He pointed toward Scott Faul and said, "He is the one for the past eighty-eight days . . . [who] has been accused of walking over to the Ram Charger and of executing U.S. Marshal Robert Cheshire.

"For the past eighty-eight days you have been allowed to think that . . . we intend to show that is not true."

When Faul got out of the car on that road north of Medina and "saw people pointing guns at his head, Scott was absolutely convinced . . . he was about to die like the guy in Utah," said Nodland. Just days before the shootout, Scott had read a magazine article about John Singer, a Utah man who was allegedly shot down and killed by law enforcement officers because he didn't wish to send his children to a local public school. Scott, too, was having disagreement with local school officials over the education of his children and he was afraid the men—who didn't identify themselves, weren't in uniform, weren't wearing badges, and didn't have red lights on their vehicles—were after him, not Gordon Kahl, said Nodland. When Scott realized he wasn't the person the men were after, continued Nodland, "he turned and started to run away. He tried to flee, or should I say retreat. He wanted to get away from there."

Only after Scott heard a shot and Yorie's scream that he was hit, only after shots were fired in his direction, did he return fire, contended Nodland. "He assumed he was the next person to be shot.

"Scott's intention was to save his own life. He was sure he was the next to die."

At the conclusion of his thirty-minute statement, Nodland reminded the jurors that Scott had not been arrested, but had turned himself over to authorities a day after the incident. Faul ran because he was scared, said Nodland. It was a human reaction.

Warren Sogard was next to address the jurors. In a short statement of only ten minutes, he said that his client, Yorie Kahl, was "presented with a nightmare. In that nightmare he saw his parents confronted by deadly force, confronted by officers making statements: 'We're going to blow your fucking heads off.'

"His initial reaction was defensive, an effort to protect his family," and in defending his family, Yorie took a shotgun blast to the stomach and suffered severe wounds. "He is lucky to be alive," said Sogard, and concluded his remarks with a plea that the jurors resist

forming any opinions until after Yorie had testified. While that
would be hard, since the government will present its case first,
there are two sides to the story, he said. "He will testify," Sogard
said of his client. "Retain an open mind, listen to the truthfulness
of his statements. You are going to determine Yorie Kahl killed
no one."

Defense lawyers Ralph Vinje and Robert Ramlo followed with
similarly short statements. Vinje contested that while David Broer
initially faced charges of murder—charges later reduced to assault—the "charges [were] made against a man who laid on the
ground and prayed.

"They [the government] can't prove there was any evil action,
any evil thought, any wrongdoings committed by David Broer," he
insisted.

Ramlo pointed out how his client, Joan Kahl, also had been
charged with murder, when the only action she took during the
whole incident was to crawl on the floor of the car to try and save
her life.

"Joan Kahl's only crime was being the loving and caring wife of
a man with an obsession against taxation," said Ramlo. "She didn't
share that view with her husband, but stayed with him for thirty-
eight years because he was a kind, loving man."

Joan Kahl wept silently at the defense table as Ramlo spoke.

Once the opening statements were concluded, Lynn Crooks set
about piecing together the jigsaw puzzle. He called his first witness,
Lynn Cheshire. She was followed by Lois Muir.

When notified that the widows of the two slain marshals would
be summoned to testify, defense attorneys registered a strong objection to Judge Benson.

"We think that the prejudicial effect and sympathetic appeal far
outweighs the use of these," argued Nodland. "The rights of victims
is a real issue and whatnot, but it has nothing to do with this trial.
It is solely and totally appealing to sympathy."

Crooks saw it a bit differently.

"This is not being done for sympathy, it's being done to put these
men into the courtroom," he argued. "Somehow or other these two

dead marshals have the right to have their personalities, to at least a limited degree, come to trial, come to light in this trial.

"These defendants are alive and well and kicking and the survivors are alive and well and kicking, and Mr. Muir and Mr. Cheshire have no way of making their presence known in this courtroom except through their widows.

"I think the government is entitled to establish through these women that these are real, living men and not just simply government agents. They have no personalities, all they have is autopsy folders and even the studio photos don't bring these men to life . . . and they are entitled to be brought to life . . . to show this jury we aren't talking about an academic legal exercise here, we are talking about a real effect on very real human action. I can't think of anyone that can do that better than a widow."

Judge Benson agreed.

Lynn Cheshire took the stand. The packed courtroom was silent.

"Would you again tell the jury your name, please?" asked Crooks.

"My name is Lynn Cheshire."

"Mrs. Cheshire, you're the widow of Robert Cheshire, are you not?"

"Yes, I am."

"How long were you and Bob married?"

"We were married for eleven years."

"And how many children do you have and what are their ages?"

"I have three children. Brian is seven, Jimmy is six, and Christy just turned two."

"Now, how long had Bob been with the U.S. Marshals Service?"

"Five years."

"And what had been his occupation before that?"

"He was in the U.S. Navy for four years and prior to that was a police officer for Foster City for a year."

"Lynn, I hand you exhibit number seven, and can you identify that for the record. Who is that picture of?"

"Picture of my husband."

"Bob Cheshire, correct?"

"Yes."

"We offer exhibit number seven and we have no further questions," said Crooks, who stood the framed, colored, studio portrait of Bob Cheshire on the railing of the jury box for the jurors to view.

Fellow prosecutor Dennis Fisher pursued a similar line of questioning with Lois Muir and, as Crooks did with Lynn Cheshire, he had Lois identify a photograph of her husband and then placed the framed picture of Kenneth Muir on the railing of the jury box.

The defense attorneys waived cross-examination of both widows, but not before Irv Nodland, a grim expression etched on his boyish-looking face, rose from his seat, walked across the courtroom to the jury box, picked up the photographs of the dead marshals, and placed them face up on the prosecutor's table in front of Crooks and Fisher.

Following her testimony, Lynn Cheshire left the courtroom and returned immediately to her home in Bismarck. It would be her only appearance at the trial.

Lois Muir, however, stepped down from the witness stand, passed through the waist-high swinging door that separated the trial's spectators and participants, and joined her son and two daughters who were seated in the second row of the gallery, directly behind the prosecution's table. Each day of the trial, Lois took the same seat and stoically listened to the hours of testimony. In the courtroom she appeared calm, tough, in complete control of her emotions. And she *was* composed in the courtroom, where people could see her. At the end of each day however, when she returned home alone, the anger and pain overwhelmed her and she cried. She cried until it was morning and it was time to return to the courtroom. "I felt a need to be there. There was a lot I didn't know," said Lois. "I needed to know what happened out there. I needed to know who these people were."

Seated directly across from Lois, in the section behind the defense tables, were Shauna Faul, Joan Broer, and Janice Kahl, the wives of Scott, David, and Yorie. Neither the wives of the defendants nor the wife of the victim so much as acknowledged the other's presence during the entire proceedings.

At the end of the first day of testimony, Judge Benson, as he would at the beginning of each recess and at the end of each trial day, admonished the jurors not to discuss anything related to the case among themselves, or with members of their families or friends or with the marshals. The jurors were then excused and escorted under heavy guard to a waiting van, which took them to the Fargo Holiday Inn on the outskirts of town, where they would be housed for the duration of the trial. The fourth floor of the motel's tower was the jurors' alone, its access closely guarded by U.S. marshals. The rooms had no television sets or radios (a television set in the lounge was closely monitored so that no news of the trial could be viewed), and trial-related stories were clipped from all newspapers before being allowed on the floor. Telephone conversations also were monitored and listening marshals could cut the connection the second a reference to the trial was made. The only information the jurors were going to get about the trial was what they heard in the courtroom.

Scott, David, and Yorie were next out of the courtroom, surrounded by eight deputy marshals, who led the defendants some twenty yards down the hall to a holding cell in the U.S. marshal's office. There, the three defendants were placed in leg irons and handcuffs before they were taken to an automobile parked at the rear of the federal building, and whisked three blocks south to the Cass County jail.

The first full day of the trial started the next morning, Friday the thirteenth, when Stutsman County deputy sheriff Bradley Kapp took the witness stand and described the actions he took that Sunday afternoon, actions which set into motion the events that ended with the shootout. He testified that Yorie Kahl had fired the first shot in the brief, intense, gun battle and that it was that bullet which had struck Cheshire in the chest. "The shot came from the left of me. The only ones to the left of me were Yorie Kahl and Robert Cheshire, and Mr. Cheshire didn't shoot," he said.

"Now, Bradley, you have described a series of events that left you without a finger. When you pulled up with Mr. Cheshire and Mr. Hopson—U.S. marshals—and announced who you were, and these men got out [of their cars] with guns, why didn't you shoot them?" Crooks asked near the end of his direct examination.

"Basically because I don't want to kill anybody," replied Kapp.

"What was your purpose of going that day?"

"To arrest Gordon Kahl."

"Did you have any intention of killing him?"

"No."

"Did you have any intention of killing Mr. Faul, Mr. Broer . . . or anyone else?"

"No."

"Did you have any intention of firing on anyone unless you were fired on?"

"No."

Ramlo placed an arm on Joan Kahl's shoulder, stood up, hitched his pants, and ambled toward the witness stand. Short, squat, with a stomach that protruded over his belt, and square-shaped wire-rimmed glasses that slid down the bridge of his nose as he talked, the forty-year-old Ramlo was a down-home, country lawyer. He excelled at arguing his case before a jury with a folksy, homespun approach that included equal blends of humor, common sense, and righteous indignation. Before he received the request to serve as legal counsel for Joan Kahl, Ramlo had seriously considered quitting law. All he had ever done was go to school and practice law. He was looking for a change. He decided, however, to delay his search.

"When you were watching the meeting with your flak jacket on, waiting to arrest Gordon, who you knew was dangerous or thought was dangerous, there was nobody else that you were interested in arresting . . . is that right?" Ramlo asked Kapp.

"That's right," Kapp replied.

"Gordon was the only one that you were after?" Ramlo again asked.

"That's correct."

"When Gordon was with those six other people, was there ever any discussion then among the police officers what should be done to protect the six other innocent people who could get hurt when you tried to arrest Gordon?" asked Ramlo.

"We had no discussion on the fact," said Kapp.

"Did you consider in you own mind that Mrs. Kahl could have been shot?"

"Yes."

"What precautions did you take for her safety?" asked Ramlo, who turned, cocked his head and looked at the fourteen jurors.

"The precaution I would have taken is not shoot at her," replied Kapp.

Nodland, Sogard, and Vinje tried repeatedly to chip away at the credibility of Kapp's belief their clients were dangerous men because of the political views they held and the fact they were heavily armed.

"You testified, with Mr. Crooks' assistance, that you weren't aware of any hunting seasons that were open at this time, didn't you?" asked Ralph Vinje, Broer's attorney.

"I don't believe there were any that were open, no," responded Kapp.

"You familiar with the animal known as a coyote?"

"Yes."

"You know whether coyote season was open at that time?"

"I don't know."

"Are you aware of whether badger season was open at that time?" Vinje again asked.

"I don't believe it was," answered Kapp.

"Are you aware whether the raccoon season was open at the time?"

"No, I don't think it was."

"I see. And if, in fact, I showed you a 1982 North Dakota Small Game, Waterfowl and Fur Bearer Guide, you imagine you could refresh your recollection as to the seasons in question?" He handed Kapp the pamphlet, and gave him a moment to peruse it.

"Have you refreshed your recollection?" asked Vinje. "Do you recall now whether or not coyote season was open at the time?"

"Yes, it was open," replied Kapp.

"Do you recall now whether or not badger season was open at that time? Raccoon?"

"Yes, they were open."

"So actually, these statements that there weren't any hunting seasons open at that time was really just you and the United States trying to make the presence of those weapons appear a little more sinister than it really was, wasn't it?" asked Vinje.

Crooks's objection to the question was sustained by Judge Benson.

"I'll withdraw the question," said Vinje.

In his haste to discredit Kapp's belief that his client was a dangerous man, however, Vinje committed a cardinal error when he asked a question to which he didn't already know the answer.

"You indicated you considered five out of the six people . . . in the two vehicles to be dangerous. I read into that, without knowing, that the one you considered not to be dangerous was Mrs. Kahl, is that correct?" asked Vinje.

"That's correct," replied Kapp.

"And therefore, you did consider David Broer to be dangerous. . . . What is the reason for that?"

"Prior knowledge, you know, . . . I had prior knowledge of some people from Cass County coming to repossess a vehicle that he owned and that he told them if they didn't leave he would kill them."

Kapp's response totally surprised Vinje who then demanded that the remark be stricken from the record based on the grounds of hearsay.

"You asked the question and it was answered," said Judge Benson, who overruled the request.

Vinje collected himself.

"Even though there was a whole batch of you out there pointing guns at him and he didn't even do anything to defend himself and just let you shoot around him?" persisted Vinje.

"He was the more sensible one," said Kapp.

"And yet you're still going to maintain the position that he was dangerous?" continued Vinje.

"Yes," Kapp replied flatly.

"Were you dangerous?" Vinje asked of Kapp.

"Yes."

"Okay. You can be dangerous no matter what side of the fence you were on that day, can't you?"

"I'm sure you can," said Kapp.

Kapp was followed to the witness stand by Susan Reardon, her brother, Jeffrey Anderson, and his girlfriend, Laurie Franks, all of whom witnessed the execution of Cheshire from a window in the trailer home. Despite the fact that evidence suggested otherwise, the three witnesses remained adamant: Faul shot Cheshire. There was no doubt. Even during Nodland's cross-examination, which, at times, seemed to be a test of wills, none of the three would so much as concede he or she might have been wrong. Although their eyewitness accounts of the execution couldn't be corroborated, Crooks called the three witnesses to the stand because they also saw the flashing red lights on the vehicles and figured the men inside must be lawmen.

Wayne Reardon didn't witness the execution, but he too saw the red lights, and watched as Scott Faul, armed with a rifle, ran toward his trailer home and took up a position at the corner of it, and then heard a series of shots fired from that location. A plainspoken man, Reardon testified that while he warned there might be a shootout, he didn't know what the hell the fight was about, or which of the two sides were right or wrong. What Reardon did know was that there were men with guns outside his home. So he got one.

It was that reaction to the situation that defense attorneys tried to exploit.

"What kind of gun did you get?" asked Sogard.

"A twelve-gauge shotgun," said Reardon.

"Why did you do that?"

"Looking out the window and seeing a man with a rifle mighty close to my home, I felt like that was the only thing I could do," said Reardon.

"You felt that the only thing you could do when threatened by people with weapons was protect your family?" asked Sogard.

"Right, sir."

"Very understandable reaction," said Sogard.

Sogard's comment brought a swift objection from the government and Benson instructed the jury to disregard it.

The court recessed for the weekend, but not before Benson dealt a major blow to Yorie Kahl's defense when he ruled that statements Kahl made in the hospital to law enforcement officers could be entered into the trial as evidence. Kahl had told authorities he may have fired first, and shot Cheshire. Sogard had argued, prior to the start of the trial, that the statements were gained by coercion and improper influence since medical personnel and law enforcement officers were the only persons allowed to see Yorie for the first ten days he was treated for his wounds.

"One part of the body of Robert Cheshire was in a bag and separately received. I mean, one of the gunshot wounds had actually blown most of the brain outside of the skull."

The words were those of Dr. Merrit Moon, who took the witness stand Monday morning, May 16. A clinical pathologist from Bismarck, North Dakota, Moon had performed the autopsies on Deputy Marshal Cheshire and U.S. Marshal Kenneth Muir.

Although the head wound was the most destructive and death was almost instantaneous, said Moon, Cheshire also suffered two earlier wounds that were "potentially fatal, given time." The chest wound Cheshire suffered entered his left arm, bypassing the bulletproof vest he wore, traveled into the chest, chipped his rib bones, severed an artery, passed through his windpipe, and lodged, finally, in his right armpit, said Moon. The other wound was to the left side of Cheshire's face, which severed an artery and veins. Cheshire would have bled to death within ten to fifteen minutes from the chest wound without immediate surgery, and the face wound would have resulted in death a short time later. "But that time had not lapsed. There is no indication he was dead before suffering the skull wound," said Moon.

A slightly built man, with glasses, Moon, who spoke in a professional tone of voice, presented his findings in a straightforward, nonemotional manner. Nonetheless, he shocked many listeners with his testimony. Spectators, who had braved bone-chilling winds and lined up outside the Old Federal Building as early as seven-thirty that morning to get a seat in the courtroom, whispered among themselves, some gasping softly during parts of Moon's more graphic testimony. A number of the jurors also seemed unnerved by Moon's remarks, and squirmed uneasily in their leather, rocker-back chairs. At the defense table, the four defendants and their attorneys sat stoically and revealed no emotion. Nor did members of the Muir family, who sat in their customary seats in the second row of the spectator gallery, betray any anger or pain, even when Moon described the wound suffered by their father and husband.

"There was a large entrance wound that was in the upper chest. The breastbone was penetrated and actually shattered. As the body was seen at the time of the autopsy, there was actually a small amount of lung protruding from this wound," said Moon.

Fragments from the breastbone severed the aorta and Muir bled to death. "The bleeding was very extensive. There was no way his life could have been saved," said Moon.

Just before the noon recess, Crooks moved to enter as evidence the seventeen X-rays and color autopsy photographs of the dead marshals which Moon had used during his testimony. After lunch Benson held the jury out of the courtroom as defense attorneys registered their vehement objections to the use of the photographs.

"They are prejudicial, inflammatory, and unnecessary," Faul's attorney, Irvin Nodland, said angrily. "They are gruesome, they are bloody."

If nothing else, said Nodland, the government could certainly use black-and-white photos.

The attorneys for Joan Kahl and David Broer were particularly offended by the government's action, since neither of their clients was charged with acts of violence. "The photographs are so shock-ing, so horrifying, the spillover effect would be so great it would make it impossible for Joan Kahl to receive a fair trial on the charges against her," argued Joan's lawyer, Robert Ramlo.

Crooks agreed that the photographs were all that the defense lawyers said they were—horrifying, gruesome, shocking—but he added, "that simply is the way these bodies were left by the defendants and I might explain to the court that we have picked the most innocuous of the death scenes.

"There are numerous other death-scene photos showing blood, gore, whatnot. We have picked the photographs that show the bodies bathed, essentially with the blood washed away."

Crooks also argued that the photographs were essential for the forensic pathologist—whom the government would summon on Wednesday—whose testimony would include the direction from which the shots were fired and the sequence of the wounds. Judge Benson allowed the admission of the color photographs.

Nodland was outraged.

"It's the lions ten and us nothing," he told a reporter at the midmorning recess. "On the crucial issues—change of venue, recusal, admissibility of evidence—you can't get Judge Benson to go along with anything except that wanted by Lynn Crooks."

When the time came to present the photographs to the jury, Judge Benson issued words of caution. "I am alerting you those photographs will not be pleasant to look at," said Benson, who added that the jurors shouldn't allow themselves to be swayed by what they saw and return a verdict based upon passion or sympathy.

It was clear, however, the jurors were not prepared for what they viewed, especially when shown the photograph that displayed the right part of Cheshire's skull blown away. One juror placed his head down into his hands and then threw himself back in his chair, letting his hands down slowly. Another juror placed a handkerchief to her mouth, while another moved uneasily in her chair. All the while, nationally known forensic pathologist Dr. Charles Petty of Dallas addressed the jury as an instructor would address his pupils, giving detailed, graphic, and even animated descriptions of the wounds suffered by the two lawmen.

The score, by Nodland's count, became eleven-to-nothing when Benson overruled objections to a photograph that purportedly depicted three distinct locations from where gunshots fired at the Ram Charger originated. Although James Hufford, the FBI agent who set up the photograph, admitted during cross-examination that he used some "poetic license" in preparing the display, he maintained the photograph fairly depicted the field of fire. Judge Benson, however, did caution the jury that the photograph "should not be taken as a reenactment or proof that three different persons fired at the vehicle."

Judge Benson did, however, deny the government's request to enter into evidence fragments from Robert Cheshire's skull. "Just to view them adds no probative value to the case," said Benson to the visible relief of several jurors who were openly unnerved by the sight of the sealed, plastic bags in Crooks's hand.

The next witnesses called by the government were Mouritz Engquist and Russell Larson. The two men testified they had gone to the February 13 meeting to ask David Broer for his help in their disputes with the federal government. Larson, in particular, was eager for advice on whatever steps he could take to save his farm from being foreclosed upon by the government.

"What in fact did the meeting turn out to be about?" continued Crooks.

"That turned out to be basically an argument on racism and religion," responded Larson.

"Did it ever turn to have . . . anything to do with farm problems, farm foreclosure type problems?" asked Crooks.

"No, it did not."

"Did there appear to be somewhat of a division that seemed to have formed during that meeting?"

"Yeah."

"Between who?"

"Between Gordon and Doc Martin," replied Larson.

"And essentially what was the division, as near as you could make out, about?" asked Crooks.

At that point, Nodland asked permission to approach the bench. He wanted to register an objection outside the earshot of the jurors. He wanted Crooks's line of questioning stopped.

"Your Honor, in our pretrial motions . . . counsel indicated that this matter was not going to be gone into in the trial," Nodland

argued. "In his opening statement he told the jury that it has nothing to do with religious matters, political matters . . .

"If the witness gets into an area having to do with religious
disagreements and having to do with racial disagreements, and this
witness gives an answer prejudicial to my client, it is my intention
to move for a mistrial," he threatened.

"Just a minute," said Crooks. "I have indicated I do not intend
to dwell on that issue, but I certainly don't in any way agree with
counsel that what happened at that meeting is not part of the . . .
crime and setting that came up to it. I don't concede for a moment
it's not relevant. Certainly anything that happened at that meeting
. . . is relevant to these offenses."

Nevertheless, Crooks agreed to rephrase the question.

"Fine," responded Judge Benson.

The defense attorneys took their seats, and Crooks returned to
questioning Larson. "I'll ask, Mr. Larson, so I don't give you quite
an open-ended question, . . . was there an obvious division between
Gordon Kahl and the people that were with him and Dr. Martin?"

"There seemed to be, yes," replied Larson.

Both Larson and Engquist testified that as the meeting drew to
a close, they were informed the clinic was being watched by a law
enforcement officer and that David Broer then called Medina police
chief Darrell Graf to find out why the group was under surveillance.
"He hung the phone up, if I remember right, and then they figured
the warrant was for Scotty. Got real excited as if they were after
him," said Larson.

After that, continued Larson, Yorie, Scott, Gordon, and David
held a conference near the back door of the clinic and discussed
how they were going to get Scott out of town.

"Now during this period of time . . . did Scott Faul make a request
of you and, or make an inquiry of you and Mouritz?" asked Crooks.

"He asked if we had weapons along and he says 'we may need
some help.' "

"What answer did either you or Mouritz give?" asked Crooks.

"We looked at each other and said no," replied Larson.

In his cross-examination of both witnesses, Nodland centered upon the state of mind of his client. "Was there any question at all in your mind that the discussion revolved around the fact that it was Scott Faul that was being sought?" Nodland asked Engquist.

"There is no doubt in my mind, no," Engquist replied.

"The discussion did not center on Gordon Kahl being wanted?" asked Nodland.

"Everything that I heard, they had an APB out on Scott Faul. He was the one they were after," said Engquist.

Larson testified it was obvious Faul feared for his life and that Faul's request for armed assistance was made after discussions about a possible ambush. "What they [defendants] figured . . . was it was trap or setup. They were definitely scared for their lives," he said.

Both men also portrayed David Broer as a peacemaker and mediator, and were emphatic about Joan Kahl's lack of involvement in any plan to evade the lawmen. "She just followed her husband . . . [and] her son. She was a wife. She didn't plot anything," insisted Larson.

The rustling of a page being turned in a reporter's notebook was the only sound Wednesday in the suddenly quiet courtroom when Lynn Crooks called the government's next witness: Deputy U.S. Marshal James Hopson. All eyes were riveted to the southeast door of the dark-paneled, third-floor courtroom as Hopson, dressed in a gray three-piece suit, entered, his left hand resting on the shoulder of his wife, Doris, for balance. Hopson's sixty-foot walk to the witness stand was slow and awkward; he stopped briefly before the deputy clerk of the court to be sworn in to testify. When Hopson reached the witness stand, located just in front of the fourteen jurors, he was helped up the two steps and into the chair by his wife.

Ninety-five days earlier Hopson had lain seriously wounded on the road north of Medina, a piece of asphalt having penetrated his skull and entered his brain. The injury left him partially disabled and unable to walk unaided; his speech was painfully deliberate and sometimes slurred. "I was a whole man when I went out of that car," Hopson told Crooks in response to a question about how the wound affected him.

Like the testimony of the two widows and the admission of the color autopsy photographs, Hopson's appearance was tense, high drama. But his testimony offered no new information as to what occurred on that road. The head injury had affected not only his speech and his coordination, it had robbed him of much of his memory. "Only highlights of that day are in my mind," the fifty-seven-year-old, bespectacled Hopson said in a soft, halting voice.

What he did remember was seeing two people, armed with rifles, get out of the car in front of him and run. One man ran behind a post or tree, while another man ran toward a wooded area. A deputy marshal left a vehicle and chased the man running toward the woods. A person asked him who they were and what they wanted. He told the person they were marshals and they wanted to arrest Gordon Kahl. He tried to talk a woman or small man (actually David Broer) out of one of the cars and urged her or him to join him in the ditch where he was located. He called for support from other marshals. Then, said Hopson, "somebody shot and that is all I remember."

All he recalled beyond that was that a helicopter was about to land and that his feet were cold.

Why, asked Crooks, didn't he and the other officers shoot the individuals when the lawmen saw them get out of their cars with guns? "Well, it wasn't Bob's [Cheshire] or my way to shoot somebody in cold blood," Hopson responded slowly. "We were there to arrest one person, a man."

In his cross-examination, Robert Ramlo asked Hopson if it was Joan Kahl he tried to talk out of the car. And, if it was, asked Ramlo, did she do anything to interfere with Hopson carrying out his duty.

"She didn't do anything," Hopson replied. "She didn't follow what I said. Probably a good thing she didn't. I got shot, she didn't."

Stutsman County chief deputy Jack Miller added a few pieces to the yet uncompleted puzzle; he interviewed Yorie Kahl while he was hospitalized and testified that Kahl said "I might have shot the guy in the white shirt. It could have been I shot first."

"What else was said by Mr. Kahl?" asked Crooks.

"He said that as they were driving north out of Medina he noticed two vehicles . . . blocking the roadway and they had the red lights going," said Miller.

"What else did he say?" asked Crooks.

"He remembered that the marshals yelled out, 'We want Gordon Kahl,' and told us he and his father changed coats and caps in order to confuse the police," testified Miller.

Other pieces of the puzzle were provided by Vernon Wegner, who testified that he knew the men who stopped them on the road were law enforcement officers, and by Darrell Graf, who said he urged his fellow lawmen to call off the arrest attempt because he had attended earlier meetings with Gordon, Yorie, and Scott and knew they wouldn't go peaceably.

"At one of the January meetings . . . did Scott Faul make a statement in your presence, which gave you that concern?" asked Crooks.

Faul said he didn't anticipate a problem because the agents or government people wanted to go home to their wives and families too, but " 'if you kill a couple of them the rest will listen a little better,' " replied Graf.

"Did Yorie Kahl . . . make a statement which gave you some additional concern?" asked Crooks.

" 'The time for talking is done, only time we have left is to use these weapons,' " said Graf.

"Referring to the weapons they had with them at the meeting?"

"Yes."

Under cross-examination by Nodland, however, Graf acknowledged that someone else may have made the comment he attributed to Scott Faul, and that Scott only answered yes or no to it.

Graf was clearly uncomfortable in the witness box. Two weeks after the shootout, Graf had been fired as police chief of Medina because he had mishandled an investigation of vandalism that involved some juveniles at the high school. At least that was the reason he was given by the mayor. Graf didn't accept it for a minute. He knew that the real cause for his dismissal was what he did—

or didn't do—that Sunday afternoon. Graf knew what people thought. They thought he was part of that group. Or worse, they questioned his courage. Graf believed that he, as much as the four defendants, was on trial.

To questions posed by both the prosecution and the defense attorneys, Graf's answers were at times vague. He couldn't recall conversations other witnesses said they had had with him. He may have told two people to "get the hell out of here, there is going to be a shootout." He may have told a fellow city employee that "there is a tax evader up there and now they are going to shoot him." He may have told Russell Larson he "was going to try to save at least Dave's [Broer] life." He couldn't remember. "I think it's unlikely, but it's possible."

Sometimes, Graf was defensive. "I can't see anyone laying their life on the line over a tax deal."

At other times, contradictory. He attended the group's meetings because he was concerned about the farming community—"When the small farming goes down, so does the small community and I wanted to see what was being done with these farm foreclosures." He attended the meeting because he was undercover. "I was concerned about who these people were. I really didn't know much about these people with guns. But I did keep an eye, if you want to call it that, wondering just who are these people and what makes them tick."

Finally, after several hours of testimony, the question Graf dreaded was put to him by Warren Sogard. "Is it your common practice not to respond to a specific radio direction to you?" he asked.

"No, it is not," Graf responded.

"Well, if it's not your common practice, why didn't you respond this day?" Sogard asked.

Graf paused. He seemed to visibly weaken in his chair. "Because," he said slowly, "I saw what could be happening and I was scared."

Stephen Schnabel followed Graf to the witness stand. Life had not been kind to Schnabel since the shootout. Like Bradley Kapp, Schnabel agreed to aid the marshals in the arrest and was wounded in the confrontation. But while Kapp had been honored for his actions by the marshals service and awarded a plaque, Schnabel didn't receive so much as a thank-you. While Kapp was promoted to sergeant, Schnabel, like Graf, was fired from his job. Later, Schnabel left Medina and moved to Fargo and returned to college. For one of his English classes, he wrote about his experience on that Sunday afternoon. He concluded his essay: "Before, I would drive by the Reardon farm and think it was such a beautiful place, with plush green grass and neatly pruned hedges. The old western-type corral made of the logs behind the trailer offset by the towering cottonwoods in the uniform shelterbelt that ran the length of the yard. And the scent of freshly cut hay in the morning dew. There was such a feeling of contentment.

"Now, when I drive by, no matter what time of year it is, all I see are bare, medieval-looking trees overshadowing a barren, rustic farmyard, set aside as a place of many unanswered questions and ridicule. The scent of freshly cut hay in the morning dew is blanketed by the aroma of death."

The next day, May 20, Deputy U.S. Marshal Carl Wigglesworth, the lone lawman to escape the shootout unscathed, took the witness stand. Wigglesworth, who had chased Scott Faul into the trees and was not involved in the gunfight, said the lawmen were wearing their badges and did identify themselves as U.S. marshals. He also testified that once the shooting stopped, he returned to the road and crawled on his hands and knees toward his boss, Kenneth Muir. "What did you find?" asked assistant prosecutor Dennis Fisher.

"There was no pulse," responded Wigglesworth; his voice dropped off, then cracked. He reached for a glass of water in front of him on the witness stand, took a sip and tried to regain his composure. He continued. He next crawled toward Hopson and told his wounded comrade not to move, help was on the way. Wigglesworth then worked his way toward the Ram Charger that was about a hundred feet away and looked inside the passenger side of it and saw "blood and tissue all over." He circled around to the driver's side. "What did you find?" Fisher asked.

"I found Bob Cheshire," responded Wigglesworth. His voice faltered. "By looking at him I knew there was no help for him"—Wigglesworth's voice started to break—"the whole top of his head was gone."

The mustachioed, bearlike Wigglesworth started to cry. He lowered his face into his large hands. The stark silence of the packed courtroom was broken only by his quiet sobs. Judge Benson ordered the court into recess for the weekend. As the courtroom cleared, Fisher rose from his seat at the prosecution table, met Wigglesworth at the foot of the witness stand, put his arm around Wigglesworth's shoulder, and squeezed it.

On Monday morning, the fourteen jurors were handed typed transcripts of the radio conversations between the lawmen just before the shooting started. On paper, the last words spoken by Robert Cheshire and Kenneth Muir seemed crisp, emotionless, sterile.

An FBI agent walked to the clerk's desk in front of the judge's bench and placed a cassette into a tape recorder. The words came to life. So did the emotion. The panic, the anger, the pain, and the fear. The jurors listened, and stared at the transcripts. Lois Muir listened too. She heard the fear in her husband's voice. He had been scared.

Robert Cheshire's voice filled the courtroom. "Let's go guys . . . I'm hit bad."

Then static. For nearly seven minutes the radio static crackled through the courtroom speakers. Finally, a voice interrupted the static. It was a woman's voice. "Five-two-oh-six, do you request any other assistance that we can provide?" the voice asked.

At 10:42 A.M., the tape recording ended and, after nearly 8 days, 39 witnesses, and 135 exhibits, so did the government's case. "At this time the United States rests," said Crooks.

17

A Case for Self-defense

After the government rested its case, Judge Benson heard defense motions for acquittal. Trial watchers speculated the judge would grant such a motion on behalf of Joan Kahl since the mention of her name had been noticeably absent from the testimony of many of the government's witnesses and, when her name was mentioned, it was usually in a favorable light. None of the witnesses saw Joan Kahl do anything wrong.

Nor was Benson convinced the government had proved its case against Joan Kahl. After the court recessed on Friday, he ordered his clerk to complete the necessary paperwork for a judgment of acquittal, but the judgment was never issued.

Crooks acknowledged the government's case against Joan Kahl wasn't as strong as those against the other defendants, and he was willing to concede on the charge of her being an accessory after a murder. But, argued Crooks, on the other two charges—conspiracy to impede arrest efforts and harboring—the circumstantial evidence was quite compelling. "Joan Kahl was very clearly acting as an intentional decoy when she got in the car with Yorie and not her husband. She did have an opportunity to stay at the clinic," he said.

Benson agreed, and denied the motions for acquittal on the charges of conspiracy and harboring. He dismissed, however, the charge of accessory after a murder. "I don't think there's any evidence in the record that Joan Kahl could have known Marshals Kenneth Muir and Robert Cheshire were murdered—if they were murdered," said Benson.

The judge denied without comment the motions for acquittal requested by the other defense attorneys.

Although not required by law to testify on their own behalf, each of the defendants took the witness stand. The first to do so was Joan Kahl. Dressed in a matching gray jacket and skirt, Joan Kahl looked tired, weary, on the verge of tears. Even with the aid of a microphone, her voice was barely audible to the spectators who packed the courtroom or to the jurors who sat only a few feet away from her. On several occasions Judge Benson asked her to speak up so her answers could be heard. Those answers included denials that she was involved with, or was even aware of, a plan to help her husband escape arrest that Sunday.

Under the gentle guidance of her attorney, Robert Ramlo, Joan drew a self-portrait of a loyal housewife, whose primary responsibilities were to raise her and Gordon's children and manage the family's finances. It was a family, she said, that did little socializing with friends or neighbors, a close-knit family whose togetherness included hunting, hence all the weapons around the house. No, she said, Gordon wasn't unkind to either her or the children, and he didn't raise a hand against her. "He was never a violent man. He was just a real good person to have around the house. He was a mild-mannered man," said Joan, who started to weep.

"So why did you plan to leave him?" asked Ramlo.

Joan's voice trembled as she admitted Gordon's mild manner changed when taxes were the subject of conversation. She tried to ignore the anti-tax talk, said Joan, but as the years progressed, so did her husband's obsession and her fear of the eventual outcome.

"So you did have an expectation that someday there would be some kind of trouble?" asked Ramlo.

"Yes. I really did, but not like that. I never thought of an ambush or anything like that," said Joan, her voice barely audible.

"Did you think that this trouble would involve just Gordon or the whole family?" Ramlo continued.

"I thought it would probably involve Gordon and myself because we drove all over the country alone," said Joan. "We had gone to Bismarck and Minot and Jamestown, all over alone, just he and I, and I always did have the vision of a roadblock and I thought they would get him because I knew they wanted him."

"What do you mean by 'get him'?"

"I thought they would get him and I really honestly thought they'd kill him, I really thought that, but I thought they'd let me go. I didn't know that it would be like this," replied Joan.

At the prosecution table, Crooks grew increasingly angry as he listened to Joan Kahl's hour-long testimony. Before she took the stand, Crooks had debated with himself over how he would handle his cross-examination of her. If he approached it too gingerly, the jury might be left with the impression the government's case against her was motivated by revenge, not justice, and that could have an adverse effect on its cases against all the defendants. Yet, if Crooks's interrogation of her was too harsh, she could break down on the witness stand and he would be left looking like the heavy. It was not an impression he wanted carried into the jury room when deliberations started. He would have to walk a fine line.

But each time Joan Kahl referred to an ambush or setup, Crooks was furious. When she completed her testimony, the course he would take was set.

To hell with that fine line, and with what the jury might think. To hell with what anyone might think. Crooks was not going to let her get away with depicting good lawmen, his friends, as cold-blooded killers.

"Let's talk about 'come and get him,' " Crooks said sharply. "What did you assume they were going to do, just come out and shoot him down in the highway? Was that your idea of what they were going to do in 'come and getting him'?"

"I thought they were going to come and kill him," Joan responded.

"They were just going to come and kill him for no reason at all?" asked Crooks.

"For the reason he violated his probation," said Joan.

"You felt that was of such high importance in the federal government that agents of the federal government, because such a horrendous deed had been done, would simply come out and shoot your husband down in cold blood?" Crooks asked in an incredulous voice. "And they weren't going to give him a chance to surrender, they weren't going to give him a chance to give himself up, they were just going to shoot him down?"

Rather than break under Crooks's brisk questioning, Joan Kahl seemed to harden. The tears disappeared. Her tone of voice became more combative. "I didn't know all about that. But I knew eventually I felt like that's what would happen. . . . It's been done before," she responded.

Crooks pressed Joan about her claims that she didn't participate in an escape plan. No, she didn't know anyone was watching the clinic, she insisted. No, it was not unusual that Vernon Wegner took her husband's place in their car and Gordon rode with David Broer, said Joan.

"Why did you think all this was happening? Did you think you were going out to hunt more rabbits or something?" Crooks demanded to know.

"No, I didn't. I was assured with my own self after Gordon told me there wouldn't be any trouble . . . was completely assured everything would be all right. I didn't think I had anything to worry about," responded Joan.

Crooks pounced upon the contradiction. "You said Gordon assured you there wouldn't be any trouble. The way you told it earlier, you had no reason to believe there was going to be trouble. Why did you ask him if there was any trouble?"

For the first time, Joan appeared rattled by Crooks's question.

"I didn't know anything about anything set up until I went out in the car after the meeting was over," she said. "They told us on the north side of the clinic we were being set up."

"You immediately took that to mean that somebody was going

to come and murder you, is that what you're having us believe?" asked Crooks.

"I don't think murder. I sure didn't think of that. I felt they was after Gordon. I knew they wanted him," she said. "I didn't ask any questions. It all happened fast. I just followed him along."

Finally, Crooks asked Joan if, just before the shooting started, she considered getting out of the car, grabbing Gordon by the arm and saying, hey, give this up, it isn't worth it.

"No way. No way. Not with all those guns pointing around. I'm not going to get my head blowed off," she replied.

"You didn't try to talk to Gordon?" asked Crooks.

"I didn't try to talk anybody out of anything," said Joan.

David Broer was next on the witness stand. Then Scott Faul. And then Yorie Kahl.

Each man offered testimony that was almost verbatim to that presented by the other. No, they didn't see any red flashing lights. No, the men who stopped them weren't dressed in police uniforms. No, they didn't wear badges, or identify themselves as lawmen.

Rather than lawmen, said the defendants, the men had acted as hooligans and terrorists. They laughed as they climbed out of their vehicles and pointed rifles and shotguns at the cornered people. They screamed and yelled obscenities.

" 'We are going to blow your goddam heads off. We are going to blow your fucking heads off,' " recalled Broer.

They put the fear of God and death into everyone on that road.

"While this was going on, what did you think?" asked Broer's attorney, Ralph Vinje.

"I was frightened. I thought I was going to die," responded Broer.

Then, testified the defendants, those lawmen started shooting like terrorists. "I didn't know at that time why I was being shot at at all. I hadn't done anything wrong," said Faul.

Faul, like Broer before him and Yorie after him, insisted the first shot "sounded like a pop, not a sharp report. It was a shot from a short-barrel weapon."

"A pistol?" asked his lawyer, Irv Nodland.

"Yes."

The only person who fired a handgun that day was Marshal Kenneth Muir, who got off one round before he was killed.

Yorie testified that the first shot hit him. And it would have struck him in the heart, said Yorie, if he hadn't been wearing a shoulder holster, which held his .45-caliber pistol. Instead of killing him, the bullet shattered the hand grip on the pistol and knocked the wind out of him. It was only after he was shot that he, or anyone else in his group, returned fire. To support the self-defense theory, the shattered, wooden hand grip of Yorie's pistol was entered into evidence. The defense would have been better served if they could have introduced the pistol itself. But after the shootout, Yorie had given the weapon to Scott, who, in turn, gave it to Gordon Kahl, who apparently took it with him when he fled.

The defendants' claim that the first shot was fired from a pistol was supported by Mark Lanenga, who had been stopped with his wife at the top of Cheese Plant Hill by Darrell Graf just before the shooting started. Lanenga, who claimed he received extensive weapons training during his four-year hitch with the U.S. Marine Corps, testified that the first shot "sounded like a pistol shot. A distinct sound, a dull pop. There is no doubt the first shot was a pistol shot."

Faul's wife, Shauna, and four of the couple's five children, sat among many of Faul's relatives and friends who packed the spectator gallery. During most of Faul's lengthy testimony, Shauna remained composed, gently touching the hair of one of her daughters who rested her head on Shauna's lap. She did start to weep once when her husband cried as he told of a minor argument the couple had prior to his leaving for the clinic that Sunday and that he had failed to kiss her good-bye and tell Shauna he loved her.

The prosecution team of Crooks and Fisher alternated the interrogations of each defendant and, through the use of sharp and sometimes caustic questioning, attempted to shred the self-defense theory.

Fisher was first.

"These men out there on the road, the madmen, the hooligans

... the ones that caused the confrontation, as you say, do you recall those people?" asked Fisher.

Yes, replied Broer.

"One of those hooligans happened to be Jim Hopson . . . one of those hooligans that you asked whether you were under arrest. Remember that?" asked Fisher.

"That's correct," said Broer, who could barely complete one answer before Fisher hurled another question at him.

"You usually ask hooligans if you're under arrest?"

"If they have a gun pointing at me."

"Do hooligans arrest people?"

"I don't know."

"Don't police arrest people, Mr. Broer?"

"I would say normally."

"Don't United States marshals arrest people?"

"Yes, they do."

Fisher handed Broer a copy of the statement Broer made to an FBI agent shortly after his arrest and asked him to read it. When Broer finished, Fisher asked, "You didn't tell him anything about a flat report which you now suspect may have been a handgun?"

"I don't recall discussing it, no," replied Broer.

"You didn't tell it to him either?"

"I don't know if I did or not."

"It's not in the report anywhere?"

"I don't see it, no."

"What it looks like here, Mr. Broer, you're just trying to help your friends and acquaintances, isn't that right?" asked Fisher.

"No. I'm telling you as I recall," insisted Broer.

"As I get from your statement you're certainly convinced that these aren't police officers . . . isn't that what you said?" asked Crooks.

"I didn't know exactly what they were," replied Faul.

"Fact he was shouting that he was a deputy U.S. marshal, apparently the wind kind of blew that away from you, on that nice windless day?" asked Crooks.

"From the distance he was, I didn't hear what he was saying," said Faul.

"At what point did you . . . become convinced that some sort of vigilante movement was now out to get you and to shoot you dead because you hadn't sent your children to public school?" Crooks asked.

"When I looked out the car door and there was a shotgun staring me in the face," said Faul.

"Now these men were laughing . . . because they were now going to succeed, apparently, in finally taking the life of a man who hadn't sent his kids to school, is that what you're trying to convince the jury of?" asked Crooks.

"I didn't know what they would be laughing about," replied Faul.

"Wasn't anything funny going on the entire day, was there?"

"I didn't think so."

"You think Bob Cheshire thought this was awfully funny?"

"He probably did."

"Didn't turn out very funny for him, did it?"

"Sure didn't."

Crooks also challenged Faul's claim he did nothing wrong in shooting back at the lawmen.

"Somebody was shooting at you?"

"That's correct."

"Didn't hit you, did they?"

"Apparently not."

"Somebody hit Marshal Muir, didn't they? Blew a hole right in his chest, dead as a stone within minutes, you know that?" asked Crooks.

"Now I do," said Faul.

"Somebody blew the top of Mr. Cheshire's head off, you know that don't you? Somebody blew off Mr. Kapp's finger? Somebody shot Mr. Schnabel in the leg?"

"Apparently they did."

"You haven't the slightest idea who did any of that other than it might be Gordon Kahl because he gave you a little letter?" asked Crooks.

"That's the idea," replied Faul.

"You didn't do any of that yourself?"

"I didn't shoot any individual that day."

"Just kind of firing in the general direction of that Ram Charger? Not intending to hit anybody?"

"That's correct."

"Just too bad if Mr. Cheshire happened to get his face right in the front of where one of those bullets came through, is that about it?" pressed Crooks.

"Terrible, yes," replied Faul.

Dennis Fisher collected his thoughts before he approached the witness box and Yorie Kahl. The contempt he had betrayed earlier during his cross-examinations of Broer and several other defense witnesses was no act. Fisher really did hate the defendants. He hated who they were, what they stood for, and what they had done on that road outside of Medina.

"You had no head wounds. Your memory is just as good as it's always been, isn't that right?" asked Fisher, with the now familiar sarcasm in his voice.

"Right now, my memory is reasonably well, yes," replied Yorie.

"Well, if you said you may have shot the first shot, wouldn't that start the onslaught . . .?" asked Fisher.

"I said that because I didn't know. Someone had suggested that to me," said Yorie.

"You're so amenable to suggestion . . . so receptive to police suggestion that you would just believe them over your own recollection, isn't that right?" continued Fisher.

"Wrong. I just didn't dispute it at that time because I couldn't remember for sure what happened," said Yorie.

The two prosecutors didn't limit their questions to the events that occurred at the shootout. They probed the political, philosophical, and religious beliefs of the defendants, the same beliefs that the prosecutors had said in their opening statements were of no importance in a murder trial. Through repeated objections, defense attorneys were able to stop most of the inquiries. But not all of them.

"You felt that you had to kind of set up your own little township all by itself somewhere?" Crooks asked.

"It's a township type of government that we were looking into," responded Faul.

"You're going to set up a township," repeated Crooks. "Is it because you don't feel that the state of North Dakota has adequate forms of government that you need your own? Is that your philosophy?"

"No. That's not my philosophy," said Faul.

"What is this going to be? At some point after the big bomb falls you're going to be there to save the day with the little township?" continued Crooks.

"No," said Faul.

"That isn't quite it either?" asked Crooks.

"No."

Fisher quizzed Yorie about which federal agency was out to kill his father. "What did you mean if the government ever got a chance to take a shot at your father that they would? Which portion of the federal government? It is very large," said Fisher.

"Yes, it is. Entirely too large," replied Yorie.

"Why do you think that?"

"Because of the extreme amount of control they have initiated over the people of the United States."

"In what form?"

"All forms."

"Tell me one," goaded Fisher.

"For example, your fifty-five-mile-an-hour speed limit," offered Yorie.

"Saves lives, doesn't it?" asked Fisher.

"I don't know that it does," replied Yorie.

No sooner had Yorie finished his answer than Fisher followed with another question.

"What other forms of control?" asked Fisher.

"Control over our children in school," said Yorie.

"You mean compulsory education?"

"Well, the requirement of the schools to teach basically non-Christian education."

"You consider geography not Christian? You consider mathematics not Christian?"

"No."

"You consider algebra and associated things non-Christian?"

"No, not necessarily."

"How about foreign languages?"

"Not necessarily."

"How about anatomy?"

"In some respects a lot of it is, yes."

"What other forms of control, Mr. Kahl?" asked Fisher.

"There is a lot of them," insisted Yorie.

Fisher questioned Yorie about the authority that gave his father the right to ignore the repeated requests to drop his weapon and turn himself over to the lawmen.

"Under the authority and duty to protect his family," replied Yorie.

"And that is written in some law someplace?" asked Fisher.

"That's written in the heart," said Yorie.

"Is it written in Ken Muir's heart which was blown out on the road?" asked Fisher.

Sogard, who had remained coiled at the edge of his seat throughout Fisher's ninety-minute cross-examination, sprang to his feet. "Objection. Argumentative."

"Sustained," said Benson.

Fisher refused to retreat. He reworded his question. "I suppose that is inscribed in your heart, too?"

"Objection. Argumentative," said Sogard.

"Overruled," said Benson.

"I do feel I have a duty to my family to protect them," replied Yorie.

"That includes shooting law enforcement officers, doesn't it?" asked Fisher.

"If I feel that anyone is going to injure any of my family, I feel it is my duty to do something about it," responded Yorie.

Fisher asked if, under Yorie's interpretation of the Constitution, there was anything wrong with the way Cheshire and Muir died. "I don't know, I didn't see them die," responded Yorie.

Fisher picked up a folder from the prosecutor's table, approached the witness stand, and placed it in front of Yorie. Inside were photographs of the wounds suffered by the slain marshals. Do you see how those marshals died, asked Fisher.

"Objection," said an exasperated Sogard.

"Sustained," said Benson.

During Fisher's interrogation, Yorie admitted that he, like his father, refused to file federal income tax returns—"The Sixteenth Amendment and the second plank of the Communist Manifesto are one and the same"—and that he didn't own a state pistol permit.

"I have a permit referred to as a constitutional arms permit. It states that if any government official denies me my Second Amendment right, they are violating the constitutional oath of office and are in violation of the law," said Yorie.

Fisher taunted Yorie. "Kind of floated down, get it in a cereal box, did you?"

Throughout most of the cross-examination, Yorie had appeared jaunty, as if he enjoyed the verbal jousting match with Fisher. But this time Fisher's sarcastic question touched a raw nerve and Yorie lost his temper and responded angrily, "I think you are getting ridiculous. It was issued by our forefathers of two hundred years ago."

"You type it up yourself and put it in plastic?" continued Fisher.

"I certainly did not," replied Yorie.

At the conclusion of the government's cross-examination of David Broer, Scott Faul, and Yorie Kahl, defense attorneys expressed outrage at what they saw as a mid-course correction in the government's approach to the trial.

The government has told us this case isn't about the philosophical, political, or religious beliefs of Scott Faul, fumed Nodland, but the prosecutors have taken a "pail of slop and walked over and poured it on Scott's head. They have started to point out the differences Scott has with other people—that he isn't the type of man who is stamped out of a cookie cutter."

An equally angered Sogard said, "The entire style of the government has been pretty vicious examination. The defendants are being nailed because they are different than the normal Joe. It is sad when the government resorts to pointing out differences as a means to influence and prejudice the jury."

The defense lawyers weren't the only ones upset by the government's tactics. Kahl's supporters railed against the injustice they claimed they saw unfolding in the courtroom. The *Dakota Update*, a weekly, four-page, typed and mimeographed newsletter, repeatedly carried references to the courtroom as "Satan's oven" and cast Benson, Crooks, and Fisher as "agents of Satan." "The government has such a weak case that the government agents are using every dirty trick in the book, and a few that aren't, to gain a conviction . . . ," its editor wrote. [The government] is determined that someone or more must be blamed for their fiasco at Medina and are pulling out all stops to be sure it isn't themselves.

"It is amazing the depths to which some Americans will lower themselves in serving their Satanic masters."

Fisher, who at times seemed to relish his role as interrogator, was singled out for attention and became a lightning rod for the hate generated by the trial. He was harassed by late-night telephone callers and, at one point, the Posse issued a warrant for the arrest of that "hateful Jew Fisher."

A former newspaper reporter in Chicago, who moved to North Dakota because his wife felt her native state offered a better environment in which to raise their family, Fisher didn't take the threats lightly. He moved his family to a secret location and started carrying a pistol. Crooks, too, received threatening phone calls and took precautions. At bedtime, he removed his old Browning shotgun from the gun rack, loaded it, and placed it near the bed. It would make Nancy feel more comfortable, Crooks told himself.

The prosecutors weren't the only persons subjected to harassment. Nodland was told by one anonymous telephone caller that if

Scott Faul was freed, Nodland would be the next person to die. There was plenty of hatred on both sides.

On Wednesday, May 25, spectators in the packed courtroom were surprised when the defense called its next witness, Harold Warren, former United States marshal for North Dakota. Warren's hulking figure filled the witness box. Still a deputy marshal, Warren didn't want to be on the stand, not as a witness for the defense. But he had been subpoenaed to appear.

Warren recounted his attempts to peaceably bring Gordon Kahl before the court, the repeated telephone calls to Kahl and Kahl's friends, the meeting in Heaton. Warren told of his efforts to convince Muir—once Muir was appointed marshal—not to try to take Kahl into custody with a head-on approach, and the two men had argued. He said it was widely known throughout the marshal's office that his research of Kahl's activities revealed that the only time Gordon Kahl was without his weapon was when he went grocery shopping with his wife.

"At that time I let it be known that was my preference, that I would take Gordon Kahl in the shopping center when he and his wife went in shopping. I would be in the aisle shopping and come around the corner, hopefully, and take custody of Gordon Kahl. There was no secret about that within the marshals service here in Fargo, whatsoever," said Warren.

Warren also suggested there wasn't a need to attempt the arrest that Sunday afternoon. He testified that in the summer of 1982, Muir was ordered by the deputy director of the marshals service to "put the file away and not to spend any more time or manpower on the attempt to apprehend Gordon Kahl because of the minor violation type of a thing and that's the last I heard about Gordon Kahl from Mr. Muir at the time."

Crooks was dismayed by Warren's testimony. He had considered Warren a friend, he called him by his nickname, Bud. No longer. Warren went too far in trying to protect his own reputation at the expense of his fallen comrades.

Others in law enforcement were more blunt in their appraisal of Warren's performance on the witness stand. "He should have his balls cut off," steamed Rodney Webb.

Crooks kept his cross-examination of Warren short.

"There certainly wasn't any disagreement among members of the marshals service that if the court wanted that warrant served, it was going to be served by the United States Marshals Service for the District of North Dakota, wouldn't that be true?" asked Crooks.

"That's true," replied Warren, who appeared ill at ease.

"And there might be some disagreement as exactly how it was going to be done, but essentially all you men in North Dakota were going to do your job?" asked Crooks.

"Yeah. There is no question about that. Had Marshal Muir ordered me along on that Sunday, I would have went, but he gave me a choice," said Warren.

"I have no further questions."

By noon Thursday, the defense rested.

The remainder of the day was used by the prosecution to rebut the testimony of Scott Faul, David Broer, and Yorie Kahl. Seven lawmen took the stand. Among them was Jack Miller, the Stutsman County chief deputy who interrogated Broer after the shootout. Miller testified that during that initial interview Broer admitted he saw the red lights on the police vehicles and that the officers had identified themselves as United States marshals. And Miller reiterated his earlier testimony that Yorie Kahl told him he may have fired the first shot in the gun battle.

At one point during the rebuttal, alarms started to ring throughout the courthouse, and outside the courtroom footsteps could be heard running up and down the hallway, as armed marshals positioned themselves. Inside, it seemed as everyone in the courtroom held his breath and wondered what was about to happen. A deputy marshal entered the courtroom and climbed the steps to the judge's bench. The fire alarms had been activated and the building was being evacuated. Judge Benson looked at the deputy, smiled and said, "Keep me informed," and then ordered Crooks to continue with his examination of the witness on the stand. It was later discovered the alarms were tripped by a malfunction.

That night, as he pored over his notes and placed the last commas and periods to his closing argument, Lynn Crooks allowed himself a moment to feel self-satisfied. There would be no flat-out acquittal. The trial had gone just as he planned, or better. There had been no high points, no low points and, most important, no surprises.

But that would change. The one person who hadn't been heard from during the three-week trial was about to make his presence known.

The prosecution split its closing arguments. Fisher opened, Crooks went last, and the pleas of the defense attorneys were sandwiched between them. In his summation, Fisher admitted that the arrest attempt had been a disaster. Men were killed, others wounded. But, he added, "The defendants took advantage of a bad plan, bad tactics, and they committed murder. The marshals didn't do anything wrong. They were just doing their jobs. The only holes in the government's case are the holes in the bodies of the dead men."

Irv Nodland likened the government's case to an abstract painting where the witnesses and lawyers came into the courtroom, lobbed gobs of paint at the canvas and then asked the jury to "look at that abstract painting and find profound truth in it."

The only truth in this case, said Nodland, is that stupidity is dripping all over it. United States marshals, out of uniform, wearing flak jackets, armed with rifles, set up a roadblock in unmarked vehicles to execute a warrant their superiors had told them to file away. "Darrell Graf knew it was insanity. Bud Warren knew it was insanity," said Nodland. "I'm asking you, pleading with you to recognize the terror Scott Faul was placed in on that road."

Ralph Vinje said he hadn't heard one whit of evidence that his client used a dangerous weapon, and asked the jury to send the government a message. "It scares me the U.S. attorney has the power and will to charge people so frivolously as they have . . . it scares me. You people on the jury have the opportunity to tell the United States government you do not believe in abusing citizens as they have in this case. By your verdict, tell them they were wrong," he urged.

Warren Sogard appealed to the jurors' midwestern sense of decency and fair play and asked them to give fair consideration to the fact that there were two sides presented in the case. The government entered the case with a preordained theory on what occurred at the roadblock and never deviated from it, he said. "They believed the marshals were bushwhacked on that road and that Yorie Kahl fired the first shot. I don't think they fairly considered any other theory. I ask that you do," pleaded Sogard.

Just minutes before Ramlo started his presentation, he, along with the rest of the court, was informed that FBI agents acting on an anonymous telephone tip, found Yorie Kahl's pistol, a bullet still lodged in its handle, in a dumpster outside a shopping mall.

Judge Benson requested all the attorneys to meet with him in his chambers. When everyone gathered, Benson told them it was clear someone—in all likelihood Gordon Kahl—was trying to manipulate the trial. He wouldn't allow it. Nor, he said, would he reopen the case to allow further testimony about the gun. With that in mind, said Benson, he wanted a consensus on how to proceed. Nodland immediately moved for a mistrial, which Benson denied. After more than one hour, the two sides agreed to have the pistol entered into evidence with an explanatory statement as to the circumstances surrounding its discovery. Crooks also agreed to stipulate that the bullet lodged in the handle was not a .223-caliber round, such as those fired from the weapons of the defendants.

Since the other defense attorneys had completed their closing arguments, it was left to Ramlo to comment about the gun, and its importance, on behalf of both Yorie Kahl and Scott Faul. He didn't want to assume that role. He wanted to keep his client as far removed as he could from the other defendants in the minds of the jurors, and his task would be made harder if he had to talk about the gun. Joan Kahl made the decision easier for Ramlo. He had to talk about it, she said.

Ramlo opened by urging the jurors to believe everything the government witnesses said about Joan Kahl. Not one had offered a single piece of evidence that suggested Joan Kahl did anything wrong. "I want you to believe those government witnesses with your whole heart and soul," exhorted Ramlo.

Ramlo then explained to the jury the position he had been placed in with the discovery of the pistol. Then, with all the requisite passion and conviction, Ramlo stepped into the role of defense attorney for both Yorie and Scott. Ramlo displayed a .223-caliber shell to the jury. This is the type of bullet the defendants had in their weapons. The bullet lodged in the handle of that pistol is clearly not a .223, he said. In all likelihood, said Ramlo, the bullet embedded in that gun handle came from Marshal Muir's .38-caliber pistol. What that strongly suggests, he continued, is that Yorie and Scott have told the truth from the beginning of the trial. The marshals started the shootout and Yorie, Scott, and Gordon only acted in self-defense.

The appearance of the pistol disrupted Crooks's well-scripted closing argument. The gun would have to be addressed, and credence now given to the defendants' self-defense claim. But Crooks didn't bother to rework his script. Instead, he set it aside and allowed emotions to speak for him. "These defendants have appeared at this trial to slander these good dead public servants, accuse them of attempting to commit murder on a North Dakota highway. For those of us who knew Kenneth Muir and Bob Cheshire, knew them as friends, associates, colleagues, that would be almost laughable if it were not absolutely heart-rending and sickening.

"What we have is a self-delusional and paranoid rationalization that Gordon Kahl was so important that these good men would abandon all their training, their reputations, their careers to go murder him on a public highway, and that is so absurd that it wouldn't deserve comment except the argument has been made. It's been made by Yorie Kahl, it's been made by Scott Faul and, to a certain extent, by David Broer."

Crooks reminded the jury that "this nation is a nation of laws . . . obviously all of us do not agree with all of those laws, but we follow them because we all believe in majority rule. When our elected and appointed representatives do not serve the public, they are removed. Even the president of the United States can be, and in recent times has been, removed simply because he did not reflect the will of the majority. But Yorie Von Kahl, in particular, would have us all dance to a different drummer, the same type of drummer that I suppose beat for Adolf Hitler when he rose to power, Mussolini when he rose to power, all of those who rose to power on the standard of setting their own laws. That is not the American way. With the help of God it never will be."

What really happened on that road, continued Crooks, was not just an assault on Ken Muir, Bob Cheshire, or any of the other law enforcement officers on that road, but an assault on their authority, nothing less than a private declaration of war by the defendants on the entire population of this country, all that we stand for and believe in.

"Those men were there to enforce our laws. They were our representatives. They were doing their duty. They were good men, honest men, loving men, and they were shot down like dogs on a highway because these men sought to shield Gordon Kahl from the will of the majority.

Crooks's voice trembled with anger as he addressed the issue of who fired the first shot. "If Ken Muir did start the shooting. So what. He had the right to start shooting the minute those persons got out of the car with weapons."

Crooks looked over at the defendants. His eyes rested on Yorie Kahl. "It does my heart good to know Ken at least shot somebody before forfeiting his own life."

At 6 P.M. on Friday, May 27, after Judge Benson completed his seventy-one pages of instructions and discharged the two alternates, the remaining seven women and five men on the jury started their deliberations. Benson told the jurors they could deliberate as long as they wanted on Friday, but that they would be expected, if no verdict was reached, to resume on Saturday, and then on Monday. When reminded that Monday was Memorial Day, Benson smiled and said that in the eyes of the court there were no holidays.

The jury ended its first round of deliberations at 9:45 P.M. that evening. They had chosen a foreman, Allan McCullough, a thirty-year-old truck driver from Hope, North Dakota, and decided to resume their duties at 8:15 A.M., the next morning, earlier than suggested by Judge Benson. For more than nine hours they debated the questions before them. Then, shortly before 6 P.M., at approximately the same time the shooting had started on that prairie road 105 days earlier, the jury informed the court they had reached a verdict. Even before the news was relayed to the large contingent of reporters and cameramen, who either lounged in the first-floor press room or took advantage of the summerlike weather and conducted their vigil on the picnic benches outside the courthouse, family members and relatives of the defendants started to arrive at the Old Federal Building and were escorted to the third-floor courtroom. Shauna Faul wept quietly as she took her seat, and a woman at her side tried to comfort her, patting Shauna's leg and saying softly, "Shauna, you said you were going to be brave." Lois Muir and her family arrived and were ushered to their customary seats.

Crooks and Fisher entered the courtroom. Neither man showed the strain the three-week trial had inflicted upon them. They appeared at ease and engaged in casual conversation with some of the news reporters. They even allowed smiles to crack the serious demeanor they had maintained throughout most of the trial. A few minutes later the defendants, accompanied by their attorneys, were led into the courtroom by four grim-faced deputy marshals. The defendants appeared tired, their mood somber. Scott Faul offered only a weak smile when he caught the eyes of his wife. The defendants were immediately followed by the jurors, who entered in single file. They appeared uncomfortable. The defendants vainly tried to read the outcome on the face of each juror that passed them, but the jury members wouldn't allow it. They either kept their heads down or looked away from the defendants toward the judge's bench as they quick-stepped past the defense table to the jury box.

At 6:20 P.M., Judge Benson entered the courtroom, his black robes which contrasted sharply with his silver hair billowing behind him. He seated himself behind the bench, turned to the jury, and asked of them the timeworn question: "Has the jury reached a verdict?" McCullough stood and responded, "We have, Your Honor."

McCullough handed over the sealed verdicts. The clerk opened the bulky white envelope, stapled the verdicts together, and handed them up to Benson, who reviewed them and then returned them to the clerk to read. Gasps filled the courtroom and friends hugged each other joyously as the clerk read the jury's findings of not guilty on both charges against Joan Kahl. Joan Kahl tipped her head into her hands and Ramlo wrapped an arm around her shoulder. But the joy was momentary. As the courtroom quieted, the clerk read that both Yorie Kahl and Scott Faul had been found guilty of two charges of second-degree murder, and of six related charges including assault. In the case of David Broer, the jury acquitted him of all seven assault charges, but found him guilty on charges of conspiracy and harboring a felony suspect.

The defendants watched stoically as Benson polled the jurors and each member affirmed the verdict. Benson then thanked the jurors—"This completes what I'm sure must have been a very difficult assignment. We appreciate you allowing us to interrupt your lives, as we must have done during these three weeks"—and ordered them escorted home by deputy marshals. He set sentencing for June 24, at which time he would comment, "I think this case has been correctly characterized as an assault on the law. I don't think the defendants had any personal feelings for or against the individual victims, but their malice was for the position the victims held and the duties that they were performing." Benson would sentence Kahl and Faul to concurrent life prison terms, and impose upon Broer consecutive five-year sentences.

As deputies moved to handcuff the just-convicted men and return them to their jail cells, Joan Kahl approached her son and lightly touched his arm twice. "You'll be all right. You'll be all right," she said. Behind Yorie, his wife, Janice, now seven months pregnant with their third child, cried uncontrollably. She collapsed when she was being led out of the courtroom by Warren Sogard and was later examined by a doctor and sedated. Shauna Faul waved off reporters. "Nothing at all," she said. Lois Muir, who showed no emotion when the verdicts were read, offered only, "I'm just glad it's over."

In the fading twilight, Crooks and Fisher stood on the courthouse steps and faced a forest of microphones. They were defiant and, particularly Fisher, not at all gracious in victory. "Not guilty doesn't mean innocent. It just means there wasn't enough evidence to convict her," said Fisher of Joan Kahl's acquittal.

He also expressed disappointment that Broer was convicted on only two charges, neither of them assault. "The jury obviously showed him more mercy than he showed either Bob or Ken on that road."

Yet neither man expressed disappointment that the first-degree murder verdicts sought by the government had been reduced. "Murder is murder. It doesn't make a bit of difference," said Crooks. "The murder verdicts, as far as I'm concerned, are satisfactory. I'm satisfied justice was done."

Richard Blay was only partially satisfied that justice had been served. Only after Gordon Kahl was apprehended and brought to trial would justice be sated. And the possibility of that occurring any time soon had dimmed considerably. The number of tips received by the FBI had slowed to a trickle, and as the tips dwindled, so did the size of Blay's investigative force. Although he insisted that MarMurs, the bureau's code name for the search, was still a high-priority case, and would remain one until Kahl was captured, his force of fifty special agents and federal marshals had been reduced to twelve. He and everyone else was frustrated. But all they needed was one solid lead, a telephone call from someone who had seen Kahl, and the investigation would be in good shape.

18

The Lake of Fire

Four days after the verdicts were returned in Fargo, North Dakota, Karen Russell Robertson paced the lobby floor of the Ramada Inn in Mountain Home, Arkansas. Her eyes darted from the glass front doors to the lobby clock and back again. Where is he? she asked herself nervously.

She had reason to be nervous. And scared. Just the day before, on May 31, Karen, with Michelle and Mary in tow, parked her old, beat-up, green International pickup truck in the lot of the E-Z Mart along Highway 5. There, she climbed out of the truck, walked toward the pay telephone, and placed a call. "I know where you can find Gordon Kahl," she told an agent at the FBI's office in Little Rock.

Within minutes, Karen was on the line with a second agent from Fayetteville, who arranged the meeting with her for today. An agent named Knox. Fort Knox, thought Karen, who smiled at her own joke. There was nothing funny, however, about what Karen was about to do. She was going to turn against her father, his cause, his friends, and his hero. If anyone found out, there wouldn't be much life left in front of her. And if there was still a reward for his capture, she wouldn't have much opportunity to spend it. But for Karen it was a chance worth taking. It wasn't her cause, they weren't her friends, and Gordon Kahl wasn't her hero. He was a killer. And he planned to kill again, this time a deputy sheriff, someone who had been at the Medina shootout, and an attorney, or was it a judge, Karen couldn't remember.

Karen was afraid for her children. She was afraid Kahl would succeed again and would return to use her father's home as a hideout. Then, eventually, the police would find him there and more people would die, possibly her father, herself, or, God forbid, her children. She wasn't going to take that chance. And there was the reward; no matter what the amount, it was more money than Karen had ever had in her life, and she was tired of being poor. She wanted enough money so she could get out of there, away from her father and his constant complaints about her housekeeping and child-raising abilities. Enough money to finish her high school education, to go on to college and find a decent job.

Karen looked at the clock. It read 6:20 P.M. Where is he?

Jack Knox entered the motel lobby. When Knox first heard of the shootout in Medina, he considered it the act of a lone, crazed gunman. But as Knox became more immersed in the search for Kahl—checking out leads on Kahl's Arkansas connection—he soon realized that while Kahl might be crazy, he wasn't alone. To his horror, Knox uncovered a subculture composed of people who not only shared Kahl's beliefs but viewed the man as a hero, a modern-day patriot who would've been welcomed with open arms by the country's Founding Fathers. Some of the people Knox met seemed nonviolent, if not exactly rational, when they talked about the Jewish-controlled conspiracy that was hell-bent on subverting the white race through the income tax and civil rights laws. Too many others, however, fell into Knox's category of psychopaths, people who, like Kahl, wouldn't stop short of killing someone seen as the enemy. They were the kind of people who believed their cause was helped by the murders of a Jewish Texarkana pawnbroker and a black Arkansas state trooper, murder committed solely in response to bigotry and prejudice.

Knox didn't know into which of those two groups of people Karen Robertson fell, but he took no chances. He asked for the meeting in the motel lobby because he wanted a lot of people around. And outside, a backup agent closely watched the individuals who followed Knox through the lobby doors.

Once inside, Knox instinctively reached behind him and felt the handgun wedged into the small of his back. Comforted with the knowledge his weapon was there, Knox's eyes searched the lobby for a woman with red-tinted brown hair, and who had two young girls with her. Knox saw her. Her face, untouched by makeup, was pale; she looked almost anemic. Yet, if somewhat plain-looking, she was also attractive. Her hair fell far down her back and, like many women in the movement, she wore an old-fashioned, floral-patterned dress that skirted her ankles and hung loosely on her extremely thin frame. Knox approached her.

"Karen Robertson?" he asked.

Karen looked at the man, who was dressed in blue jeans and wore a windbreaker over a plaid shirt. He stood approximately five feet ten inches tall, had a medium build that carried 165 pounds, gray hair, and appeared to be in his late forties. He didn't look like an FBI agent, but his smile told her not to be afraid.

"Yes," Karen replied.

"Jack Knox, FBI," he said.

Knox took the woman's hand to shake it, and noticed it tremble. A closer look told him that her whole body was shaking. This woman wasn't here to set him up, thought Knox. This woman is scared for her life.

Knox suggested they go into the restaurant, where they were seated by the hostess. It was suppertime, and the tables near them were filled with diners, many of whom were engaged in lively and loud conversations. It was obvious to both Knox and Karen that it was too busy to talk without being overheard, a risk neither was willing to take. Across the street was the city park. Knox suggested they meet there to talk. He reached into his pocket, pulled out a twenty-dollar bill and handed it to Karen with instructions to buy some sandwiches and soft drinks for Michelle and Mary. Karen took the money and tried her Fort Knox joke out on the agent. A smile creased Knox's face.

Karen and her daughters entered the park with a bucket of fried chicken. Knox stood next to a picnic table and watched as Karen readied her children's dinner on another table next to a set of swings where the two girls would play between bites of chicken and sips of soft drinks. When Karen joined Knox, the agent set out a tape recorder and sat himself across from her. In his twenty years as an agent, Knox had learned a person's facial expressions could reveal as much as the spoken word.

Karen spoke first. She told Knox that Gordon Kahl had stayed at her father's house until just a few days ago. She wondered if it were possible for her father to receive immunity from prosecution. "I'm scared to death that my father . . . I sometimes think he is the sanest man in the world, and other times he just acts [kind] of crazy and I'm scared of him," said Karen.

"I can't give you any guarantees your father wouldn't be arrested and charged with something, if your story is true," replied Knox. "What I will guarantee is that you and your daughters will be protected. No harm would come to any of you."

Karen looked toward the swings and watched as Michelle and Mary played.

"How do you know the man who stayed with you is Gordon Kahl?" asked Knox.

Karen offered a weak smile. "He told me."

Karen recounted Kahl's arrival at her father's home, what Kahl looked like, her father's insistence that she not tell anyone who was living with them and—after Kahl and she had watched a news story about the shootout—that she had asked Kahl if he had really killed the marshals. "He told me they were looking to kill him, not arrest him," said Karen.

"Do you have any proof the man was Gordon Kahl?" pressed Knox. "Anything that he might have left fingerprints on? A letter?"

Karen reached into her large handbag, pulled out the book *One Straw Revolution,* and placed it in front of Knox. This is a book he read while he stayed with us, she said. As Knox reached for the book, Karen looked at Knox's hands. She panicked. "You're one of them," she blurted. "You work for the Jews."

Knox was startled. "One of whom?" he asked.

Karen pointed at the Masonic ring Knox wore on his little finger. She said Gordon Kahl warned her against trusting a Mason, that Masons were dominated by rich Jews who sought to weaken the United States and bring it under the control of their one-world-government rule. Kahl had even drawn her a picture of the seven-headed beast from Revelation and explained to Karen that the beast's body represented the Satanic Jews, and the Masons represented one of its heads.

Knox was dumbfounded. How could she believe that crap? More important, how was he going to convince her that it was crap? He was losing her and he hadn't yet found out where Kahl—if it was Kahl—was now hiding. In his soft, southern-accented voice, Knox tried to alleviate her concern. "I'm a lawman," he said. "I work for the FBI, not the Jews, the Masons, or anyone else. If such a conspiracy exists, I am not aware of it or a party to it."

But, Knox promised, if such a conspiracy existed he would uncover and expose it. Right now, however, his only job was to find and arrest Gordon Kahl for the murders of two U.S. marshals. And the only way he could do that was with Karen's help. Knox reminded Karen of the danger she felt both she and her daughters faced with Kahl on the loose and the only way to make that danger go away was to help Knox find Kahl.

Knox watched as Karen relaxed and the tension left her body. She believed him. He asked his next question.

"If Kahl isn't at your father's home, where is he?"

Karen wasn't positive, but she believed he was at the home of Leonard and Norma Ginter. On Memorial Day, said Karen, Ginter and another man who she thought was Ed Udey arrived at her father's home and were met outside by Kahl. As Karen unloaded her pickup and readied herself to run some errands, she overheard the three men say that the FBI were closing in and that they needed to get some guns and ammunition. "I asked them if they were going to use the CSA and get their guns and ammo from them," said Karen.

Knox didn't like what he heard. During his investigation of Kahl's activities in Arkansas, he had uncovered the CSA, hard-core true believers with more than their share of crazies and psychopaths.

The CSA, or Covenant, Sword and Arm of the Lord, operated a two-hundred-acre compound outside of Mountain Home, near the Missouri-Arkansas border that was home to approximately one hundred inhabitants. A ragtag collection of farmers, carpenters, office clerks, machinists, ex-cons, and ex-cops, led by a charismatic preacher named James Ellison, the group worked to complete the construction of their safe haven, or survival zone, against the nuclear Armageddon they were certain would soon occur.

Like many in the Identity movement, CSA followers believed mankind had entered Tribulations—that period of war, famine, and economic collapse—which would end with the Battle of Armageddon and be followed by Christ's return to earth. The CSA members believed they had been chosen by God to spearhead the fight during this period against the Jewish-led anti-Christ forces that repeatedly violated God's law. Those violations included allowing blacks to marry whites, homosexuals to practice sodomy, and communists to speak and move freely in society. To fulfill its duty in the struggle, the CSA established itself as the paramilitary arm of the Identity movement, and assumed the responsibility of training its members and other Identity followers in the art of guerrilla and urban warfare. Seminars on Christian military truths, as well as courses in the use of automatic weapons, explosives, and small arms were regularly offered at the compound, which had a shooting range that included wooden, pop-up targets of state troopers who wore badges shaped like the Star of David. Along with food, water, and other essentials for survival in event of a holocaust, the group also stockpiled large caches of weapons and ammunition.

If Kahl had been accepted into the bosom of such a group as the CSA, thought Knox, it would be no easy feat to extract him without a lot of people getting hurt in the process.

"Were they going to use the CSA?" Knox asked.

Karen didn't know. The men hadn't answered her question, but turned away from her and entered a small mobile home that was parked near the house. She left to do her errands, and when she returned, Ginter, Udey, and Gordon Kahl were gone.

After two hours, the interview ended. Night had fallen and a chilled breeze rustled the leaves on the trees. Michelle and Mary were played-out and wanted to go home, as did Karen. Knox turned off his tape recorder. He was satisfied with the information he had collected. If the man wasn't Gordon Kahl, he was someone who knew Kahl well and, either way, it was a good, strong lead.

"Is there a reward?" Karen asked.

Knox was surprised by the question. He assumed Karen knew of the reward and that it was what motivated her to call the FBI, not her expressed concern for the well-being of her daughters. Maybe he had been a cop for too long, had grown too cynical in his judgment of what motivated people to turn informant. Yes, he said, something like $10,000 or $15,000, and she would probably receive it if her story led to Kahl's arrest.

Karen also wanted to know how she could remember Knox's name if she had to call him with additional information. You can remember Fort Knox, can't you, he joked. Karen smiled and nodded her head.

When Knox returned to Fayetteville, he immediately called his supervisor in Little Rock, James Blasingame, and told him he was convinced that his source was telling the truth and that Kahl had, in all likelihood, taken refuge at the Ginter residence. Blasingame noted, however, Knox's source had given them two other suspect locations, the home of Ed Udey and the CSA compound. Blasingame wanted to be positive of Kahl's location before he made a move. Should lawmen go to the wrong location, they would lose the element of surprise and Kahl could escape.

At 4 P.M. the next day, a single-engine, two-seater airplane circled lazily over the lush, heavily wooded Arkansas hill. Blasingame peered through his field glasses down onto a narrow clay-and-dirt road that wound its way to a clearing about a mile off state highway 115 where Leonard and Norma Ginter had their home.

It looked more like a military bunker than someone's home. Only the porch, supported by four rough-hewn beams, and the concrete front of the structure were exposed. The rest of the house was built into the side of a hill, air vents poking through the grass-covered roof. To the right of the house was a garage that had a plywood second story built on to it. In front of the garage sat a cream-colored Dodge Omni that matched the description of the car Karen Robertson had seen Ginter driving the day Gordon Kahl left her father's home.

The airplane passed over the clearing twice more. Blasingame had caught a brief glimpse of two men outside of the house, and was sure one of the men was Gordon Kahl. They had their man; it was time to move.

On the ground, Ginter and Kahl shaded their eyes against the sun and watched as the airplane repeatedly flew over the area. "It's the police. They're coming here to get you," said Ginter.

Kahl said nothing as he watched the aircraft make its last pass over the area and fly away. Ever since the verdicts were returned, Ginter had watched his friend become more and more despondent. He wouldn't talk to anyone. He walked in the woods or sat in front of the television set, the volume turned up loud so he could hear. To Ginter, Kahl seemed tired of running and hiding, perhaps even of living.

A retired carpenter, whose only visible income was a $160-a-month pension, the wiry-built, sixty-one-year-old Ginter had met Kahl several years before when they both attended patriot meetings in western Arkansas. During those meetings, the two men found they shared a common interest in the Posse Comitatus; Ginter had been a member of the Posse when he lived in Wisconsin, but quit in the late 1970s, when he and his wife moved from Wisconsin and its high tax rates. When the couple moved to Arkansas, Ginter joined the Association for Constitutional Enforcement, a group, like the Posse, that opposed personal income taxes and was steeped in the religious teachings of the Identity movement. The house Ginter built was on land leased from a fellow ACE member.

In the years he had known Kahl, Ginter had come to admire the man for his intelligence and understanding of the problems facing the country. He saw Kahl as a patriot and true hero to the cause. But for Kahl to remain a hero, he had to stay alive.

"You have got to get out of here, you know," said Ginter. "They're closing in."

Kahl turned and walked back toward the woods without a word.

James Blasingame surveyed the government assault team as its members donned their bulletproof vests and checked their weapons. It was an impressive concentration of manpower and firepower including SWAT teams from the FBI and U.S. Marshals Service, state troopers, deputy sheriffs, and members of the Arkansas Criminal Investigation Division. The task force started to assemble on a road outside of Smithville, a few miles from the Ginter home, shortly after Blasingame had completed his aerial surveillance. So as not to draw attention to themselves, the lawmen arrived separately in teams of two and three officers throughout the evening of June 2, and into the morning of June 3. By midafternoon, the task force swelled to nearly forty men and women and, when it started toward the Ginter home, was joined by an ambulance and fire truck.

Back in Minneapolis, Dick Blay busied himself in his office and awaited word on the outcome of the arrest attempt. As soon as Kahl's presence in Arkansas had been confirmed, the U.S. Marshals Service requested Blay be sent into the state to handle the investigation. The request was denied. Blay wanted to go and later he wished he had been there, but that wasn't how the FBI operated. Blay had headed the investigation in North Dakota because he was agent-in-charge of the district. When the probe switched to Arkansas, the responsibility for the search fell to Blasingame. It would be a slap in the face to have an agent from an outside district take over for another agent-in-charge.

But the two agents did discuss the arrest attempt the night before the task force moved on the Ginter home. "All the psychological studies I've seen suggest Kahl is the most vicious criminal you'll ever come up against," Blay told his Arkansas counterpart.

"You can't walk up to the house, knock on the door, and ask him to surrender," Blay cautioned Blasingame. "Kahl is a true believer, a fanatic, who will go down in a gun battle."

With twenty-nine years with the FBI under his belt, Blasingame had no intention of doing something so foolhardy. When the task force arrived at the dirt road that led to the Ginter house, Blasingame ordered the two SWAT teams to travel through the woods and close in on the house so that they would cut off any escape routes, allowing the state troopers and deputy sheriffs to remain on the highway for backup. Blasingame positioned himself and three other lawmen—Lawrence County sheriff Gene Matthews, Deputy U.S. Marshal Jim Hall, and state investigator Ed Fitzpatrick—at a bend in the dirt road just out of the sight of the house. There they would wait for word that the SWAT teams were in position before they approached the house.

The sky was overcast and the humidity hung heavy in the air. It looked and felt like rain. "The fish should be biting in this weather," said Leonard Ginter.

He pushed himself away from the kitchen table, where he had just finished his dinner of green beans and hot dogs. Norma was already at the kitchen sink cleaning the dishes, while Gordon Kahl turned his attention toward the television set. Kahl said nothing when Ginter grabbed his fishing rod and rifle and headed out the door.

Ginter wasn't interested in fishing, but in who might be outside his house. Earlier that day he had driven into Smithville and had seen a lot of strangers around, some who drove vehicles that looked a lot like police cars. If the police had discovered Kahl's whereabouts, they would come for him, and soon. Ginter wanted to give his friend whatever lead time he could. He wanted to give him a chance to survive. Ginter opened the trunk of his car and placed his fishing rod and rifle inside. Inside, he reached underneath the front seat, pulled out a .22-caliber pistol, and placed it on the passenger's seat, before starting the engine.

Blasingame watched in frustration as Ginter pulled his car out of the driveway. The SWAT teams hadn't yet radioed that they were in position. Well, he couldn't wait for them, he would have to take

Ginter down now and hope the teams would be in position by the time he himself and the others reached the house. Blasingame checked his watch; it was 5:55 P.M.

Ginter drove only a few hundred yards when he saw the car and pickup truck approaching. He stopped, reached over, and placed the pistol in his lap, then put the car in reverse and started to back into the driveway. He stopped his car when the two vehicles were upon him. Four men, armed with pistols and shotguns, jumped out and pointed their weapons at him.

Ginter's hands froze on the steering wheel, and he sat rigid in his seat as Blasingame approached the car. In one hand he carried his revolver, in the other he held out his FBI identification. "FBI. Out of the car."

Ginter remained frozen in his seat, his pistol on his lap. When Blasingame neared the driver's side, Ginter rolled down his window halfway. "What are you doing?" asked Blasingame, who kept his revolver pointed at Ginter.

"Going fishing," Ginter replied.

Blasingame moved closer to the door, looked into the window, and recoiled when he saw the pistol on Ginter's lap. "Do you always have a pistol across your lap when you go fishing?" Blasingame asked.

Ginter didn't respond.

"Get out of the car. Now!" yelled Blasingame.

Ginter placed the pistol on the passenger's seat and got out of the car. Blasingame frisked Ginter and whipped his arms behind him and handcuffed the man. The cuffs bit into Leonard's wrists.

"Who else is in the house?" asked Blasingame.

"Just my wife," replied Ginter.

"Tell her to come out," ordered Blasingame.

Ginter led the officers to the front door of his house, where he stopped and shouted, "Norma, come on outside! The FBI wants to talk to you!"

At the sink, Norma heard her husband's voice but couldn't make out the words over the sound of the TV. She wiped her hands on a towel and walked through the utility room to the door that led into the garage. Norma gasped. Two men with guns were at the door waiting for her. They escorted Norma to her husband and Blasingame. "Was anyone else in the house?" asked Blasingame.

"No," the couple replied in unison.

"I'd like to search the house," said Blasingame.

"Got a search warrant?" asked Ginter.

"Yes, we do," said Blasingame.

He was opening the manila folder to show the warrant when a shot rang out.

Then another.

Then a shotgun blast.

"Down on the ground! Next to the garage!" Blasingame yelled at the couple.

He took cover next to the concrete garage wall and fumbled in the folder for a Wanted poster. "Is this the man in the house?" demanded Blasingame. The poster had Gordon Kahl's picture on it.

Ginter, who feared he was about to die, nodded his head.

Deputy U.S. Marshal Jim Hall ran from inside the house to the garage door entrance. His shirtsleeves were covered with blood. "The sheriff's been shot!" he yelled.

The sheriff was Gene Matthews, serving his second two-year term as Lawrence County's chief law enforcement officer.

Matthews and Hall had met Norma Ginter as she left the house through a door that led into the garage. After they directed Norma toward her husband and Blasingame, Matthews, followed by Hall, entered the utility room and proceeded toward the kitchen.

No orders were given to enter the house. The plan was to get the Ginters out of the house, then use the public address system in Blasingame's car to order Kahl to surrender. If Kahl refused, he would be forced out of the concrete bunker with tear gas.

But the brawny, thirty-seven-year-old Matthews wasn't used to waiting for orders. He was used to giving them.

Matthews, his .41-caliber handgun drawn, entered the kitchen, while Hall remained near the door. When Matthews got within three feet of the refrigerator, Gordon Kahl, armed with a mini-14 rifle, stepped out from behind the appliance and the two men fired almost simultaneously.

The rifle bullet passed through Matthews's left arm, pierced the seam of his bulletproof vest, and ricocheted up and entered his chest at the armpit. The force of the bullet's impact spun Matthews around and he stumbled toward Hall. A shotgun blast, fired through a front window by another officer, peppered the back of Matthews's bulletproof vest as he lunged at Hall, who caught him in his arms. "I'm hit, but I think I killed him," Matthews told Hall. "Help me stop the bleeding."

Hall dragged Matthews through the utility room and into the garage, where Matthews collapsed and sent Hall sprawling against the car. "Help me, Jim. Help me," pleaded Matthews. "I think I'm dying."

Hall whipped off his belt and applied it as a tourniquet around Matthews's arm. He tried to drag Matthews out of the garage, but he couldn't move the much heavier man. Hall ran to the garage door and screamed for help.

As Matthews was carried to a squad car and rushed to the ambulance that waited on the highway, the situation at the scene turned chaotic. A dozen lawmen, ordered to wait at the highway, streamed toward the house when they received word of the shooting. Together with the two SWAT teams, they laid down a withering barrage of gunfire and tear gas cannisters that shattered the windows and left the concrete front of the building pockmarked. One officer climbed to the roof of the home and placed a can of diesel fuel over an air vent, while another lawman shot two holes into the can that allowed the fuel to leak down the vent and into the house. Soon, flames were dancing amid the heavy smoke and tear gas, and within minutes the house was ablaze.

For more than two hours the lawmen fired thousands of rounds of ammunition into what had surely become Kahl's funeral pyre. Shortly after 8 P.M., the shooting stopped, and the rains started. But even the heavy rain couldn't dampen the conflagration that consumed the structure. The flames leaped out of the windows and reached toward the darkened sky. An eerie silence, broken only by an occasional explosion from inside the house and the crackle of the raging fire, draped the scene. By 9 P.M., word arrived that Matthews was dead. He had lost consciousness during the ambulance ride to the hospital and never regained it. He died from a loss of blood. The mood at the scene grew more sullen.

Blasingame ordered the fire truck to approach the house. The flames were doused, and within an hour lawmen entered the building where they found, near a chair in the kitchen, a badly charred body, its legs and one of its hands seared off by the extreme heat of the blaze. A mini-14 rifle lay underneath the body. Matthews was right, he had killed Kahl, or someone, with a single shot to the head.

19

The Aftermath

Shortly before midnight Lynn Crooks received word at his Fargo home that Kahl might have been killed in the Arkansas shootout. When he had left his office that afternoon, Crooks knew there would be an attempt to arrest Kahl, and that night he was so anxious about the outcome of the attempt that he found it impossible to go to bed. He wondered whether Kahl would still be at the house when the task force moved against him. The man had always seemed to have nine lives, the ability to disappear into thin air.

The news that Kahl had been trapped at the Ginters' home and was now dead left Crooks with mixed feelings. He was relieved and pleased that Kahl had finally been apprehended, and it bothered him little that Kahl was killed in the process. Crooks wasn't surprised by the outcome, having always suspected the final chapter in the Kahl saga would be written in Kahl's own blood. But it was just too damn bad that it couldn't have been completed without the blood of yet another lawman.

Four men dead, two men in prison for the rest of their lives, another man in jail for ten years, and umpteen families destroyed. Crooks repeated the litany of carnage in his mind as he entered his bedroom, picked up the shotgun that had rested near his bed since before the start of the trial, unloaded it, and returned it to the gun cabinet. "For what?" he asked himself out loud. A tornado couldn't cause that much damage.

Crooks prepared for bed, kissed his wife good night, and wrestled himself to sleep. Over and over it played in his mind, "What the hell was in a man's mind to wreak that kind of havoc . . . because he didn't want to pay his taxes?"

Dick Blay also had known of the arrest attempt, but had decided not to lose sleep over it. The early-morning telephone call that carried the news, as well as more detailed information on the operation, awakened him. After Blay received the agent's report, he too thought what occurred was a tragedy, but for reasons other than the death of a fellow police officer.

He was disappointed that the arrest attempt was accomplished in such a wasteful way. Blay wanted Gordon Kahl in custody, alive. He wanted Kahl to have his day in court so that the government could show the world who Kahl really was, a murderer rather than a hero. Blay didn't want a martyr, but the way the whole operation was handled gave the extremist movement just that.

Blay was angered and embarrassed by the fact that lawmen deliberately set the house on fire. It didn't matter that officers feared Kahl had donned a gas mask and hidden in a corner of the house. Anytime law officers set a place on fire when there is a person trapped inside would lead to real problems, speculated Blay. "We are more professional than that. We don't want to be put in the same category as them. They are the killers," he said later. "There is no way to justify it."

Nor were Blay's fears assuaged by the knowledge that law enforcement's public statement was that the tear gas had accidentally started the fire. The truth would come out, and when it did, the lawmen would appear to be liars as well as vigilantes gone amok. All in all, thought Blay, the operation reflected badly on law enforcement.

Within days of the shootout, press conferences were called by leaders of various extremist groups around the country. As Blay expected, the conferences were used to depict Kahl as a martyr and the government as rabid, mad-dog executioners.

Ed Gran, a physics professor at the University of Arkansas and founder of the Central Arkansas Patriots, called the government's action against Kahl an "outright execution."

Gran demanded the arrest attempt be investigated by a grand jury because there were indications that the blaze was no accident, that the Ginter home had actually been firebombed by the authorities. "I am fearful that this tragedy may be part of a government program to label peaceful constitutionalist groups as violent by provoking isolated individuals through the use of unbearable pressure," said Gran, an articulate, distinguished-looking man with white hair, thick muttonchop sideburns, and glasses.

"Although we did not know Mr. Kahl, and we disapprove of violence, we feel that he and Sheriff Matthews may both have been pawns in a larger scheme to neutralize political constitutionalist groups."

It was a charge that would resurface and assume more credibility eleven months later when the *Arkansas Democrat,* a Little Rock newspaper, printed a series of stories that concluded it was unlikely Kahl and Matthews killed each other. The newspaper based its conclusions on the autopsy reports of state Medical Examiner Fahmy Malk, which indicated that both Kahl and Matthews were shot to death from behind, and the fact that authorities could not find a spent shell casing from Kahl's rifle.

Lawmen, however, have remained firm in their contention that Matthews shot Kahl and Kahl shot Matthews. Anything else, said Deputy U.S. Marshal Hall, is "just speculation on the part of Kahl sympathizers."

Press conferences similar to the one held by Gran in Arkansas, where similar rhetoric was employed, were held in Wisconsin, Virginia, Oregon, North Dakota, and Montana. In some cases, extremist leaders who did not yet want their hero to become a martyr for the cause, suggested Kahl had not been killed in the shootout, despite findings issued by the Arkansas medical examiner indicating that the charred remains were indeed those of Kahl.

Donald Laverne Hollenbeck of Portland, Oregon, the self-proclaimed national commander of the Posse, told reporters he believed Kahl was still alive. His reasons were simple. "The word of any law enforcement officers can't be trusted," insisted Hollenbeck. Nor, he added, would Kahl be "stupid enough to hide in a building with no rear exits.

"He is in hiding, and he is going to show up."

Joan Kahl also wanted to believe her husband was still alive. Although for more than twenty years she had feared and even expected her marriage to Gordon to end this way, she wasn't now ready to accept that he was dead. The names of the owners of the house weren't familiar to her, and the scene of the shootout was hundreds of miles from where Joan would have expected Gordon to be hiding if he were in Arkansas. She wanted a second autopsy, performed by a pathologist chosen by the family. The findings were the same: the body belonged to Gordon Kahl.

It was over. There would be no more sleepless nights spent wondering what happened to Gordon. The tears rushed from her. But no matter how hard she cried, Joan couldn't wash away the guilt she felt for having sided with the government during so many arguments with Gordon. He had been right all along. The government had been out to destroy him and all that good Christians believed to be true. He had been right and she had waited too long to tell him. A bitter hatred toward her government, her country, filled her.

While the extremists' movement attempted to place Gordon Kahl upon a pedestal, and Joan Kahl mourned and made funeral arrangements, the government moved quickly to arrest Kahl's sympathizers in Arkansas. Leonard and Norma Ginter, along with Arthur Russell, seventy-four, and Ed Udey, seventy, and his wife, Irene, sixty-one, were arrested on federal charges of conspiracy to harbor Kahl. The Ginters were arrested also on state charges of murder in the death of Sheriff Matthews.

The federal trial for the five defendants was held in October, and the star witness for the prosecution was Karen Robertson. The trial did not go smoothly, despite heavy security. On the days Robertson testified, the trial was repeatedly interrupted by bomb threats. When those attempts failed to stop her testimony, which ultimately led to convictions against all except Irene, the CSA entertained more drastic measures.

The day after Christmas, an assassination team was dispatched from the CSA's compound along Bull Shoals Lake with orders to kill Robertson, as well as FBI agent Jack Knox and federal judge H. Franklin Waters, who presided over the trial. The motive was now revenge. After guilty verdicts were returned, Judge Waters had sentenced both Leonard Ginter and Ed Udey to five years in prison, Arthur Russell to six months in jail, and placed Norma Ginter on five years' probation. Fortunately for the intended victims, the van that carried the hit squad skidded off the road and the mission was aborted.

Robertson also was scheduled to testify at the state trial of the Ginters. But the murder charge against Norma Ginter was dropped and her husband entered a guilty plea to a harboring charge in exchange for the state dropping the murder charge against him. Leonard received an additional eight-year prison sentence on the lesser charge.

Karen Robertson eschewed a government offer to enter the federal witness protection program and, after having collected the $25,000 reward, left the area to establish a new identity and a new life for herself and her two daughters.

20

A Simple Wooden Cross

Alone, atop a rise that overlooked the scuffed North Dakota prairie, stood the Bowdon Country Seventh-Day Adventist Church. Although it was not a house of worship frequented by Gordon Kahl when he was alive, the family requested the use of the 250-seat church in order to accommodate the number of mourners expected at the funeral.

The hot, dry June air penetrated the modern, brick and oak-beamed structure and threatened to wilt the array of eleven large floral arrangements that stretched from the front pew to the foot of the pulpit. At the pulpit, the Reverend Peter Dyck watched somberly as the last of the more than 250 family members, friends, and admirers—some who had traveled from as far as Texas, Georgia, Wisconsin, Iowa, and Montana to be on hand for the service—squeezed into their seats. Inside the glassed-in crying room at the back of the church, forty members of the news media shared space with parents who shushed and rocked their fussing children, while their ears strained to hear the words delivered to them through a speaker inside the room.

Dyck nodded an acknowledgment to Joan Kahl who sat in a front pew with her four daughters and youngest son—all but Yorie who was denied court permission to attend the funeral. Law enforcement authorities were concerned about security at the funeral and feared the service would present the Posse, or some other extremist group, with a once-in-a-lifetime opportunity to free Yorie. So distraught when he heard that his father had been killed, Yorie was placed under a suicide watch, which would be continued past the funeral.

A Baptist minister noted for his bombastic delivery, Dyck quietly welcomed the people gathered before him, and opened his eulogy in a subdued tone of voice. "On this quiet, humble community today, we have the eyes and ears of the entire nation. As we all realize, the events surrounding this funeral are most unusual in nature. And, I think it behooves us to have an unusual funeral since the circumstances, the man, and the events are unusual."

If in truth the eyes and ears of the nation were on the service, what the nation would see and hear from inside that church would be more than unusual, would strain the bounds of credibility.

Dyck's right hand shot upward and pierced the air. His voice rose, and now trembled as he spoke. The time for muted words was past. "I would like to say that we honor this country," his voice boomed. There would be no further need for a PA system in order to hear his words.

"We teach the great American history to our youngsters. We tell them the tremendous stories of early American history, such as the story behind the Star-Spangled Banner, the flag under which so many of our men on foreign soils have fought. It is a tremendous story, heart moving. So, we love this country, and we can say that this man really loved his country."

Dyck, who admitted to frequent disagreements with Kahl over certain issues, insisted, however, that his friend was grossly misunderstood and was not the violent or dangerous man portrayed by the media. What Kahl was, said Dyck, was a controversial man, a dedicated man, and a sacrificial man who "paid a great price . . . in his attempt to awaken a pacifistic public to the dangers facing these great United States of America."

In his eulogy, Dyck recalled illustrious figures from American history, famous patriots. He referred to Patrick Henry's stirring speech that decried the British government's policy of publicly flogging ministers who preached without a license, and how those licenses served as chains on a man's freedom. His voice filled the church as he repeated Henry's famous closing line, "Give me liberty or give me death."

"I believe I can say here today that Gordon Kahl really believed that, and he felt that by speaking up, he could resist the rising despotism that he saw in our nation," said Dyck.

"Paul Revere rode through the night and cried in a loud voice to arouse people that 'the British are coming. The British are coming.'

"This man has traveled all across this country and, in his way and bound by his conscience, cried 'the tyrants are coming, the tyrants are coming.' Hardly anyone paid any attention to the warning. People didn't believe in a lot of his political and religious beliefs, so they discounted everything he said."

As he looked down from his pulpit at the flag-draped casket that contained Kahl's body, Dyck asked, "Is this here today mute and eloquent evidence that the tyrants did come?"

Dyck placed the blame for the shootout upon the government, and contended that in all his battles with authorities Kahl only used words, never violence.

The minister was too generous in his praise of Kahl. To a vast majority of Americans, Kahl wasn't a hero, but a man who should be condemned to infamy. Rather than be likened to Patrick Henry or Paul Revere, he could be compared to the Islamic fanatics who rule Iran or the terrorists who have torn asunder the once peaceful land of Lebanon. Gordon Kahl was a man who left behind an epitaph of needless violence and death, not peace and goodwill.

Dyck anticipated such a sentiment. "If this man must be buried in infamy, perhaps I am, and sir, perhaps you are, partially to blame for being too uninvolved in seeking to rectify some of our evils," he said.

At the end of the seventy-minute service, the mourners filed out of the church amid strains of organ music, climbed into their cars, and followed the hearse to a small, country cemetery several miles away. There, Joan Kahl bowed her head and wept as her husband's body was lowered into a grave marked by a simple wooden cross. Kahl was buried next to his parents.

Facing a stand of ancient evergreens that towered above them, a makeshift American Legion honor guard gave Kahl a respectful, if awkward, military salute—four of the six attempted gunshots misfired, while a young boy struggled to play taps. The six Legionnaires—four from Sykeston, and one each from Heaton and Minot—were not there to honor Kahl's most recent actions, said Darrell Hansen, a past commander of the Sykeston post. Instead, he said, they were there to pay tribute to Kahl for what he did nearly forty years earlier while a gunner in the U.S. Army Air Corps. "I think it should have been a military funeral. He served his country when it called," said Hansen.

The honor guard was hastily organized just the day before when the United States Air Force and state veterans groups turned down the family's repeated invitations to attend the funeral.

Marion Bjerk peered around the corner of the tent that shaded the Kahl family from the blistering sun. She and Mark Anderson had traveled from Grand Forks to pay respects to a man they saw as a hero. "He is one of the greatest men since Nathan Hale and George Washington. He is a patriot who gave his life to straighten out the crooked taxers," said Anderson, who shaded his eyes from the sun with his hands.

Bjerk chimed in, "He did what a lot of us would like to do, but don't dare to."

So, it hadn't died with Kahl—the hate, the violence, the twisted logic he epitomized. It lived on, and continued to fester in the hearts and minds of people frightened by the disorder, chaos, and displacement they saw around them.

The afternoon sun glowered from the sky and the heat simmered over the parched, tormented soil. Slowly, the mourners turned away from the grave and left the cemetery.

Cast of Characters

The True Believer

GORDON KAHL A farmer, war hero, and leader of the extremist anti-tax organization known as the Posse Comitatus, Gordon used the Bible and God's name to justify the murder of three lawmen before he too was killed.

Kahl's Family, Friends, and Supporters

JOAN KAHL Gordon's wife.

YORIE KAHL Gordon's son and fanatical follower. To him, there was no truth until it was spoken by his father. He was convicted of murder and sentenced to two life terms, plus fifteen years, in prison.

SCOTT FAUL Gordon's friend and a fellow farmer, Scott, too, was convicted of murder and sentenced to two life terms, plus fifteen years, in prison.

DAVID BROER A Posse member, he was sentenced to ten years in prison for his part in the murders of the United States marshals.

VERNON WEGNER A one-time lawman and Posse enthusiast, he became a prosecution witness at the trial of Yorie Kahl, Scott Faul, and David Broer. In return for his cooperation, Vernon was placed on two years' probation.

CLARENCE MARTIN A doctor, and Gordon's closest friend, he attempted to dissuade Gordon from using violence to further the cause of the extremist views held by both men.

JAMES WICKSTROM The self-proclaimed director for counterinsurgency of the Posse Comitatus, he threatened to complete the job Kahl started.

The Lawmen

KENNETH MUIR The United States marshal for North Dakota. He was killed during the first arrest attempt against Gordon Kahl.

ROBERT CHESHIRE A deputy United States marshal. He was killed during the first arrest attempt against Gordon Kahl.

GENE MATTHEWS The Lawrence County, Arkansas, sheriff. He was killed during the second arrest attempt against Gordon Kahl.

JAMES HOPSON A deputy United States marshal. He was critically wounded during the first arrest attempt against Gordon Kahl.

BRADLEY KAPP A deputy county sheriff, he was wounded during the first arrest attempt against Gordon Kahl.

STEVE SCHNABEL A police officer for the city of Medina, he was wounded during the first arrest attempt against Gordon Kahl.

CARL WIGGLESWORTH A deputy United States marshal, he was the only lawman to escape unscathed during the first arrest attempt against Gordon Kahl.

HAROLD "BUD" WARREN The former United States marshal for North Dakota, he attempted to talk Gordon Kahl into turning himself over to authorities. Later, he was asked by Muir to go on the arrest attempt against Gordon Kahl. He refused.

DARRELL GRAF The police chief for the city of Medina, he refused to accompany lawmen on the arrest attempt against Gordon Kahl.

RICHARD BLAY The FBI agent who was in charge of the nearly four-month search for Gordon Kahl.

JACK KNOX The Arkansas-based FBI agent who received the tip on Gordon Kahl's whereabouts.

JAMES BLASINGAME The FBI agent who led the government's assault against Kahl in Arkansas.

The Prosecutors

RODNEY WEBB The United States attorney for North Dakota.

LYNN CROOKS The assistant United States attorney and chief prosecutor for the murder trial of Yorie Kahl and Scott Faul.

DENNIS FISHER The assistant United States attorney and assistant prosecutor for the murder trial of Yorie Kahl and Scott Faul.

The Defenders

WARREN SOGARD The attorney representing Yorie Kahl.

IRV NODLAND The attorney representing Scott Faul.

RALPH VINJE The attorney representing David Broer.

ROBERT RAMLO The attorney representing Joan Kahl.

JONATHAN GARAAS The attorney representing Vernon Wegner.

Source Notes

The following source notes are by no means a complete listing. They are simply an attempt to indicate the principal published works consulted for this book.

Books

Barker, William E. *The Aryan Nations: A Linkage Profile*. Written and published by William E. Barker, 1986.

Coates, James. *Armed and Dangerous: The Rise of the Survivalist Right*. New York: Noonday Press, 1987.

Cunningham, Douglas. *U.S. Citizens Handbook for Justice*. N.p., n.d.

Elletson, Roger C. *The Highlights of the Power of Parameters of Money*. N.p., 1979.

Emry, Sheldon, *Billions for the Bankers, Debts for the People*. Phoenix: America's Promise, 1983.

Goodwyn, Lawrence. *The Populist Moment: A Short History of the Agrarian Revolt in America*. New York: Oxford University Press, 1978.

Gunther, John. *Inside USA*. New York: Harper & Bros., 1947.

Hicks, John D. *The Populist Revolt*. Lincoln: University of Nebraska Press, 1961.

Martin, Len. *The Attack on Gordon Kahl at Medina*. Detroit Lakes: Constitutional Defense, 1985.

Robinson, Elwyn B. *History of North Dakota*. Lincoln: University of Nebraska Press, 1966.

Sevareid, Eric. *Not So Wild a Dream*. New York: Alfred A. Knopf, 1946.

Turner, Capstan, and A. Jay Lowery. *There Was a Man: The Saga of Gordon Kahl*. Nashville: Sozo Publishing, 1985.

Wickstrom, James. *The American Farmer: 20th Century Slaves*. Written and published by James Wickstrom, n.d.

Zeskind, Leonard. *The Christian Identity Movement: A Theological Justification for Racist and Anti-Semitic Violence*. The Division of Church and Society of the National Council of the Churches of Christ in the U.S.A., 1986.

Articles

Clark, Timothy. "Borrowing Trouble," *National Journal*, September 7, 1985.

Cook, Kenneth A., and Susan E. Sechler. "Agricultural Policy: Paying for Our Past Mistakes." *Issues in Science and Technology*, fall 1985.

"Crisis in Agriculture," a special section produced by the staff of *The Forum*, February 3, 1985.

Fowler, Veronica. "Ultra-Right Farm Groups Taking Root." *Des Moines Register*, September 29, 1985.

Frazier, Deborah. "Farmers Warned of Extremist Promises." *Rocky Mountain News*, December 7, 1985.

Gebert, Chet. "Lonnie Kahl: 'They're Hunting Him Like a Dog.' " *The Forum*, February 15, 1983.

Helgeland, John. "The Religion of Terrorism and the Mind of Gordon Kahl." *Terrorism, Violence and Insurgency Journal*, summer 1987.

"How the Jewish Question Touches the Farm," in *Primrose and Cattleman's Gazette*, May 1983. Adapted from *The International Jew*, by Henry Ford, Sr.

Jacobs, Mike. "Shooting Affects All of Us." *Grand Forks Herald*, February 19, 1983.

King, Wayne. "Right-Wing Extremist Seeks to Recruit Farmers." *New York Times*, September 20, 1985.

Levitas, Daniel. "Violence on the Rise." Prairefire Rural Action, Inc. N.d.

Lewthwaite, Gilbert. "Tax Protestor Kahl Still Eluding Dragnet." *Baltimore Sun*, February 27, 1983.

Marsden, Victor E., trans. (from the Russian text). *Protocols of the Meetings of the Learned Elders of Zion*. N.p., 1922.

Maxwell, Bruce. "Radical Right Wing on the Rise in Midwest," a six-part series. *Rochester Post-Bulletin,* November 1984.

The Monitor (a publication for the Center for Democratic Renewal). "Right-Wing Extremists Organize Midwestern Farmers." January 1986.

———. "The Christian Identity Movement: A Theology Rooted in Racism." March 1986.

———. "Constitutional Fundamentalism: Hiding Bigotry Behind the Red, White and Blue." March 1987.

"An Open Letter to the American Farmer." *The White Patriot,* edited by Thom Robb, May 1985.

Rauch, Jonathan. "Writing a Blank Check." *National Journal,* March 23, 1985.

———. "A Rock and a Hard Place." *National Journal,* September 7, 1985.

Robbins, William. "No End in Sight for Annual Harvests of Debt." *New York Times,* January 4, 1987.

Stokes, Bruce. "A Divided Farm Lobby." *National Journal,* March 23, 1985.

"The Tragic Medina Shootout." *The Forum,* editorial, February 18, 1983.

Unger, Robert. "Death Kept Its Appointment in a Dakota Town." *Kansas City Times,* March 5, 1983.

"What We Believe." *CSA Journal* of the Covenant, Sword and Arm of the Lord. N.d.

Research Reports

The American Jewish Committee. "Anti-Semitism, Extremism and the Farm Crisis: A Background Memorandum." September 1985.

Anti-Defamation League of B'nai B'rith/Civil Rights Division. "The American Farmer and the Extremists: An ADL Special Report." January 1986.

North Dakota State University, Fargo, Department of Agricultural Economics. "Selected Financial and Other Sociological Characteristics of North Dakota Farm and Ranch Operators." Agricultural Economics Report No. 199, July 1985.

———. "Off-Farm Income and Employment of North Dakota Farm Families." Agricultural Economics Miscellaneous Report No. 88, October 1985.

Prairiefire Rural Action, Inc. "The Continuing Crisis in Rural America: Fact vs. Fiction." Des Moines, Iowa: May 15, 1985.

————. "Rural Radical Right Updates: Confidential Memorandum." January, May, and August 1986; August 1987; and April 1988.

Vogel, Sarah M. "The Law of Hard Times: Debtor and Farmer Relief Actions of the 1933 North Dakota Legislative Session." *North Dakota Law Review* 60, no. 3 (1984).

Zeskind, Leonard. "Background Report on Racist and Anti-Semitic Organizational Intervention in the Farm Protest Movement" and "Far-Right Racist and Anti-Semitic Organizations Active in the Middle West and Iowa." Center for Democratic Renewal, 1985.

———— and Daniel Levitas, "Update on Anti-Semitic and Racist Intervention in the Farm Protest Movement." Center for Democratic Renewal, 1986.

Responding to the Rural Crisis, a conference in New York City on February 28, 1988, that offered perspectives on the rural crisis and discussed the directions of American agricultural policy. Among the speakers were: Jim Hightower, Texas commissioner of agriculture; Jim Nichols, Minnesota commissioner of agriculture; Peter C. Myers, deputy secretary for the U.S. Department of Agriculture; Helen Waller, chairperson for the National Save the Family Farm Coalition; Mary Ellen Lloyd, director of the Office of Domestic Hunger and Poverty for the National Council of Churches; Daniel Levitas, research director for Prairiefire Rural Action; and Leonard Zeskind, research director for the Center for Democratic Renewal.

Index